THE POSITIVE SECOND AMENDMENT

The Second Amendment is among the most recognizable provisions of the Constitution. It is also perhaps the most misunderstood. Common misconceptions about the Amendment – what it forbids, what it permits, how it functions as law – distort the gun debate and American constitutional culture. In *The Positive Second Amendment*, Blocher and Miller provide the first comprehensive post-*Heller* account of the history, theory, and law of the right to keep and bear arms. Their aim is not to pick sides in the gun debate, but rather to show how a positive account of the constitutional Second Amendment differs from its political cousin. Understanding the right to keep and bear arms as constitutional law will challenge many deeply held beliefs. But it may also provide a better way to negotiate the seemingly intractable issues that afflict the gun debate.

Joseph Blocher is the Lanty L. Smith '67 Professor of Law at Duke University School of Law. As an associate at O'Melveny & Myers LLP, he coauthored the briefs for the District of Columbia in *District of Columbia v. Heller*. His Second Amendment scholarship has been published in the *Yale Law Journal, Stanford Law Review, NYU Law Review, University of Chicago Law Review*, and many other journals.

Darrell A. H. Miller is the Melvin G. Shimm Professor of Law at Duke University School of Law. He is a graduate of Harvard Law School and Oxford University and is a former Marshall Scholar. His scholarship has been cited by the Supreme Court of the United States, the United States Courts of Appeals, the United States District Courts, and in congressional testimony and legal briefs.

CAMBRIDGE STUDIES ON CIVIL RIGHTS AND CIVIL LIBERTIES

This series is a platform for original scholarship on US civil rights and civil liberties. It produces books on the normative, historical, judicial, political, and sociological contexts for understanding contemporary legislative, jurisprudential, and presidential dilemmas. The aim is to provide experts, teachers, policymakers, students, social activists, and educated citizens with in-depth analyses of theories, existing and past conditions, and constructive ideas for legal advancements.

General Editor: Alexander Tsesis, *Loyola University, Chicago*

The Positive Second Amendment

RIGHTS, REGULATION, AND THE FUTURE OF *HELLER*

JOSEPH BLOCHER
Duke University School of Law

DARRELL A. H. MILLER
Duke University School of Law

CAMBRIDGE
UNIVERSITY PRESS

University Printing House, Cambridge CB2 8BS, United Kingdom

One Liberty Plaza, 20th Floor, New York, NY 10006, USA

477 Williamstown Road, Port Melbourne, VIC 3207, Australia

314–321, 3rd Floor, Plot 3, Splendor Forum, Jasola District Centre, New Delhi – 110025, India

79 Anson Road, #06-04/06, Singapore 079906

Cambridge University Press is part of the University of Cambridge.

It furthers the University's mission by disseminating knowledge in the pursuit of education, learning, and research at the highest international levels of excellence.

www.cambridge.org
Information on this title: www.cambridge.org/9781107158696
DOI: 10.1017/9781316666029

© Joseph Blocher and Darrell A. H. Miller 2018

This publication is in copyright. Subject to statutory exception and to the provisions of relevant collective licensing agreements, no reproduction of any part may take place without the written permission of Cambridge University Press.

First published 2018

Printed in the United States of America by Sheridan Books, Inc.

A catalogue record for this publication is available from the British Library.

Library of Congress Cataloging-in-Publication Data
NAMES: Blocher, Joseph, 1979-author. | Miller, Darrell A. H., 1972- author.
TITLE: The Positive Second Amendment: Rights, Regulation, and the Future of *Heller* / Joseph Blocher, Darrell A. H. Miller.
DESCRIPTION: Cambridge; New York: Cambridge University Press, 2018. |
SERIES: Cambridge studies on civil rights and civil liberties | Includes bibliographical references and index.
IDENTIFIERS: LCCN 2018012826| ISBN 9781107158696 (hardback) | ISBN 9781316611289 (paperback)
SUBJECTS: LCSH: Firearms—Law and legislation—United States. | United States. Constitution. 2nd Amendment. | Gun control—United States. | Constitutional history—United States. | Heller, Dick Anthony. | BISAC: LAW / Constitutional.
CLASSIFICATION: LCC KF3941 .B56 2018 | DDC 344.7305/33–dc23 LC record available at https://lccn.loc.gov/2018012826

ISBN 978-1-107-15869-6 Hardback
ISBN 978-1-316-61128-9 Paperback

Cambridge University Press has no responsibility for the persistence or accuracy of URLs for external or third-party internet websites referred to in this publication and does not guarantee that any content on such websites is, or will remain, accurate or appropriate.

For Marin, Ben, and Sam.
– J.B.

For my family.
– D.A.H.M.

Contents

Acknowledgments

We have been writing about the Second Amendment since the day *District of Columbia v. Heller* was decided. During that time, we have accumulated far too many debts of gratitude to enumerate here. We deeply appreciate the support, encouragement, and disagreements that have shaped our understanding of the Second Amendment in the last decade. This book is a product of those conversations, exchanges, and debates.

The book would not have been possible without the extraordinary help we have received from our friends and colleagues at Duke Law School. We owe special thanks to Dean David Levi, and to the colleagues who have helped guide us. Jamie Boyle, Maggie Lemos, Marin Levy, and Jeff Powell went far beyond the call of duty, reading and commenting on most or all of the manuscript – the structure and argument of the book owe a great deal to their wise counsel. Research librarians Jane Bahnson, Jennifer Behrens, and Cas Laskowski helped us locate and confirm some incredibly hard-to-find sources, from old books and articles to the century-old handwritten gun regulations of Tombstone, Arizona. Besides our friends and colleagues in Durham, we received especially insightful thoughts, comments, and criticisms from Saul Cornell, Mark Frassetto, Eric Ruben, and Adam Skaggs. And of course we are deeply grateful to Alex Tsesis, editor of this series, for shepherding it along.

Our students have been a truly remarkable resource, and some in particular deserve special mention. In the spring of 2017, we taught a research seminar based on an early version of the manuscript, and were fortunate enough to enroll a fantastic set of students: Ali Jessani, Boykin Lucas, Jon Ng, Nicolas Thomson, Emily Taft, Courtney Thomson, Bowen Wang, and Jake Wasserman. They helped us with everything from intra-chapter organization to the identification of case studies. Luke Morgan spent the better part of a summer doing book-related tasks, and we are especially grateful for his hard work and contributions. And as the manuscript neared completion, Rich Hatch, Erin Mack, and Kelsey Smith joined the team to help us check every citation. Marlyn Dail and Leanna Doty managed innumerable administrative tasks, including the final preparation of the manuscript.

Although we've refined the expressions and argumentation through the many revisions of this book, many of the arguments and the supporting sources first found voice in our previous work, some of it coauthored, including the following:

- Eric Ruben & Joseph Blocher, *From Theory to Doctrine: An Empirical Analysis of the Right to Keep and Bear Arms after* Heller, 67 Duke L.J. 1433 (2018)
- Darrell A. H. Miller, *Institutions and the Second Amendment*, 66 Duke L.J. 69 (2016)
- Joseph Blocher & Darrell A. H. Miller, *What is Gun Control? Direct Burdens, Incidental Burdens, and the Boundaries of the Second Amendment*, 83 U. Chi. L. Rev. 297 (2016)
- Joseph Blocher & Darrell A. H. Miller, *Lethality, Public Carry, and Adequate Alternatives*, 53 Harv. J. Leg. 279 (2016)
- Darrell A. H. Miller, *Second Amendment Traditionalism and Desuetude*, 14 Geo. J. L. & Pub. Pol'y L.J. 223 (2016)
- Joseph Blocher, *Hunting and the Second Amendment*, 91 Notre Dame L. Rev. 133 (2015)
- Joseph Blocher, *Good Cause Requirements for Carrying Guns in Public*, 127 Harv. L. Rev. F. 218 (2014)
- Darrell A. H. Miller, Peruta, *the Home-Bound Second Amendment, and Fractal Originalism*, 127 Harv. L. Rev. F. 238 (2014)
- Joseph Blocher, *Gun Rights Talk*, 94 Boston U. L. Rev. 813 (2014)
- Darrell A. H. Miller, *Text, History, and Tradition: What the Seventh Amendment Can Teach Us About the Second*, 122 Yale L.J. 852 (2013)
- Joseph Blocher, *Firearm Localism*, 123 Yale L.J. 82 (2013)
- Joseph Blocher, *The Right Not to Keep or Bear Arms*, 64 Stan. L. Rev. 1 (2012)
- Darrell A. H. Miller, *Guns, Inc.*: Citizens United, McDonald, *and the Future of Corporate Constitutional Rights*, 86 N.Y.U. L. Rev. 887 (2011)
- Darrell A. H. Miller, *Retail Rebellion and the Second Amendment*, 86 Ind. L.J. 939 (2011)
- Joseph Blocher, *Categoricalism and Balancing in First and Second Amendment Analysis*, 84 N.Y.U. L. Rev. 375 (2009)
- Darrell A. H. Miller, *Guns as Smut: Defending the Home-Bound Second Amendment*, 109 Colum. L. Rev. 1278 (2009)

We gratefully acknowledge those journals and their editors. We also made use of the Duke Repository of Historical Gun Laws, https://law.duke.edu/gunlaws/, an interactive resource for historical materials on gun regulation and rights.

Finally, we acknowledge in advance the scholars, students, lawyers, judges, fellow citizens, and others who will continue to shape the Second Amendment, and from whom we will continue to learn. One of the themes of this book is that the Second Amendment demands – and rewards – the kind of careful, reasoned discussion and debate that constitutional law can, at its best, deliver. We hope this book provides a blueprint for that kind of productive engagement.

Introduction

The Gun Debate and the Constitution

On the morning of December 14, 2012, Adam Lanza shot his way through a glass panel in front of Sandy Hook Elementary School in Newtown, Connecticut. Entering the building, he worked his way from room to room, methodically killing twenty young children and six adults with more than 150 shots from a Bushmaster semiautomatic rifle. The massacre ended, as it had begun, with a gunshot, as Lanza – standing in the middle of a classroom – placed a handgun to his head and pulled the trigger.[1]

The immediate reaction to Sandy Hook was horror. During a televised address that afternoon, President Barack Obama paused twice to wipe away tears, and later said that visiting Newtown was the "toughest day of my presidency."[2] National Rifle Association Executive Vice President Wayne LaPierre held a press conference a week later, saying that the organization's "4 million mothers, fathers, sons and daughters join the nation in ... outrage, grief and earnest prayer for the families of Newtown, Connecticut."[3]

Congressional leaders soon drafted legislation designed to help keep guns away from people like Lanza. The most notable proposal would have expanded existing federal background checks to cover most commercial sales of firearms, including gun shows and online sales. It was known as the Manchin-Toomey Amendment, after its sponsors, Senator Joe Manchin (a Democrat from West Virginia) and Senator Pat Toomey (a Republican from Pennsylvania).[4] The idea was broadly popular. Polls

1 *See* CNN Library, *Connecticut Shootings Fast Facts*, CNN (Dec. 7, 2017), www.cnn.com/2013/06/07/us/connecticut-shootings-fast-facts/; Edmund H. Mahoney & Dave Altimari, *A Methodical Massacre: Horror and Heroics*, The Hartford Courant, Dec. 16, 2012, at A1.

2 *See* Dylan Stableford, *Obama: Going to Newton was the 'Toughest day of my Presidency'*, Yahoo News (Jan. 5, 2017), www.yahoo.com/news/obama-going-to-newtown-was-the-toughest-day-of-my-presidency-164748871.html.

3 *See NRA Press Conference Transcript*, The Record, Dec. 22, 2012, at News Section (ellipses in original).

4 S. Amdt. 715, 113th Cong. (2013), 158 Cong. Rec. S2613-18 (daily ed. Apr. 11, 2013).

indicated that more than 90 percent of Americans favored "universal" background checks, including 74 percent of NRA members[5] – an almost unimaginable degree of support for any legislative proposal, let alone one involving guns. It seemed, for the first time in decades, that Democrats and Republicans would find common ground on a major gun law.

But not everyone supported the proposal. After a meeting with Vice President Joe Biden to discuss possible regulations, NRA leaders expressed "disappoint[ment] with how little [the] meeting had to do with keeping our children safe and how much it had to do with an agenda to attack the Second Amendment."[6] The NRA's fundamental position was that "the only thing that stops a bad guy with a gun is a good guy with a gun."[7] The way to prevent another Sandy Hook, the NRA argued, was not to further limit guns, but to ensure that they were in the proper hands – to emphasize gun rights, rather than gun regulation. "[A]bsolute protection" would mean putting "armed police officers in every single school in this nation."[8] That suggestion was widely derided by others.[9]

Despite strong public support for the background check requirement, the Senate rejected the Manchin-Toomey Amendment.[10] Why? Lobbying groups like the NRA are certainly a part of the explanation. But how were those groups able to sink legislation that seemed to have so much going for it? What accounts for the strong opposition to otherwise popular regulations such as expanded background checks?

According to a Gallup poll, the most common reason for opposition to the Manchin-Toomey Amendment was not that background checks would be ineffective, but that they would violate the Second Amendment or the "right to own

[5] Scott Clement, *90 Percent of Americans Want Expanded Background Checks on Guns. Why Isn't This a Political Slam Dunk?*, WASH. POST (Apr. 3, 2013), www.washingtonpost.com/blogs/the-fix/wp/2013/04/03/90-percent-of-americans-want-expanded-background-checks-on-guns-why-isnt-this-a-political-slam-dunk, archived at http://perma.cc/X8E3-KM68 ("Nine in 10 Americans support expanding background checks on gun purchases."). After the Senate vote, 65 percent of Americans believed the Senate should have passed the provision to expand background checks. Frank Newport, *Americans Wanted Background Checks to Pass Senate*, GALLUP (Apr. 29, 2013), www.gallup.com/poll/162083/americans-wanted-gun-background-checks-pass-senate.aspx, archived at http://perma.cc/Y3S9-DNXS (showing that only "29% agree with the Senate's failure to pass the measure").

[6] *See* Stephanie Condon, *NRA "Disappointed" with Biden Gun Meeting*, CBS NEWS (Jan. 10, 2013), www.cbsnews.com/news/nra-disappointed-with-biden-gun-meeting/.

[7] *See* Peter Overby, *NRA: 'Only Thing That Stops A Bad Guy With A Gun Is A Good Guy With A Gun,'* NPR-ALL THINGS CONSIDERED (Dec. 21, 2012), www.npr.org/2012/12/21/167824766/nra-only-thing-that-stops-a-bad-guy-with-a-gun-is-a-good-guy-with-a-gun (quoting Wayne LaPierre).

[8] *See* David Nakamura, *Put Armed Police in Every School, NRA urges*, WASH. POST, Dec. 22, 2012, at A1.

[9] Eric Lichtblau and Motoko Rich, *N.R.A. Envisions 'A Good Guy With a Gun' in Every School*, N.Y. TIMES, Dec. 22, 2012, at A1 ("The N.R.A.'s plan ... was met with widespread derision from school administrators, law enforcement officials and politicians....").

[10] 158 CONG. REC. S2740 (daily ed., Apr. 17, 2013); *see also* Ted Barrett & Tom Cohen, *Senate Rejects Expanded Gun Background Checks*, CNN POLITICS (Apr. 18, 2013), www.cnn.com/2013/04/17/politics/senate-guns-vote, archived at http://perma.cc/C9M3-4EP7.

guns."[11] Congressional rejection of universal background checks – an overwhelmingly popular proposal floated at a time of extraordinary national attention – speaks volumes about the power of constitutional rhetoric in the American gun debate. Policy preferences concerning guns are frequently framed by one's understanding of constitutional law. To make sense of the political debate, then, not to mention the current state of the law, one must also understand the Constitution itself.

Popular beliefs about constitutional law have always undergirded America's national political conversation. But the gun debate is unique in the degree to which constitutionalism is the starting point, and often the ending point, of political argument. And the version of the Second Amendment invoked in political discussions often diverges sharply from the Second Amendment recognized as constitutional doctrine. Under current law, for example, there is no reason to suppose that an equitably administered system of background checks would violate the Second Amendment. Still, many describe those checks as infringements of Second Amendment rights.

Divergence between popular discussion of the Second Amendment and constitutional law was once even more extreme. After all, it was only in 2008, with the Supreme Court's holding in *District of Columbia v. Heller*,[12] that the Second Amendment became plausibly enforceable in the way that most Americans understand constitutional rights. In a 5-4 decision, the Court found that the Amendment was not limited to members of the organized militia, but protects an "individual" right to keep and bear arms for private purposes such as self-defense, thereby pushing the law closer to the popular conception of the right. But *Heller* also emphasized that the individual right to keep and bear arms is subject to a broad set of potential regulations.

Heller ushered in a new era for the Second Amendment. Indeed, it is no exaggeration to say that we are witnessing the nativity of a fundamental constitutional right – one whose development will, in turn, affect the future of gun policy in the United States. Still, though *Heller* may have helped bridge the gap between law and popular understanding of the Amendment, it has done little so far to decrease the political polarization concerning guns. Discussions of the Amendment often exhibit the same venom, blame, and misunderstanding that characterize the broader gun policy debate.

Some supporters of broad gun rights believe that the right to keep and bear arms encompasses an individual right not just to defend against would-be criminals, but also the right to resist whatever governmental tyranny the individual may detect. On this

[11] *See* Frank Newport, *Americans Wanted Background Checks to Pass Senate*, GALLUP (Apr. 29, 2013), www.gallup.com/poll/162083/americans-wanted-gun-background-checks-pass-senate.aspx, archived at http://perma.cc/Y3S9-DNXS (showing that only "29% agree with the Senate's failure to pass the measure") (reporting that when asked an open-ended question about why they opposed expanding background checks, 40 percent of people answered "Violates Second Amendment/People have right to own guns").

[12] District of Columbia v. Heller, 554 U.S. 570 (2008).

account, gun regulation – or, more ominously, gun "control" – is a modern invention out of step with American tradition and identity. The Amendment is "absolute" and immune to regulation. Supporters of this view essentially ask, "What part of 'shall not be infringed' do you not understand?"

Some advocates of gun regulation, by contrast, consider the Second Amendment an anachronism at best and an outright constitutional evil at worst. Because of it, they say, we are unable to pass gun regulations to address the epidemic of firearm death in the United States – a plague that claims roughly 30,000 lives (mostly by suicide) and causes 70,000 injuries every year.[13] Some say that *Heller* lacks historical support and must be overturned. More strident voices call for the repeal of the Second Amendment itself.[14]

The extremists are wrong about the Second Amendment. They are wrong about what the other side believes, and they are often just as wrong about what *they* believe. They are wrong about what they disagree about, and they are wrong about what they agree about. They are wrong to conflate support for the Second Amendment with opposition to gun regulation, wrong to equate support for gun regulation with rejection of the Second Amendment, and wrong to treat agreement with *Heller* as a litmus test for supporting the Second Amendment. Most of all, they are wrong to believe these things with such certainty.

The Second Amendment is complicated and nuanced. There are no easy answers, and nothing in this book will fully satisfy the extremists. To the contrary, we hope to show that aside from a few broad certainties – that the right protects some private purposes, and that it is and has always been subject to regulation – the Second Amendment resists the kinds of simplistic arguments lobbed for or against it by gun rights absolutists or gun prohibitionists.

We will support this position with evidence rooted in history, doctrine, and jurisprudence, but our conclusions are not limited to the academy – far from it. A solid majority of Americans – like the Constitution itself – reject the extremes, and embrace the legitimacy of both gun rights and gun regulation. More than three-quarters of Americans believe, as *Heller* held, that the Second Amendment protects an individual right to keep and bear arms.[15] And yet, as the debate over

[13] Centers for Disease Control and Prevention, National Center for Health Statistics, www.cdc.gov/nchs/fastats/injury.htm.

[14] *See* David S. Cohen, *Why It's Time to Repeal the Second Amendment*, ROLLING STONE (June 13, 2016), www.rollingstone.com/politics/news/why-its-time-to-repeal-the-second-amendment-right-bear-arms-20160613; Kurt Eichenwald, *Let's Repeal the Second Amendment*, VANITY FAIR (Jan. 3, 2013), www.vanityfair.com/news/politics/2013/01/kurt-eichenwald-lets-repeal-second-amendment; Hollis Phelps, *The Second Amendment Must Go: We Ban Lawn Darts. It's Time to Ban Guns*, SALON (Dec. 4, 2015), www.salon.com/2015/12/04/the_second_amendment_must_go_we_ban_lawn_darts_its_time_to_ban_guns/; Bret Stephens, *Repeal the Second Amendment*, N.Y. TIMES (Oct. 5, 2017), www.nytimes.com/2017/10/05/opinion/guns-second-amendment-nra.html; John Paul Stevens, *Repeal the Second Amendment*, N. Y. TIMES (Mar. 27, 2018), www.nytimes.com/2018/03/27/opinion/john-paul-stevens-repeal-second-amendment.html.

[15] Jeffrey M. Jones, *Public Believes Americans Have Right to Own Guns*, GALLUP (Mar. 27, 2008), www.gallup.com/poll/105721/public-believes-americans-right-own-guns.aspx.

Manchin-Toomey revealed, even more Americans support universal background checks.[16] It is these overlapping groups – the quiet, consistent middle of the gun debate – who have the Second Amendment on their side, rather than those who make such broad and confident claims for or against it.

The Second Amendment as a matter of constitutional law is not the bogeyman feared by some, nor the invincible champion imagined by others. Though the gun debate tends to drive participants to political extremes, the *law* of the Second Amendment respects rights and regulation in the way that most Americans do.

In addition to explaining the substance and method of Second Amendment law, we hope to help point a way forward in the gun debate by giving a *positive account* of the Second Amendment that is true to law, history and theory, even if it does not satisfy everyone. By "positive," we mean a vision of the Second Amendment that is affirmative and constructive, a creature of constitutional rather than natural law, and also one that provides some right and wrong answers. We do not suppose that any account of the Second Amendment can fully satisfy all of these goals, and we do not claim to have answered all of the hard questions. But we hope to show that the Second Amendment can be understood through the kind of reasoned debate to which law aspires, rather than the extremism that gun politics too often deliver. And, to be sure, Second Amendment extremism has consequences. It hobbles productive political discussion, it blocks reasonable firearm policy, and it distorts our understanding of constitutional law.

It wasn't always like this, and it doesn't have to be. The Second Amendment, the Constitution, and the country should recover a discourse and doctrine that can accommodate both the fundamental right to keep and bear arms and the imperative of reasonable regulation. Consider three ways in which a better understanding of constitutional law might resolve unnecessary disagreements in the gun debate, thereby making room for the many disagreements that matter.

First, gun debate partisans often misunderstand or misrepresent the content of constitutional doctrine, for example in assuming – with either relief or resentment – that the Second Amendment is "absolute," and permits only minimal gun regulation, or perhaps none at all. One often hears people saying that they oppose gun regulation because they support the Second Amendment, or vice versa.

In fact, the history of gun rights and regulation is primarily one of accommodation and coexistence, and nothing in *Heller* demands otherwise. The proper debate is about how, not whether, to accommodate rights and regulation. Although the constitution undoubtedly restricts policy choices, no constitutional right is entirely immune to regulation. As Justice Antonin Scalia emphasized in *Heller*, the right to keep and bear arms is "not unlimited."[17] The right to keep and

[16] Newport, *supra* note 11.
[17] *Heller*, 554 U.S. at 595.

bear arms does not allow a person to do whatever he or she wants with a gun, just as the right to free speech does not give a person a right to say whatever he or she wants to say.

The boundaries of constitutional rights manifest in different ways. Constitutional law can establish thresholds for a principle's applicability (what counts as "speech," for example) and it can explain what the principle, if applicable, demands (the conditions under which "speech" be regulated). This means that there are at least two ways in which a constitutional claim can fail. A challenge might fall outside the scope of the asserted right altogether. If a white-collar criminal argues that his securities fraud is constitutionally protected, a court will respond that fraud is simply not "speech" for First Amendment purposes.[18] But even constitutionally covered activity (speech in a public park, for example) can be regulated, pursuant to one of the many types of scrutiny that form the bread and butter of constitutional doctrine. Following Fred Schauer's now-familiar terminology, these two categories of limitation can be called "coverage" limitations – those in which the right does not even come into play – and "protection" limitations – those in which the right can be invoked, but also modulated based on the type and strength of government interests.[19] These categories of limitation form the conceptual backbone of post-*Heller* Second Amendment doctrine. For example, courts have overwhelmingly held that concealed carrying falls outside the scope of the Second Amendment, and that banning it therefore raises no constitutional questions. By contrast, most courts have held or assumed that some form of public carrying is covered by the Second Amendment, but that it is subject to various forms of regulation.

Second, gun debate partisans often distort not only the substance but also the *method* of constitutional law. In American constitutional law, not all forms of argument are legitimate. One can usually invoke precedent, history, and tradition in support of a particular legal position, for example, but not bare political preference. The latter is not simply unpersuasive, but inapt – like using the Bible to prove a mathematical theorem, or particle physics to analyze a Renaissance poem.[20] Like any specialized language, American constitutional law has a grammar – rules that govern not just what one says, but how one says it. A goal of this book is to affirm that constitutional reasoning has rules, and that the gun debate would benefit from respecting them.

Participants in the gun debate regularly conflate personal, partisan, or policy preferences with constitutional law. Constitutional doctrine is not the same as sound public policy, although the former may coincide with or even incorporate the latter.

[18] Frederick Schauer, *The Boundaries of the First Amendment: A Preliminary Exploration of Constitutional Salience*, 117 Harv. L. Rev. 1765, 1806 (2004). *But see* Wendy Gerwick Couture, *The Collision Between the First Amendment and Securities Fraud*, 65 Ala. L. Rev. 903, 905–06 (2014) (questioning this conclusion).

[19] Schauer, *supra* note 18, at 1806.

[20] *See* Chapter 5.

It is perfectly sensible to conclude that a particular regulation is desirable and yet unconstitutional, or constitutional and yet undesirable. One might, for example, believe that a ban on assault weapons would save lives and is forbidden by the Second Amendment, or that a blanket prohibition on concealed carry would be constitutional and also completely ineffective. In fact, if one's constitutional conclusions and policy preferences regularly converge, one should stop to ask how much work constitutional law is actually doing.

Most pernicious, perhaps, is the extent to which the Second Amendment is routinely invoked to address issues that aren't even constitutional. For example, with a few exceptions not relevant here, only government actors are subject to constitutional rules. As a matter of law, then, it is simply wrong to invoke the Second Amendment against private companies like Starbucks who forbid guns on their property.[21] Our employer, Duke University, bans personal guns on campus.[22] Because Duke is a private institution, this stringent rule does not even implicate, much less violate, the Second Amendment. By contrast, when public universities ban guns, they are subject to constitutional lawsuits.[23] Gun rights advocates can of course argue that allowing firearms onto private property is good policy, and supporters of gun regulation can argue the opposite, but that debate has nothing to do with Second Amendment law.

Finally, the misunderstanding and misuse of the Second Amendment tends to aggravate geographical and political divisions. More than any other constitutional right, the Second Amendment reflects the country's urban/rural divide – a split that has received a great deal of attention in the wake of the 2016 election.[24] Many rights have varying degrees of constitutional salience in different geographic areas. The religion clauses, for example, might matter more (or less) in areas of varied religious practice. But little compares to the Second Amendment when it comes to regional difference. Study after study has shown that "[g]un ownership is more common among those residing in small cities and towns and in the suburbs compared to those living in large cities."[25] The precise figures vary, but one representative survey found that only 29 percent of urban residents own a gun, compared to 56 percent of

[21] For instance, 2ACheck.com (tagline: "Don't Check Your Rights At Their Door") maintains a Second Amendment Check Boycott List of "Anti-Gun Companies." www.2acheck.com/the-boycott-list/ (accessed Dec. 30, 2017).

[22] Duke University Policies, *Weapons/Firearms/Explosives*, (Aug. 3, 2016), http://policies.duke.edu/students/universitywide/weapons.php.

[23] *See, e.g.*, DiGiacinto v. The Rectors & Visitors of George Mason Univ., 704 S.E.2d 365 (Va. 2011) (prohibition of firearms on campus did not violate visitor's Second Amendment or state constitutional right to bear arms).

[24] *See, e.g.*, Robert Leonard, *Why Rural America Voted for Trump*, N.Y. TIMES, Jan. 5, 2017, at A23.

[25] JAN E. DIZARD, ROBERT MUTH & STEPHEN P. ANDREWS, *The War over Guns: Introduction: Numbers Don't Count*, in GUNS IN AMERICA: A READER 165, 169 (Jan E. Dizard, Robert Muth & Stephen P. Andrews, eds., 1999); *see also* DAVID C. WILLIAMS, THE MYTHIC MEANINGS OF THE SECOND AMENDMENT: TAMING POLITICAL VIOLENCE IN A CONSTITUTIONAL REPUBLIC 71 (2003) ("American gun owners ... reside primarily in rural areas.").

rural residents.[26] This difference in gun ownership unsurprisingly echoes differing views about the desirability of gun regulation. One recent study found that while 56 percent of urban residents favored stricter gun control, only 34 percent of rural residents did – numbers roughly comparable to those for non-gun owners (59 percent) and gun owners (31 percent).[27]

Moreover, the gun debate has become almost completely partisan,[28] in a way that amplifies and reinforces common misunderstandings of the Second Amendment. In May 2016, Donald Trump told a crowd, "Hillary Clinton wants to take your guns away, and she wants to abolish the Second Amendment."[29] Democrats had very little to offer other than denials. Responding to a question at one of the presidential debates, Hillary Clinton insisted that she did not want to do away with guns or the Second Amendment, and then followed up with a qualifier: "Well, first of all, I support the Second Amendment ... But I also believe that there can be and must be reasonable regulation."[30]

What was missing from Clinton's response was a positive constitutional account of the Second Amendment, as opposed to a series of exceptions to it. There is, we think, a serious difference between saying, "I support the Second Amendment, *but* I also support reasonable gun regulations," and saying, "I support the Second Amendment *and* reasonable regulations." Until liberals offer an account *of* the Second Amendment, as opposed to a defense *against* it, they will

[26] Carl T. Bogus, *Gun Control and America's Cities: Public Policy and Politics*, ALB. GOV'T L. REV. 440, 464 (2008) (citing The Gallup Poll: Public Opinion 2005, at 141 (Alec M. Gallup & Frank Newport, eds., 2006)); *see also* Gary Langer, *Some Gun Measures Broadly Backed but the Politics Show an Even Split*, LANGER RESEARCH (Mar. 12, 2013), www.langerresearch.com/uploads/1147a2GunControl.pdf (reporting that gun ownership is "nearly doubly common in rural compared with urban areas"); Chuck Raasch, *In Gun Debate, It's Urban vs. Rural*, USA TODAY (Feb. 27, 2013), www.usatoday.com/story/news/nation/2013/02/27/guns-ingrained-in-rural-existence/1949479 ("A compilation of December [2012] Gallup polls showed that rural Americans – roughly one-sixth of the population – are more than twice as likely to have a gun in the home than those living in large cities."). The General Social Survey found that only 23 percent of urban households had guns in the 2000s, compared to 56 percent in rural areas; the same study found that 22 percent of households in the Northeast had guns, compared to roughly 40 percent in the comparatively rural South and mountain regions. Sabrina Tavernise & Robert Gebeloff, *Share of Homes with Guns Shows 4-Decade Decline*, N.Y. TIMES, Mar. 10, 2013, at A1.

[27] Public Opinion on Gun Control Laws (Feb. 2013), TEX. POL., http://laits.utexas.edu/txp_media/html/poll/features/gun_control_feature/slide1.html (dataset and methodology described at Sampling and Weighting Methodology for the February 2013 Texas Statewide Study, TEX. POL., http://texaspolitics.laits.utexas.edu/11_9_16.html).

[28] Nate Cohn & Kevin Quealy, *Nothing Divides Voters Like Owning a Gun*, N.Y. TIMES (Oct. 5, 2017), www.nytimes.com/interactive/2017/10/05/upshot/gun-ownership-partisan-divide.html; Baxter Oliphant, *Bipartisan support for some gun proposals, stark partisan divisions on many others*, PEW RESEARCH CENTER (June 23, 2017), www.pewresearch.org/fact-tank/2017/06/23/bipartisan-support-for-some-gun-proposals-stark-partisan-divisions-on-many-others/.

[29] Jeremy Diamond, *Trump Says Clinton Wants to Abolish the 2nd Amendment*, CNN (May 7, 2017), www.cnn.com/2016/05/07/politics/donald-trump-hillary-clinton-second-amendment/index.html.

[30] The American Presidency Project, Presidential Debate at the University of Nevada in Las Vegas (Oct. 19, 2016), www.presidency.ucsb.edu/ws/index.php?pid=119039.

continue to lose constitutional debates. And as long as liberals choose to ignore or reject the Second Amendment, they lose a chance to shape it – ceding that authority to gun rights partisans who systematically underestimate and minimize its limits.

Conservatives must come to grips with a new reality as well: A world in which their central reading of the Second Amendment is the law, recognized by *District of Columbia v. Heller* and enforced by the courts. That is a victory, but also a change in substance and style. The constitutional Second Amendment cannot bear all of the weight that some gun rights partisans would place on it. It is enforceable by courts, but also answerable to doctrine, and not simply to imagined histories and values.

The gun debate maps on to some of the deepest divisions in American life – between individual and society, between present and past, between rural and urban, between Republican and Democrat. If these divisions can be bridged, the Second Amendment must be part of the solution. To oversimplify a bit: Liberals must take the law of the Second Amendment seriously; conservatives must take the Second Amendment seriously *as law*.

Skeptics may doubt that a clarification of constitutional law will be of much help in such a contentious debate and, to be fair, they have reasons for their skepticism. Many gun rights absolutists know perfectly well that *Heller* leaves ample room for most gun regulations, ranging from registries and concealed carry regulation to outright bans on dangerous and unusual weapons. Justice Scalia made that fact quite clear. On the other side, of course, there are supporters of gun regulation who play down the historical evidence favoring an individual right to keep and bear arms. Wildly exaggerated (or misleadingly minimizing) claims about the extent of constitutional rights are nothing new in American popular discourse and nothing here will end them. We do not suppose that we will reach the skeptics or the extremists, and our object is not to confirm preconceived notions of what the Second Amendment means.

Instead, we think that – beyond the realm of passionate insiders, with their prepared talking points about the Second Amendment – there is an interested and engaged population of citizens who would actually like to know what the law of the Second Amendment says and doesn't say. When we have discussed these issues in public fora, we've been struck by the degree to which people, whatever their particular commitments regarding guns, are genuinely interested in constitutional law.

Exploring the Second Amendment requires engaging with history, politics and controversy in ways that can be profoundly illuminating. The past decade has seen the development, almost from scratch, of a new constitutional right – a remarkable opportunity and challenge for anyone interested in constitutional doctrine. The Second Amendment also serves an important symbolic role; it valorizes and re-imagines a particular relation of the citizen to arms and to the state. As a symbolic matter, *Heller* was rightly seen to embrace a particular narrative and set of norms about American identity. To make sense of the Second Amendment's many roles – as a constitutional rule, a political banner, and a cultural symbol – one must situate it in a larger story about gun rights, gun regulation, and constitutional law.

The story begins with the history of gun rights and regulation in the United States, a history in which the two have always coexisted (Chapter 1). That broad proposition is historically uncontestable, and yet debate abounds concerning the proper boundary between rights and regulation and the tools with which it should be drawn. Before the Second Amendment became judicially enforceable as a personal right, some legislators regulated as if there were no rights, and some rights-advocates responded as if there was no legitimate regulation. That helped generate the first major debate for the right to keep and bear arms: Whether it is limited to arms, people, and activities bearing some connection to the militia, or whether it includes certain private purposes such as self-defense against crime. That was the central question in *District of Columbia v. Heller* (Chapter 2). The Supreme Court endorsed the latter view, and ultimately extended its application beyond federal law; it also reiterated the constitutionality of many forms of gun regulation and left open a broad range of difficult questions (Chapter 3).

Heller's constitutionalization of the gun debate means that questions previously left to politics must now answer to the Constitution, as courts continue to map the boundaries and internal terrain of the Second Amendment (Chapter 4). In doing so, they – and any faithful participant in the debate – must respect the fundamental rules of constitutional argument; the "grammar" or "language" of constitutional law (Chapter 5). In addition to abiding by those rules, full elaboration of Second Amendment doctrine requires a clearer view of the Amendment's underlying value – one that might be grounded in personal safety, autonomy, or the prevention of tyranny (Chapter 6). Though it is not easy, gaining a clearer understanding of the Second Amendment can help minimize some of the gun debate's pathologies (Chapter 7).

We are not so naïve as to think that understanding the Second Amendment as constitutional law will supply ready answers to every question surrounding firearms. Nor does it guarantee that gun partisans on either side will respect or respond to legal arguments,[31] although we hope they will. At the very least, we want to provide a framework for Second Amendment theory – to approach the myriad problems left unresolved by *Heller* with the kinds of legal tools used for other constitutional rights.

[31] Dan M. Kahan & Donald Braman, *Cultural Cognition and Public Policy*, 24 YALE L. & POL'Y REV. 149 (2006) (arguing that individual's public stances on policy issues are not formed by empirical evidence).

Judges, lawyers, and legal scholars are the obvious and hopefully the most receptive audience for this approach. Much of this book, especially the middle chapters, deals with specific doctrinal challenges, and we attempt to show how they can be addressed using standard tools of legal reasoning.

For students and scholars of the law, the Second Amendment demands and rewards – but generally has not received – the kind of careful intellectual attention given to other amendments. Of the hundreds of law professors teaching at the nation's top law schools, only a handful identify the Second Amendment as a primary academic interest. Many others have written on it, some very well; we rely on their scholarship throughout this book. But most of the existing scholarship is not focused on the Second Amendment as such. To the degree that the Amendment is discussed in legal scholarship, it is typically raised as a banner for a particular interpretive methodology or wielded as a cudgel against it; a pawn in the interpretive battles, rather than an independent subject of inquiry.

This is a loss for the Second Amendment, but also for constitutional scholarship. To make sense of the Second Amendment means operating at the very limits of the law. That is true in the obvious sense, inasmuch as it means answering novel doctrinal questions for what is essentially a new constitutional right. But it is also true in the sense that the Second Amendment exists in the borderlands between politics and law, individuals and the state. Rarely are constitutional scholars presented with such a challenge or opportunity.

But as the aftermath of Sandy Hook demonstrates, the rules, rhetoric, and opportunities of constitutional law are not the sole bailiwick of courts, lawyers, and scholars. Nor are the tools of constitutional reasoning. One need not be a law professor to recognize and evaluate claims about constitutional structure, text, history, or doctrine. And our hope is that making these tools more broadly accessible will, if even to a small degree, bring discipline to the gun debate.

We recognize the magnitude of the challenge. Attempting to move the debate from a political to a constitutional register has risks, in part because the Second Amendment both encapsulates and stokes the fear and anger that are so prominent in American politics.[32] Faith in institutions appears to be plummeting;[33] isolation and individualism are on the rise.[34] And nothing better expresses the notion of the man-unto-himself – standing not only apart from his neighbor, but

[32] *See, e.g.*, YUVAL LEVIN, THE FRACTURED REPUBLIC (2016); Molly Ball, *Donald Trump and the Politics of Fear*, THE ATLANTIC (Sep. 2, 2016), www.theatlantic.com/politics/archive/2016/09/donald-trump-and-the-politics-of-fear/498116/; Lynn Vavreck, *American Anger: It's Not the Economy. It's the Other Party.*, N.Y. TIMES (Apr. 2, 2016), www.nytimes.com/2016/04/03/upshot/american-anger-its-not-the-economy-its-the-other-party.html?_r=0.

[33] Bill Bishop, *Americans Have Lost Faith in Institutions. That's Not Because of Trump or 'Fake News,'* WASH. POST, Mar. 5, 2017, at B4.

[34] JACQUELINE OLDS & RICHARD S. SCHWARTZ, THE LONELY AMERICAN: DRIFTING APART IN THE TWENTY-FIRST CENTURY (2009).

against him – than the Second Amendment.[35] There's always a danger that constitutionalizing a political debate will only bring more turmoil, polarization, and intransigence.

But this is a risk we think is worth taking. A positive vision of the Second Amendment, and with it, a better gun politics and a better constitutional discourse, is impossible until the Second Amendment is understood as law.

[35] Kate Masters, *Fear of Other People is Now the Primary Motivation for American Gun Ownership, A Landmark Survey Finds*, THE TRACE (Sept. 19, 2016), www.thetrace.org/2016/09/harvard-gun-ownership-study-self-defense/.

1

Gun Rights and Regulation in American History

For 200 years, the Second Amendment was mostly inert as a matter of constitutional law. The Supreme Court rarely acknowledged its existence, and not a single federal case struck down a law on Second Amendment grounds during that time.[1] Then, in 2008, the Supreme Court held in *District of Columbia v. Heller* that a Washington, D.C. handgun regulation violated the "individual" right to keep and bear arms for private purposes like self-defense.

The majority in *Heller* wrote that it was doing nothing more than refusing "to pronounce the Second Amendment extinct."[2] That position has strong rhetorical appeal, especially among gun rights advocates; it portrays *Heller* as a conserver rather than innovator. But as a matter of constitutional doctrine, it is a hard position to defend. Whether or not one agrees with *Heller*, it represented a sea change in the law. Before 2008, there was no enforceable federal constitutional right to keep and bear arms for private purposes. After 2008, there was.[3]

[1] Clark Neily, District of Columbia v. Heller: *The Second Amendment Is Back, Baby*, 2007–2008 CATO SUP. CT. REV. 127, 140. A single district court opinion, United States v. Emerson, 46 F. Supp. 2d 598 (N.D. Tex. 1999), *rev'd and remanded*, 270 F.3d 203 (5th Cir. 2001) declared 18 U.S.C. § 922(g)(8) (criminalizing possession of a firearm while under a restraining order) unconstitutional on its face and held that the Second Amendment guarantees an individual right to bear arms. The Fifth Circuit agreed with the District Court that the Second Amendment guarantees an individual right to bear arms, but found that the statute was constitutional regardless. Additionally, some state courts struck down laws on the basis of the Second Amendment. *See, e.g.*, In Re Brickley, 8 Idaho 597 (1902) (striking down a total ban on publicly carrying firearms in towns and cities); Nunn v. State, 1 Ga. 243 (1846) (striking down a total ban on public carry, but finding a valid a prohibition on concealed carry).

[2] District of Columbia v. Heller, 554 U.S. 570, 636 (2008); Neily, *supra* note 1, at 127, 148, 154.

[3] That *Heller* was novel doesn't make it wrong. After all, those who criticize the newness of the right recognized in *Heller* may simultaneously celebrate rights of even more recent vintage, such as the right of same sex couples to marry. Obergefell v. Hodges, 135 S. Ct. 2584 (2015). As Justice Scalia noted in *Heller*, even the freedom of speech was hardly enforced for the first 150 years of the First Amendment's existence. *Heller*, 554 U.S. at 625–26. *See also* Frederick Schauer, *Towards an*

Heller claimed to be preserving a preexisting right long recognized in the historical record,[4] but long neglected by federal judges. That makes accurate reconstruction of the history of gun rights and regulation crucial. Understanding this history is not only necessary to evaluate *Heller* on its own terms, but also important to address the Second Amendment questions *Heller* left open.

The historical record is frequently misunderstood. The story of guns in America has always involved both gun rights and gun regulation. One would not know it from the shrillness of the modern gun debate, but agreement – or at least compromise – on the vast majority of gun-related issues has been the rule, not the exception, throughout history. Neither history, nor policy, nor the Second Amendment requires an absolute choice between rights and regulation.

Although the story is primarily one of law, judges and lawyers are not the only characters. Millions of people, over hundreds of years, outlined the right to keep and bear arms – and also sketched its limits – long before the justices of the Supreme Court did. The creators of the modern right include English monarchs and Protestant chauvinists, the minutemen and the Black Panthers, Wyatt Earp and Al Capone, John Brown and John Hinckley, and the Brady Center and the National Rifle Association. It has been said that the use of history in legal interpretation is the equivalent of looking out into a crowd of people and picking out one's friends.[5] If so, this is quite a crowd from which to pick.

Our story begins with a zealot in a port city in the west of England.

ENGLISH FOUNDATIONS

In the spring of 1686, Sir John Knight stepped out into the streets of Bristol, England, armed for confrontation. King James II's ascent to the throne had plunged the nation into bitter political and sectarian conflict, pitting the Crown against Parliament and Catholics against Protestants. Earlier that April, Knight, had broken up a Catholic conventicle at a private residence with the aid of local officials.[6] Fearing retaliation, Knight

Institutional First Amendment, 89 MINN. L. REV. 1256, 1278 n.97 (2005) (noting, but disagreeing with, the popular view that "the First Amendment started in 1919" with Abrams v. United States, 250 U.S. 616 (1919)).

4 Treatises, books, collections, law review articles, online articles, and newspaper articles account for 94 of the 175 sources cited by the majority. Dictionaries account for another six. The remainder includes all federal and state cases, all state and federal statutes, state constitutions, and legislative history. Those 94 sources make up 136 of the 270 citations in the opinion (150 if one counts dictionaries). We are grateful to Alyssa Rutsch, Duke Law Class of 2015, for reviewing the citations in *Heller* and *McDonald*.

5 Patricia M. Wald, *Some Observations on the Use of Legislative History in the 1981 Supreme Court Term*, 68 IOWA L. REV. 195, 214 (1983); *see also* Samuel Issacharoff, *Pragmatic Originalism?*, 4 N.Y.U. J.L. & LIBERTY 517, 534 (2009) (noting that the criticism can be applied to some versions of originalism as well).

6 Tim Harris, *The Right to Bear Arms in English and Irish Historical Context*, in FIREARMS AND THE COMMON LAW: HISTORY AND MEMORY (Jennifer Tucker, ed., Smithsonian Institute Scholarly Press, forthcoming) (on file with authors).

equipped himself with a sword and gun, and, according to the prosecution, walked about the city before entering the Anglican church of St. Michaels.[7]

In doing so, Knight had potentially broken the law. In 1328, King Edward III had enacted the Statute of Northampton, which read:

> [N]o man great nor small, of what condition soever he be, except the king's servants in his presence, and his ministers in executing of the king's precepts, or of their office, and such as be in their company assisting them, and also [upon a cry made for arms to keep the peace, and the same in such places where such acts happen,] be so hardy to come before the King's justices, or other of the King's ministers doing their office, with force and arms, nor bring no force in affray of the peace, nor to go nor ride armed by night nor by day, in fairs, markets, nor in the presence of the justices or other ministers, nor in no part elsewhere, upon pain to forfeit their armour to the King, and their bodies to prison at the King's pleasure.[8]

Although the Statute of Northampton was centuries old by the time of Knight's adventure, the idea of preventing armed persons in the streets was even older. Edward I (Edward III's grandfather) had declared in 1299 that, "under pain of forfeiture" of life, limb, and property, no one should go armed in the realm "without the King's special license"; an injunction later reiterated by his son, Edward II.[9]

The notion of regulation of public weapons had become so accepted that William Blackstone, whose name is almost synonymous with English common law, would later explain that the "offence of riding or going armed, with dangerous or unusual weapons, is a crime against the public peace, by terrifying the good people of the land." In this respect, the Statute of Northampton was merely a confirmation of a common law tradition traceable all the way to the "laws of Solon," under which "every Athenian was finable who walked about the city in armour."[10]

The Tudor monarchs added to this ancient prohibition, concerned as they were with new lethal (and concealable) technology. Henry VIII restricted certain weapons called "hagbutts" – a kind of muzzle-loading gun – and set a minimum length for guns to prevent concealment.[11] His son followed suit.[12] Henry's daughter,

[7] *Id.*; *see also* Rex v. Knight, 87 Eng. Rep. 75 K.B. (1686).

[8] Statute of Northampton, 1328, 2 Edw. 3, c. 3 (Eng.).

[9] 4 Calendar of the Close Rolls, Edward I, 1296–1302, at 318 (Sept. 15, 1299, Canterbury) (H. C. Maxwell-Lyte, ed., London, Mackie & Co., 1906); 1 Calendar of the Close Rolls, Edward II, 1307–1313, at 52 (Feb. 9, 1308, Dover) & 553 (Oct. 12, 1312, Windsor) (H. C. Maxwell-Lyte, ed., London, Mackie & Co., 1892).

[10] 4 William Blackstone, Commentaries on the Laws of England *149; *see also* State v. Huntly, 25 N.C. 418, 420 (1843) (statute of Northampton does not create the offense, but merely recognizes a common law crime).

[11] 33 Hen. 8, c. 6, § 2 (1541–42) (Eng.); *see* Lois G. Schwoerer, Gun Culture in Early Modern England 59 (2016). There were exceptions to these regulations for individuals in the country or the coasts. *Id*; *see also* Lois G. Schwoerer, *To Hold and Bear Arms: The English Perspective*, 76 Chi.-Kent L. Rev. 27, 34–37 (2000).

[12] Schwoerer, *supra* note 11, at 61 (describing Edward VI's proclamation banning any one from carrying a small concealed handgun within a perimeter of three miles of court).

Queen Elizabeth I, later ordered "all Justices of the Peace" to enforce the Statute of Northampton "according to the true intent and meaning of the same," which included a prohibition on "car[r]ying and use of Gunnes ... and especially of Pistols, Birding pieces, and other short pieces and small shot" that could be easily concealed.[13]

Elizabeth's successor King James I also emphasized the dangers of concealed weapons in a January 1613 proclamation: "[T]he bearing of Weapons covertly, and specially of short Dagges, and Pistols, (truly termed of their use, pocket Dagges, that are apparently made to be car[r]ied close, and secret) hath ever beene, and yet is by the Lawes and policie of this Realme straitly forbidden, as carying with it inevitable danger in the hands of desperate persons..."[14]

With their references to royal servants and ministers, and their use of hoary terms like affray and dagges, the Statute of Northampton and its ilk call to mind a very different legal system in a very different world. But stripped of the archaic language, and taking account of technological changes in weaponry, these laws are recognizable as regulations designed to prevent armed violence, especially in public places, and especially with concealable weapons. Such regulations are part of a tradition that stretches from ancient Athens, through seventeenth-century England, to the modern day.

As early as the thirteenth century, London's statutes provided that no person shall "be found going or wandering about the Streets ... after Curfew tolled ... with Sword or Buckler, or other Arms for doing Mischief ... nor ... in any other Manner, unless he be a great Man or other lawful Person of good repute, or their certain Messenger, having their Warrants to go from one to another, with Lantern in hand."[15] Another fourteenth-century London law proclaimed that "for keeping the peace in the city and suburbs" it was decreed that "no stranger or privy person, save those deputed to keep the peace, shall go armed therein after they shall come to their lodgings."[16] That law's fifteenth-century successor "forb[ade] any man of whatsoever estate or condition to go armed within the city and suburbs, or any except lords, knights and esquires with a sword."[17] Even Sir John Knight remarked that his habit ordinarily was

[13] By the Queene [Elizabeth I]: A *Proclamation Prohibiting The Use and Carriage of Daggers, Birding Pieces, And Other Gunnes, Contrary To the Law* (London, Robert Barker 1600).

[14] By the King [James I]: A *Proclamation Against The Use Of Pocket–Dags* (London, Robert Barker, 1613).

[15] Statutes for the City of London, 1285, 13 Edw. (Eng.).

[16] 2 Calendar of the Close Rolls, Richard II 1381–85, at 92 (Nov. 2, 1381, Westminster) (H. C. Maxwell-Lyte, ed., 1920); *see also* JOHN CARPENTER, LIBER ALBUS: THE WHITE BOOK 335 (Henry Thomas Riley, ed., 1861) (1419) (specifying "[t]hat no one, of whatever condition he be, [may] go armed in the said city or in the suburbs, or carry arms, by day or by night," except certain people connected to "great lords" or the royal family or when commanded to keep the peace).

[17] 3 Calendar of the Close Rolls, Henry IV 1405–09, at 485 (Jan. 30, 1409, Westminster) (A. E. Stamp, ed., 1931).

to leave his weapons "at the end of the Town when he came in" and pick them up again "when he went out."[18]

Regulations on hunting and the use of guns for that purpose were also longstanding in England.[19] Many of the earliest legal restrictions imposed property requirements on hunters,[20] thereby preserving hunting as a pastime for the nobility and aristocracy. These laws became increasingly stringent during the reign of James I, raising the property requirements and prohibiting the use of particular weapons for taking certain game,[21] and there is good reason to think that these changes were motivated by James I's fear of insurrection[22] and desire to disarm the supposedly violent lower classes.[23]

Restrictions became even more severe after the Restoration under Charles II.[24] Perhaps most notorious was the 1670 Game Act, which historian Joyce Lee Malcolm has described as having "deprived the great majority of the community of all legal right to have firearms."[25] The history of the law is disputed, but it has been said that it was later invoked by James II as grounds for ordering the militia to search private homes for "muskets or guns" because "a great many persons not qualified by law under pretence of shooting matches keep muskets or other guns in their houses."[26] Fifty years later, the Black Act was passed, nominally to prosecute poachers (who would blacken their faces for purposes of disguise, hence the Act's name) in the Waltham forests.[27] It, too, is frequently described as repressive – not necessarily because hunting itself was central to the right to keep and bear arms, but because regulations that were nominally about hunting were actually designed to restrict the lower classes' ability to bear arms.[28] Because it is unclear how much these laws

[18] Harris, *supra* note 6.

[19] The discussion in these two paragraphs is taken from Joseph Blocher, *Hunting and the Second Amendment*, 91 NOTRE DAME L. REV. 133, 158–60 (2015).

[20] David B. Kopel, *It Isn't About Duck Hunting: The British Origins of the Right to Arms*, 93 MICH. L. REV. 1333, 1340 (1995) (discussing fourteenth-century laws); *see also* JOYCE LEE MALCOLM, TO KEEP AND BEAR ARMS 72, 198 n.83 (1994) (citing a law providing that "[n]one shall hunt but they which have a sufficient living").

[21] MALCOLM, *supra* note 20, at 13 (describing the 1604 Act, 1605 Act, and 1609 Act).

[22] *See, e.g.*, Schwoerer, *supra* note 11, at 35.

[23] *See, e.g.*, T. Markus Funk, *Is the True Meaning of the Second Amendment Really Such a Riddle? Tracing the Historical "Origins of an Anglo-American Right,"* 39 HOW. L.J. 411, 421 n.36 (1995) (book review); *see also generally* Kopel, *supra* note 20, at 1340.

[24] Robert Hardaway, Elizabeth Gormley and Bryan Taylor, *The Inconvenient Militia Clause of the Second Amendment: Why the Supreme Court Declines to Resolve the Debate over the Right to Bear Arms*, 16 ST. JOHN'S J. LEGAL COMMENT. 41, 65 (2002).

[25] MALCOLM, *supra* note 20, at 65; L. A. Powe, Jr., *Guns, Words, and Constitutional Interpretation*, 38 WM. & MARY L. REV. 1311, 1347 (1997).

[26] William S. Fields & David T. Hardy, *The Militia and the Constitution: A Legal History*, 136 MIL. L. REV. 1, 13 (1992) (quoting 2 Calendar of State Papers, Domestic, James II, 1212, at 314 (Dec. 6, 1686)).

[27] *See generally* E. P. THOMPSON, WHIGS AND HUNTERS: THE ORIGIN OF THE BLACK ACT (1975).

[28] *See, e.g.*, MALCOLM, *supra* note 20, at 64–71 (describing the Black Act as "draconian" and "repressive"); *see also generally* P. B. MUNSCHE, GENTLEMEN AND POACHERS: THE ENGLISH GAME LAWS 1671–1831 (1981).

were aimed at protecting game and how much they represented efforts at political control, opponents of contemporary gun regulation often cite them as evidence that seemingly sensible gun regulations may be pretexts for general disarmament.

But it was the strife of James II's kingship that motivated Knight's armed foray in the streets of Bristol. James II's short reign was dominated by a power struggle with Parliament over religion, and he would be the last Catholic to wear the English crown.[29] Knight's actions must be understood against the backdrop of this political and religious turmoil. Indeed, in one historian's account, Knight's prosecution had less to do with his decision to walk about the city armed, and more to do with his suggestion that the King was not willing or able to protect his Protestant subjects within St. Michael's church.[30] Whatever the motivation, the Attorney General pursued Knight for violating the Statute of Northampton, resulting in the spectacularly named case of *Rex v. Knight*. The charges alleged that Knight was a "very disloyall and Seditious and ill affected man" who "had caused Musketts or Armes to be carried before him in the Streets, and into the Churck to publick service to the terrour of his Majesties Leige people, etc. and to the Scandall of the Government."[31]

In the end, Knight was acquitted. Centuries later, the question is *why*. What the Statute of Northampton forbade, the significance of *Rex v. Knight*, and what the Framers of the Second Amendment understood the Statute to prohibit, are all matters of significant historical debate. Some scholars conclude that the Statute banned armed travel in public places,[32] while others say it "cover[ed] only those circumstances where carrying arms was unusual and therefore terrifying."[33] As historian Saul Cornell notes, one finds different interpretations of the law in Blackstone (cited to support the former view) and in the earlier work of Sir William Hawkins (cited to support the latter view). Since "the Founders were familiar with both English commentators ... it seems likely that there may have been a range of views on interpreting this question."[34]

The Glorious Revolution of 1689 brought James II's tumultuous reign to an end and installed the Protestants William III and Mary II in his place. William and Mary, in turn, promised to respect the rights of Englishmen, an agreement codified

[29] *See generally* DAVID WOMERSLEY, JAMES II: THE LAST CATHOLIC KING (2015).

[30] Harris, *supra* note 6.

[31] *Id.*

[32] *See, e.g.*, Patrick J. Charles, *Faces of the Second Amendment Outside the Home: History Versus Ahistorical Standards of Review*, 60 CLEV. ST. L. REV. 1, 8 (2012); Darrell A. H. Miller, *Guns as Smut: Defending the Home-Bound Second Amendment*, 109 COLUM. L. REV. 1278, 1317–18 (2009) (citing 4 WILLIAM BLACKSTONE, COMMENTARIES ON THE LAWS OF ENGLAND *149).

[33] Eugene Volokh, *The First and Second Amendments*, 109 COLUM. L. REV. SIDEBAR 97, 101 (2009).

[34] Saul Cornell, *The Right to Carry Firearms Outside of the Home: Separating Historical Myths from Historical Realities*, 39 FORDHAM URB. L.J. 1695, 1713 (2012). Historian Tim Harris is skeptical that anything meaningful can be gathered from Knight's acquittal, since it pertained more to Knight's aspersions on the King than to the incidents of traveling armed. *See* Harris, *supra* note 6.

in the English Declaration of Rights – an important predecessor of the American Bill of Rights. Among other things, the Declaration guaranteed: "Subjects which are Protestants may have Arms for the Defence suitable to their Conditions and as allowed by law."[35] In *Heller*, Justice Scalia wrote that this provision "has long been understood to be the predecessor to our Second Amendment,"[36] and Blackstone himself described it as "a public allowance, under due restrictions, of the natural right of resistance and self-preservation, when the sanctions of society and laws are found insufficient to restrain the violence of oppression."[37] The underlying balance between that "natural right" and "due restrictions" would soon become manifest in the colonies. In many ways, it was baked into the common law.[38]

GUN RIGHTS AND REGULATION IN THE COLONIES

Guns were a part of life in the American colonies. They were used for hunting, pest control, self-protection, and the struggle for independence – all of which are now central to the cultural and historical mythology of guns in the United States. And yet that history is more complicated and nuanced than the mythology might suggest.

Colonial Gun Regulation

One persistent myth, widespread in public commentary and scholarship,[39] is the notion that gun regulation is a modern development. When people refer to the "modern orthodoxy" supporting gun regulation,[40] they are implicitly contrasting it with a time when guns were supposedly unrestricted. The assumption is that because gun regulation did not exist in the colonies, it is constitutionally suspect today.[41]

[35] 1 W. & M., c. 2, § 7, in 3 Eng. Stat. at Large 441 (1689). These same sovereigns passed "An Act for the Better Securing the Government by Disarming Papists and Reputed Papists." 1 W. & M., c. 15, § 7, in 3 Eng. Stat. at Large 441 (1689).

[36] *Heller*, 554 U.S. at 593.

[37] 1 William Blackstone, Commentaries on the Laws of England *139.

[38] Saul Cornell, *The Right to Keep and Carry Arms in Anglo-American Law: Preserving Liberty and Keeping the Peace*, 80 Law & Contemp. Probs. 11, 14–15 (2017).

[39] *See, e.g.*, Glenn Harlan Reynolds, *A Critical Guide to the Second Amendment*, 62 Tenn. L. Rev. 461, 487 (1995) ("[I]n truth there is more historical precedent in this country for the requirement to own a gun than for a prohibition against doing so."); Ed Apple, *A Layman's Short History of Gun Control in America*, Keep And Bear Arms.com, www.keepandbeararms.com/information/XcIBViewItem .asp?ID=2428 ("Most people think that gun control is a recent phenomenon in America, and in a way, they're right."); Nelson Lund, *The Second Amendment and the Inalienable Right to Self-Defense*, Report #16-CGL on Political Thought, Heritage Foundation (Apr. 17, 2014), www.heritage.org/research/reports/2014/04/the-second-amendment-and-the-inalienable-right-to-self-defense ("At the time of the Framing, gun control laws were virtually nonexistent, and there was no reason for anyone to discuss what kinds of regulations would be permitted by the Second Amendment.").

[40] Nicholas Johnson, Negroes and the Gun: The Black Tradition of Arms 14, 286–97 (2014).

[41] *See supra* note 39 and sources cited therein.

History belies this assumption. As legal scholar Adam Winkler notes, "Gun safety regulation was commonplace in the American colonies from their earliest days."[42] Some colonies more or less copied the Statute of Northampton wholesale,[43] and versions of it remain on the books in some of those places even today.[44] Some colonial cities – including Philadelphia, New York, and Boston – regulated the storage and use of firearms and ammunition within city limits. Boston's law, for example, provided that "the depositing of loaded Arms in the Houses of the Town of Boston, is dangerous" and that no loaded firearms were allowed in any "Dwelling-House, Stable, Barn, Out-house, Store, Ware-house, Shop or other Building."[45] Commercial enterprises handling gunpowder within cities had to comply with safe storage laws. Cornell and fellow historian Nathan DeDino note that "New York City required ships to unload gunpowder at a magazine within twenty-four hours of arrival in the harbor and before the ship 'hawl[ed] along side of any wharf, pier or key within the city,'" while "Boston subjected any 'Gun Powder ... kept on board any ship or other vessel laying to, or grounded at any wharf within the port of Boston' to confiscation."[46] The prevalence of these regulations in cities is notable. The urban–rural divide in the colonial era – which echoes the Statute of Northampton's focus on public places like fairs and markets – persists today, as there are still significant differences between urban and rural areas with regard to the costs, benefits, and regulation of guns.[47]

Of course, the fact that some of these laws have modern analogues does not mean that all of them are worthy of emulation. For example, some early regulations imposed racial qualifications for the purchase of possession of arms.[48] Such

[42] Adam Winkler, Gunfight: The Battle Over the Right to Bear Arms in America 115 (2009).

[43] *See, e.g.*, Act of Jan. 29, 1795, ch. XXV, *reprinted in* 2 The Perpetual Laws of the Commonwealth of Massachusetts 259 (I. Thomas & E. T. Andrews, eds., 1801); An Act Forbidding & Punishing Affrays, Nov. 27, 1786, ch. XXI, *reprinted in* 1 A Collection of All Such Acts of the General Assembly of Virginia, of a Public and Permanent Nature, as Are Now in Force 30 (Samuel Pleasants, Jr. & Henry Pace, 1803); Francois-Xavier Martin, A Collection of Statutes of the Parliament of England in Force in the State of North Carolina 60–61 (Newbern 1792); *see also* Moore v. Madigan, 702 F.3d 933, 944 (7th Cir. 2012) (Williams, J., dissenting) (noting the Statute of Northampton's influence on the colonies, in particular Massachusetts, North Carolina, and Virginia).

[44] *See, e.g.*, State v. Dawson, 272 N.C. 535, 541–42 (1968) (describing common law offense of "going armed with unusual and dangerous weapons to the terror of the people," and citing the Statute of Northampton and Sir John Knight's case); N.C. Gen. Stat. § 14-269.4 (banning carrying dangerous weapons on "certain State property and in courthouses"); *id.* § 14-277.2 (banning "carrying weapons at parades and other public gatherings").

[45] Act of Mar. 1, 1783, chap. XIII, 1783 Mass. Acts 218 (cited in *Heller*, 554 U.S. at 631).

[46] Saul Cornell & Nathan DeDino, *A Well Regulated Right: The Early American Origins of Gun Control*, 73 Fordham L. Rev. 487, 512 (2004) (quoting Act of Apr. 13, 1784, ch. 28, 1784 N.Y. Laws 628; Act of June 19, 1801, ch. XX, 1801 Mass. Acts 507).

[47] This division, and its implications for Second Amendment doctrine, are the subject of Joseph Blocher, *Firearm Localism*, 123 Yale L.J. 82 (2013).

[48] An Act Concerning Free Negroes and Mulattoes, Act of Feb. 4, 1806, LXXXIII, *reprinted in* A Collection of All Such Acts of the General Assembly of Virginia 108–09 (Samuel Pleasants

laws would be impermissible today for reasons analytically distinct from the Second Amendment – they clearly violate the Constitution's Equal Protection Clause, for one thing. But they are still significant, because they show that guns were subject to legal regulation from the country's earliest days, and also that gun regulations, like any other laws, can be crafted or applied in ways that place particular burdens on disfavored groups.

The relationship between gun rights, regulation, and politics helped precipitate the Revolutionary War. By the mid-1770s, tensions between the colonies and the Crown had boiled over to the point that royal officers sought to disarm the colonists. General Thomas Gage, the Military Governor of the Massachusetts Bay Colony, did so with particular aplomb. On April 18, 1775, he sent a force of some 700 men to seize a large cache of arms rumored to be in Concord, 20 miles northwest of Boston. Unfortunately for Gage and his men, word of this plan leaked, and by the time the British began to move that night, Paul Revere had already sent his signal and begun his famous ride. When the British made it to Lexington the next morning, they found a group of armed and defiant colonists, and the first shots of the Revolution were fired. In that sense, as Winkler puts it, the Revolution itself was – within the larger context of oppression by the Crown – "a war ignited by a government effort to seize the people's firearms."[49] That said, it would be too much to say that the colonists' opposition to the British march was tantamount to a broad repudiation of gun regulation.

The Militia

Even as resistance to gun confiscation helped spark the Revolution, embrace of gun regulation – albeit of a very different kind than we see today – helped facilitate it. Specifically, the colonies adopted militia regulations that generally required all eligible members to report for muster with their own weapons and ammunition at the ready. New York's law, for example, provided for the colonel or commanding officers of the militia to call a regimental parade twice a year, at which they would examine "the arms, ammunition and accoutrements of each man"; "defaulters" would be identified and subject to fines.[50] The specificity of the militia acts and similar laws is notable: those serving in the militia were not permitted to bring whatever arms they desired, but only those specified.[51]

Jr., 1808) (forbidding the unlicensed "keep[ing] or carry[ing]" of firearms by "Negroes and mulattoes"); An Act for Regulating the Indian Trade and Making it Safe to the Publick, No. 269, § IV (1707), *in* 2 The Statutes at Large of South Carolina 310 (Thomas Cooper, ed., Columbia, A.S. Johnston, 1837).

[49] Winkler, *supra* note42, at 105.

[50] 1778 N.Y. Laws at 62 (discussed in Saul Cornell & Nathan DeDino, A *Well Regulated Right: The Early American Origins of Gun Control*, 73 Fordham L. Rev. 487, 509–11 (2004)).

[51] Saul Cornell & Kevin M. Sweeney, *All Guns Are Not Created Equal*, Chron. Higher Educ., Feb. 1, 2013, at B4.

In the romantic myth, training and familiarity with firearms made the minutemen into a dead-eyed, sharpshooting military force. Guns were thought to reflect the "civic virtue and military prowess of the yeoman" as compared to the "degeneration of England and ... the sharp decline of the 'liberties of Englishmen.'"[52] As Dan Kahan noted, even prior to *Heller*, "[t]hese connotations became institutionalized in the Second Amendment."[53]

Although the civic virtue of the colonial soldiers is undoubted, their military prowess is often overstated. As one historian put it, "[t]his force, though armed, was largely untrained, and its deficiencies were the subject of bitter complaint."[54] George Washington himself disparaged the militia as undisciplined and unreliable, likely to "fly from their own shadows" in the confusion of battle.[55]

Responding to the militias' deficiencies, Congress passed the Militia Act of 1792, which provided that "every citizen so enrolled [in the militia] and notified, shall, within six months thereafter, provide himself with a good musket or firelock, a sufficient bayonet and belt," various other accoutrements, "or with a good rifle, knapsack," and ammunition, "and shall appear, so armed, accoutred and provided, when called out to exercise, or into service, except, that when called out on company days to exercise only, he may appear without a knapsack."[56] But, as the Supreme Court noted nearly 200 years later in *Perpich v. Department of Defense*, the Militia Act "was virtually ignored for more than a century."[57]

By 1901, President Theodore Roosevelt concluded, "Our militia law is obsolete and worthless."[58] That same year, Congress used its Militia Clause power to pass the Dick Act, which divided the class of able-bodied male citizens between 18 and 45 years of age into an "organized militia" – the National Guard of the several States – and the "reserve militia," which later became known as the "unorganized

[52] Dan M. Kahan, *The Secret Ambition of Deterrence*, 113 HARV. L. REV. 413, 454 (1999) (quoting Richard Hofstadter, *America as a Gun Culture*, 21 AM. HERITAGE, Oct. 1970, at 4, 82).

[53] *Id.*

[54] Frederick Bernays Wiener, *The Militia Clause of the Constitution*, 54 HARV. L. REV. 181, 182 (1940); Carl T. Bogus, *The Hidden History of the Second Amendment*, 31 U.C. DAVIS L. REV. 309, 340–41 (1998); CHARLES ROYSTER, A REVOLUTIONARY PEOPLE AT WAR: THE CONTINENTAL ARMY AND AMERICAN CHARACTER, 1775–76, at 59 (1979) (describing Washington's complaints about the militia).

[55] George Washington, GEORGE WASHINGTON: A COLLECTION 77–78, compiled and edited by W. B. Allen (Liberty Fund Inc., 1988) ("To place any dependance upon Militia, is, assuredly, resting upon a broken staff. Men just dragged from the tender Scenes of domestick life; unaccustomed to the din of Arms; totally unacquainted with every kind of Military skill, which being followed by a want of confidence in themselves, when opposed to Troops regularly train'd, disciplined, and appointed, superior in knowledge, and superior in Arms, makes them timid, and ready to fly from their own shadows.").

[56] Militia Act of May 8, 1792, ch. 33, § 1, 1 Stat. 271, 271, repealed by Dick Act of 1903, ch. 196, § 25, 32 Stat. 775, 780.

[57] Perpich v. Dep't of Def., 496 U.S. 334, 341 (1990).

[58] *Id.* (quoting First Annual Message to Congress, Dec. 3, 1901, 14 Messages and Papers of the Presidents 6672).

militia." Fifteen years later, in the shadow of World War I, Congress "federalized" the National Guard. It provided greater federal control and funding of the Guard, and also required every guardsman to take a dual oath to support the nation as well as his state, and to obey the President (who was empowered to draft them into federal service) as well as the Governor. As the Court put it in *Perpich*, "The draft of the individual members of the National Guard into the Army during World War I virtually destroyed the Guard as an effective organization. The draft terminated the members' status as militiamen, and the statute did not provide for a restoration of their prewar status as members of the Guard when they were mustered out of the Army."[59]

In 1933, Congress remedied this problem by separating the National Guard of the various states from the National Guard of the United States. Today, all persons who enlist in the former are automatically enlisted in the latter, which in turn makes them a part of the Enlisted Reserve Corps of the Army. But unless and until ordered into active duty in the Army, they retain their status as members of a separate state Guard unit. Those ordered into federal service for "active duty or active duty for training" revert to their status in the state Guard upon conclusion of that service.

The evolution of the militia since the late 1700s has largely been a story of statutory change. But it is also intertwined with constitutional law, because the fortunes of the militia as an institution have had a significant influence on the interpretation of the Second Amendment.

THE CONTEXT OF THE AMENDMENT'S DRAFTING

The states that emerged from the Revolutionary War were not united. Bound loosely together by the Articles of Confederation, they were nominally governed by a Congress that had virtually no power to regulate domestic affairs and only limited authority to raise revenue. The national government depended mostly on voluntary financial contributions from the states, meaning that debts to foreign nations and Revolutionary War soldiers remained outstanding nearly a decade after independence.[60]

Unpaid for their service, yet subject to sometimes-oppressive taxation by their own states, some colonists found themselves caught in an economic whipsaw. Daniel Shays, a farmer from Massachusetts who had fought for the Continental

[59] *Id.* at 345.

[60] Gordon S. Wood, Empire of Liberty: A History of the Early Republic, 1789–1815 95–96 (2009). James Madison would later say that "The radical infirmity of the Articles of Confederation was the dependence of Congress on the voluntary and simultaneous compliance with its Requisitions, by so many independent communities, each consulting more or less its particular interests and convenience and distrusting the compliance of others." Clayton P. Gillette, *The Exercise of Trumps by Decentralized Governments*, 83 Va. L. Rev. 1347, 1417 n.73 (1997).

Army at Lexington, Concord, Bunker Hill, and Saratoga, was among them. As petitions to the state government went unanswered, Shays and others like him took up arms and went on the march – an uprising known as Shays' Rebellion. Hampered by the weakness of the Articles of Confederation, the federal government could not summon a force sufficient to block the thousands of rebels making their way to the federal armory in Springfield, Massachusetts. Boston's merchants, who dominated the state government, instead hired a private militia, dispersed the rebels with cannon shots, and then pursued them as they melted back into the countryside over the following months.[61]

Though it caused few casualties, Shays' Rebellion helped solidify the sense that the Articles were inadequate, and that a stronger government was needed. Reflecting on the Rebellion in early 1787, John Jay wrote that "the inefficiency of the Federal government [became] more and more manifest."[62] (Thomas Jefferson, ever quotable, was sanguine about the threat of armed rebellion: "[W]hat country can preserve it's liberties if their rulers are not warned from time to time that their people preserve the spirit of resistance? [L]et them take arms ... the tree of liberty must be refreshed from time to time with the blood of patriots & tyrants. [I]t is it's natural manure."[63]) In February, the Continental Congress called for a group of delegates to meet in May "to devise such further provisions as shall appear to them necessary to render the constitution of the Federal Government adequate to the exigencies of the Union."[64]

Throughout the course of a sweltering Philadelphia summer, those delegates produced the document we now know as the Constitution. Entire courses are taught about individual clauses of the Constitution (this book, after all, is about a twenty-seven word amendment) but the basic outline is familiar enough: enumerated federal power, separation of powers, a division of authority between the states and the federal government, supremacy of federal law, and so on.

As comfortingly foundational as those principles seem to modern Americans, the very idea of the written Constitution was radical at the time, and no provision more so than the one authorizing a standing federal army. As Governor Edmund Randolph of Virginia noted, "With respect to a standing army, I believe there was not a member in the federal Convention, who did not feel indignation at such an institution."[65] The military provisions of the Constitution therefore embody a compromise, one that – like the document as a whole – divides power among different

[61] *See generally* DAVID P. SZATMARY, SHAYS' REBELLION: THE MAKING OF AN AGRARIAN INSURRECTION (1980).

[62] *Id.* at 123.

[63] Letter from Thomas Jefferson to William Stephens Smith (Nov. 13, 1787), Jefferson, Thomas, 1743–1826: Papers of Thomas Jefferson, *microform*, Reel 13 (Library of Congress).

[64] *See* 1 JOHN VILE, THE CONSTITUTIONAL CONVENTION OF 1787: A COMPREHENSIVE ENCYCLOPEDIA OF AMERICA'S FOUNDING, 20 (2005).

[65] 3 JONATHAN ELLIOT, THE DEBATES IN THE SEVERAL STATE CONVENTIONS ON THE ADOPTION OF THE FEDERAL CONSTITUTION 401 (2d ed., 1836) (hereinafter ELLIOT).

branches of the federal government, and between those branches and the states. Congress was allowed to raise and support a national Army and Navy, and also to organize, arm, discipline, and provide for the calling forth of "the Militia," as well as to govern "such Part of them as may be employed in the Service of the United States."[66] The President, meanwhile, would serve as "Commander in Chief of the Army and Navy of the United States, and of the Militia of the several States, when called into the actual Service of the United States."[67] And the states retained the power to appoint officers and to train and discipline the militia according to rules prescribed by Congress.[68]

Of course, in order for any of this to take effect, the Constitution had to first win ratification by at least nine of the thirteen states. Supporters of ratification (most prominently the Federalists) argued in speeches, meetings, and public papers (the most famous of which are the *Federalist Papers*) that security, freedom, and prosperity depended on the creation and recognition of a federal government with broadened powers.[69] But the existence of a federal standing army and the precarious place of the state militia remained central concerns for ratification opponents, the Anti-Federalists. "The militia may be here destroyed by that method which has been practised in other parts of the world before; that is, by rendering them useless – by disarming them,"[70] Anti-Federalist George Mason warned. "Under various pretenses, Congress may neglect to provide for arming and disciplining the militia; and the state governments cannot do it, for Congress has an exclusive right to arm them."[71]

In those same debates, Anti-Federalist Patrick Henry thundered, "The great object is, that every man be armed" – a quote that some embrace as evidence that gun ownership was a right and even a duty in the Founding Era.[72] As Michael Waldman notes, "The eloquent patriot's declaration provided the title for the ur-text for the gun rights movement, Stephen Halbrook's 1984 book, *That Every Man Be Armed* ... The Second Amendment professorship at George Mason University is named after Henry. A $10,000 gift to the NRA makes you a 'Patrick Henry Member.'"[73]

66 U.S. CONST., Art. I, § 8, cls. 12–16.

67 Art. II, § 2.

68 Art. I, § 8.

69 THE FEDERALIST NO. 46 (James Madison) ("Let a regular army, fully equal to the resources of the country, be formed; and let it be entirely at the devotion of the federal government; still it would not be going too far to say, that the State governments, with the people on their side, would be able to repel the danger.").

70 THE COMPLETE BILL OF RIGHTS: THE DRAFTS, DEBATES, SOURCES, AND ORIGINS 286 (Neil H. Cogan ed., 2015); 3 ELLIOT, at 379.

71 *Id.*

72 *See* SAUL CORNELL, A WELL-REGULATED MILITIA 53–55 (2006) (describing Henry's Second Amendment rhetoric in the context of the Virginia ratification debates).

73 Michael Waldman, *How the NRA Rewrote the Second Amendment*, BRENNAN CENTER FOR JUSTICE (May 20, 2014), www.brennancenter.org/analysis/how-nra-rewrote-second-amendment.

But as Waldman demonstrates, Henry made his comment in the course of objecting to the *cost* of having both the federal government and the state arm the militia. Here is the full quote:

> May we [the States] not discipline and arm them [the militia], as well as Congress, if the power be concurrent? [S]o that *our militia* shall have two sets of arms, double sets of regimentals, &c.; and thus, at a very great cost, we shall be doubly armed. The great object is, that every man be armed. But can the people afford to pay for double sets of arms, &c.?[74]

"Far from a ringing statement of individual gun-toting freedom," Waldman concludes, "it was an early American example of a local politician complaining about government waste."[75]

Eventually, the Federalists prevailed and New Hampshire's vote on June 21, 1788, ensured the Constitution's ratification. But the battle over the scope of federal power, and specifically over its power regarding the military and the militias, did not end with ratification. Many states – especially those with strong Anti-Federalist sentiments such as Virginia, New York, and North Carolina – proposed Amendments directed at Mason's concern.

The relevant proposals sent by the Virginia Ratifying Convention, and endorsed by North Carolina, read as follows:

> 17th. That the people have a right to keep and bear arms; that a well-regulated militia, composed of the body of the people trained to arms, is the proper, natural and safe defence of a free state; that standing armies, in time of peace, are dangerous to liberty, and therefore ought to be avoided, as far as the circumstances and protection of the community will admit; and that, in all cases, the military should be UNDER strict subordination to, and be governed by, the civil power.
>
> 19th. That any person religiously scrupulous of bearing arms ought to be exempted, upon payment of an equivalent to employ another to bear arms in his stead.[76]

New York's proposal was largely identical:

> That the people have a right to keep and bear Arms; that a well regulated Militia, including the body of the People capable of bearing Arms, is the proper, natural, and safe defence of a free State .... That standing Armies, in time of Peace, are dangerous to Liberty, and ought not to be kept up, except in Cases of necessity;

[74] Patrick Henry, *Remarks at the Virginia Convention Debates* (June 14, 1788), *reprinted in* 3 ELLIOT, at 386 (emphasis added).

[75] Waldman, *supra* note 73.

[76] Documents Illustrative of the Formation of the Union of the American States, H.R. Doc. No. 69-398, at 1036 (1927); *see also* Eugene Volokh, *The Commonplace Second Amendment*, 73 N.Y.U. L. REV. 793, 803 n.32 (1998).

> and that at all times, the Military should be kept under strict Subordination to the civil Power.[77]

By directly embedding the "right to keep and bear arms" in a military context and by raising the specter of "standing Armies," the Virginia and New York proposals (as well as minority proposals from places like Maryland)[78] suggested that the Second Amendment right to keep and bear arms is tied to militia service, not to private uses like individual self-defense.

Other constitutional proposals appeared to take a different approach. The proposals of New Hampshire and Pennsylvania, for example, did not contain express militia-based language, and have often been cited to support an alternative reading of the Second Amendment that includes a right to arms for private purposes such as self-defense, and perhaps even hunting and recreation. New Hampshire's proposal read simply: "Twelfth, Congress shall never disarm any Citizen unless such as are or have been in Actual Rebellion."[79] (This proposal, it should be noted, appeared nearly immediately after another regarding the standing army.[80])

A minority proposal from Pennsylvania was written even more broadly. That proposal stated:

> [T]he people have a right to bear arms for the defence of themselves and their own state, or the United States, or for the purpose of killing game; and no law shall be passed for disarming the people or any of them, unless for crimes committed, or real danger of public injury from individuals; and as standing armies in the time of peace are dangerous to liberty, they ought not to be kept up; and that the military shall be kept under strict subordination to and be governed by the civil powers.[81]

[77] *Id.*

[78] *See Heller*, 554 U.S. at 657–58 (Stevens, J., dissenting) ("The proposals considered in the other three States, although ultimately rejected by their respective ratification conventions, are also relevant to our historical inquiry. First, the Maryland proposal, endorsed by a minority of the delegates and later circulated in pamphlet form, read: '4. That no standing army shall be kept up in time of peace, unless with the consent of two thirds of the members present of each branch of Congress .... 10. That no person conscientiously scrupulous of bearing, arms, in any case, shall be compelled personally to serve as a soldier.'") (citing 3 ELLIOT at 729, 735).

[79] *See Heller*, 554 U.S. at 657 (Stevens, J., dissenting) ("By contrast, New Hampshire's proposal, although it followed another proposed amendment that echoed the familiar concern about standing armies, described the protection involved in more clearly personal terms. Its proposal read:

> 'Twelfth, Congress shall never disarm any Citizen unless such as are or have been in Actual Rebellion.'").

[80] *See Heller*, 554 U.S. at 657 n.22 (Stevens, J., dissenting) ("Tenth, That no standing Army shall be Kept up in time of Peace unless with the consent of three fourths of the Members of each branch of Congress, nor shall Soldiers in Time of Peace be quartered upon private Houses with out the consent of the Owners.") (citing 3 ELLIOT at 761).

[81] Proposition 7, "Right to Bear Arms," The Address and Reasons of Dissent of the Minority of the Convention of Pennsylvania to Their Constituents (Dec. 18, 1787), *reprinted in* THE CASE AGAINST THE CONSTITUTION 77 (John F. Manley & Kenneth M. Dolbeare, eds., 1987).

Advocates for a broad Second Amendment right often point to the Pennsylvania minority proposal as support for the "individual rights" view of the Amendment,[82] since it refers to "a right to bear arms for the defence of themselves and their own state." Others object that a rejected proposal put forward by a dissenting faction in a single state is slim support for such an interpretation of the right.[83]

As primary draftsmen of the Constitution and of the Second Amendment, James Madison could draw upon all of this material. He was also writing against the backdrop of the extensive gun regulations described above, and which he showed little indication of disapproving. It is notable, then, that Madison's first draft did not include the "for the defense of themselves" language from the Pennsylvania minority proposal. Instead, it employed the language from Virginia and New York: "The right of the people to keep and bear arms shall not be infringed; a well armed, and well regulated militia being the best security of a free country; but no person religiously scrupulous of bearing arms, shall be compelled to render military service in person."[84] The latter clause eventually dropped out during Senate debate, although the reason why remains lost to history. But during debates in the House, Mason's concern re emerged, as Elbridge Gerry expressed the fear that Congress "can declare who are those religiously scrupulous, and prevent them from bearing arms."[85] Perhaps this explains why the third clause was removed from Madison's original draft, and the first two rephrased and reordered, before the Second Amendment as we know it was sent to the states for ratification.

The battles over the Second Amendment's phrasing set the stage for what would be the most significant constitutional debate about the Amendment's meaning: namely, whether the right it protects is limited to militia service, or whether it encompasses private and personal uses such as self-defense against criminals. That was the question at the heart of *Heller*, and is the focus of Chapters 2 and 3.

[82] *See, e.g.*, *Heller*, 554 U.S. at 604 ("[T]he highly influential minority proposal in Pennsylvania ... with its reference to hunting, plainly referred to an individual right."); David B. Kopel & Clayton E. Cramer, *Credentials Are No Substitute for Accuracy: Nathan Kozuskanich, Stephen Halbrook, and the Role of the Historian*, 19 Widener L.J. 343, 371 (2010); Thomas B. McAffee & Michael J. Quinlan, *Bringing Forward the Right to Keep and Bear Arms: Do Text, History, or Precedent Stand in the Way?*, 75 N.C. L. Rev. 781, 847 (1997).

[83] *See, e.g.*, Paul Finkelman, *"A Well Regulated Militia": The Second Amendment in Historical Perspective*, 76 Chi.-Kent L. Rev. 195, 208 (2000).

[84] Neil Cogan, The Complete Bill of Rights: The Drafts, Debates, Sources, and Origins 263 (2015).

[85] 1 Annals of Congress 749–50 (Joseph Gales ed., 1834) (statement of Rep. Gerry). The proposal that Representative Gerry opposed provided: "A well regulated militia, composed of the body of the people, being the best security of a free state, the right of the people to keep and bear arms shall not be infringed; but no person religiously scrupulous shall compelled to bear arms." Cogan, *supra* note 84, at 169.

GEOGRAPHIC VARIATION IN THE RIGHT TO KEEP AND BEAR ARMS

Ratification of the Second Amendment made it a federal guarantee, which meant that it applied throughout the United States. But that did not mandate strict national uniformity in gun rights and regulation. For one thing, prior to *Heller*, the Second Amendment did not apply to regulation of the private use of arms – it was a national guarantee, but only for matters involving the organized militia. Moreover, as Chapter 3 explains, until the middle of the twentieth century the Bill of Rights generally did not apply to non-federal law, leaving states and cities free to strike their own balance with regard to gun rights and regulation.

The Supreme Court's 2010 decision in *McDonald v. City of Chicago*[86] changed that, by making the Second Amendment applicable to state and local regulation. And yet even federal constitutional rights can be context-sensitive, meaning that a constitutional challenge that would succeed in one place might well fail in another. For example, the First Amendment permits obscenity prosecutions in Mississippi that it would forbid in Manhattan.[87] The Fifth Amendment protects property, but property is defined by state law, which differs in important respects from state to state.[88] *Heller* itself held that governments may not ban handguns everywhere, but can prohibit them in government buildings, which tend to be concentrated in some cities (like the District of Columbia) more than others.[89]

The existence of a federal constitutional right therefore does not necessarily generate a one-size-fits-all regime of legal rights and restrictions. The history of gun regulation after ratification of the Second Amendment demonstrates how pronounced and longstanding geographic variation regarding gun rights and regulation really was.

Regional Histories

Guns have long played a prominent role in Southern culture and politics. Southerners are far more likely to grow up with guns, to use them for recreation, to oppose restrictions on their possession and use, and to profess support for the Second Amendment.[90] But like so many other elements of Southern history, the

86 561 U.S. 742 (2010).

87 Miller v. California, 413 U.S. 15, 32 (1973) ("It is neither realistic nor constitutionally sound to read the First Amendment as requiring that the people of Maine or Mississippi accept public depiction of conduct found tolerable in Las Vegas, or New York City.").

88 Bd. of Regents of State Colls. v. Roth, 408 U.S. 564, 577 (1972) ("Property interests, of course, are not created by the Constitution. Rather, they are created and their dimensions defined by existing rules or understandings that stem from an independent source such as state law....").

89 *Heller*, 554 U.S. at 626 ("[N]othing in our opinion should be taken to cast doubt on longstanding prohibitions on the possession of ... laws forbidding the carrying of firearms in sensitive places such as schools and government buildings....").

90 *See* ROBERT J. SPITZER, THE POLITICS OF GUN CONTROL 13 (1st ed., 1995) ("Those who compose and support the active gun culture are overwhelmingly white males, live in rural areas (especially in

place of guns is surprisingly complicated, and is frequently misunderstood even by the people who celebrate it the most.

On the one hand, as historian Saul Cornell and legal scholar Eric Ruben have shown, the South did embrace, albeit with variation, aspects of the right to keep and bear arms that other regions of the country rejected.[91] In particular, courts in southern states were more likely to accept the existence of a Second Amendment right to keep and bear arms in public. And yet as Cornell and Ruben point out, those cases emerge from "a time, place, and culture where slavery, honor, violence, and the public carrying of weapons were intertwined"[92] – a heritage that might not be the best candidate for contemporary constitutional respect. Moreover, there is some indication that, as a social practice, open carry was rare even in the antebellum South. As the North Carolina Supreme Court said in 1843, "[A] gun is an 'unusual weapon,' wherewith to be armed and clad. No man amongst us carries it with him ... as a part of his dress."[93] The justices went on, "[N]ever we trust will the day come when any deadly weapon will be worn or wielded in our peace loving and law-abiding State, as an appendage of manly equipment."[94]

More importantly for Second Amendment interpretation, even assuming a Southern tradition of broad public carry rights, that tradition was not followed nationwide. An alternative model permitted public carry only in certain circumstances. Massachusetts, for example, allowed a person to carry guns publicly if he had "reasonable cause to fear an assault or other injury, or violence to his person, or to his family or property"[95] – a predecessor of modern "good cause" public-carry permits. The Massachusetts statute also provided that any person publicly carrying a weapon could be arrested upon the complaint of any other person (or a justice of the peace or constable without complaint) "having reasonable cause to fear an injury, or breach of the peace."[96] Gun carriers could be required to provide "sureties for his

the South), are likely to be Protestant, and are from 'old stock.'"); David C. Williams, The Mythic Meanings of the Second Amendment: Taming Political Violence in a Constitutional Republic 175 (2003) ("[T]he gun culture has a core constituency–white, rural males with conservative values, especially in the South.").

[91] Eric M. Ruben & Saul Cornell, *Firearm Regionalism and Public Carry: Placing Southern Antebellum Case Law in Context*, 125 Yale L.J. Forum 121, 125–27 (2015).

[92] *Id.* at 125.

[93] State v. Huntly, 25 N.C. 418, 422 (1843).

[94] *Id.*

[95] Ruben & Cornell, *supra* note 91, at 133. Other jurisdictions soon adopted laws similar to Massachusetts'. *See, e.g.*, An Act to Prevent the Commission of Crimes, § 16, *reprinted in* Statutes of the Territory of Wisconsin 379, 381 (1839); Me. Rev. Stat. ch. 169, § 16 (1840), *reprinted in* The Revised Statutes of the State of Maine 707, 709 (1841); Mich. Rev. Stat., title XXXI, ch. 162, § 16, *reprinted in* The Revised Statutes of the State of Michigan 690, 692 (Stanford M. Green, ed., 1846) (all cited in Ruben & Cornell, *supra* note 91, at 132 n.61).

[96] Title II, Ch. 134, § 16, *reprinted in* The Revised Statutes of the Commonwealth of Massachusetts 748, 750 (1836) ("If any person shall go armed with a dirk, dagger, sword, pistol, or other offensive and dangerous weapon, without reasonable cause to fear an assault or other injury, or violence to his person, or to his family or property, he may, on complaint of any person having

keeping the peace"[97] – a financial guarantee, roughly akin to bail, which would be forfeited if the person failed to keep the peace.[98]

Concealed carry was a wholly different matter, both socially and legally. Even in the South, where open carry might have been more acceptable, stringent regulation of concealed carry was the norm. Although restrictions on concealed carry have roots as far back as England – recall the Statute of Northampton and its successors[99] – in the United States they first became prominent in the South. It seems plausible that such regulations were designed, at least in part, to respond to the prevalence of dueling and other "honor-restoring" types of violence.[100]

For example, in an 1850 case called *State v. Chandler*, the Louisiana Supreme Court upheld a ban on concealed carry, concluding that "the right guaranteed by the Constitution of the United States ... is calculated to incite men to a manly and noble defence of themselves, if necessary, and of their country, without any tendency to secret advantages and unmanly assassinations."[101] Some states, including Georgia and Tennessee in the 1830s, would go even farther, prohibiting the sale of certain concealable weapons.[102] By the nineteenth century, restrictions on concealed carry had spread from the South and had become so much the national norm that the Supreme Court in *Heller* – citing both historical Southern cases and national commentaries – could conclude that the majority of nineteenth century authorities considered "prohibitions on carrying concealed weapons ... lawful under the Second Amendment or state analogues."[103]

The Court's reference to "state analogues" is notable. At the time of the Founding or soon thereafter, more than a dozen states had Second Amendment analogues in

reasonable cause to fear an injury, or breach of the peace, be required to find sureties for keeping the peace...."); *see also* Acts, 1794-ch. 26 [Jan. Sess., ch. 2], *reprinted in* ACTS AND RESOLVES OF MASSACHUSETTS 1794–95, at 66–67 (1896).

97 Acts, 1794-ch. 26 [Jan. Sess., ch. 2], *reprinted in* ACTS AND RESOLVES OF MASSACHUSETTS 1794–95, at 66–67 (1896).

98 Ruben & Cornell, *supra* note 91, at 131.

99 *See supra* notes 17–28 and accompanying text.

100 *See generally* CLAYTON E. CRAMER, CONCEALED WEAPON LAWS OF THE EARLY REPUBLIC: DUELING, SOUTHERN VIOLENCE, AND MORAL REFORM (1999). *But see* Sally Hadden, Book Review, 44 AM. J. LEGAL HIST. 323, 325 (2000) (reviewing Cramer's work and concluding that while it "provides basic information about the pre-1840 laws in eight states, it remains for another scholar to dig beneath the surface and discover what truly prompted legislators in these states to pass their concealed weapons laws").

101 State v. Chandler, 5 La. Ann. 489, 490 (1850).

102 An Act to Guard and Protect the Citizens of this State, Against the Unwarrantable and Too Prevalent Use of Deadly Weapons, Act of Dec. 25, 1837, 1837 Ga. Laws 90–91 (1838); An Act to Suppress the Sale and Use of Bowie Knives and Arkansas Tooth Picks in this State, Act of Jan. 27, 1838, ch. CXXXVII, § 1, 1837–1838 Tenn. Pub. Acts 200–01 (1838).

103 *Heller*, 554 U.S. at 626. Notably, some of the national commentaries relied entirely on Southern cases. *See, e.g.*, THOMAS MCINTYRE COOLEY, A TREATISE ON THE CONSTITUTIONAL LIMITATIONS WHICH REST UPON THE LEGISLATIVE POWER OF THE STATES OF THE AMERICAN UNION 350 (1868) (reprint 1972).

their own constitutions.[104] But those analogues were adopted simultaneously with sometimes-extensive regulation of guns.[105] And in keeping with that early practice, nearly all states today guarantee some version of the right to keep and bear arms in their state constitutions,[106] though the overwhelming majority also conclude that the right is subject to "reasonable" regulation.[107]

The Wild West and the Urban–Rural Divide

On a chilly October afternoon in 1881, Wyatt Earp was walking outside the courthouse in Tombstone, Arizona, when he bumped into Tom McLaury, a member of the "Cowboys" gang.[108] The Cowboys were notorious for cattle rustling, horse-thieving, heavy drinking, and threatening the Earps, with whom they had a bitter feud. What escalated the conflict on that particular afternoon, and precipitated one of the most famous shoot-outs in American history, was a gun regulation. Tombstone required visitors without a license to deposit their pistols at their destination – a regulation far stricter than that found anywhere in the United States today.[109] Wyatt, who

[104] McDonald v. City of Chicago, 561 U.S. 742, 769 (2010) (plurality opinion) (referring to "the four States that had adopted Second Amendment analogues before ratification, [and] nine more States [that] adopted state constitutional provisions protecting an individual right to keep and bear arms between 1789 and 1820").

[105] *Id.* at 870 n.13 (Stevens, J., dissenting); *id.* at 930 (Breyer, J., dissenting) (noting that "many States have constitutional provisions protecting gun possession" but that "those provisions typically do no more than guarantee that a gun regulation will be a reasonable police power regulation").

[106] Eugene Volokh, *State Constitutional Rights to Keep and Bear Arms*, 11 TEX. REV. L. & POL. 191, 192, 206–07 tbl.1 (2006) (noting that forty-four states recognize an individual right to bear arms).

[107] Adam Winkler, *Scrutinizing the Second Amendment*, 105 MICH. L. REV. 683, 687 (2007). In some states, there has been a push (usually pursued through ballot initiatives) to require strict scrutiny of all gun regulations. How far those laws will be adopted and whether they will have much legal impact remains to be seen. *See* Paul Purpura, *Gun Law That Excludes Felons is Upheld by Louisiana Supreme Court*, NOLA.com (July 1, 2014) www.nola.com/crime/index.ssf/2014/07/louisiana_supreme_court_uphold_4.html (noting that Louisiana's felon-in-possession law survived a constitutional challenge even after that state's adoption of a strict scrutiny amendment).

[108] The material in this subsection is taken from Blocher, *supra* note 47, at 84.

[109] There is some discrepancy in the wording of the ordinance. Paul Lee Johnson has identified it as stating as follows:

Section 1: It is hereby declared to be unlawful to carry, in the hand or upon the person, or otherwise, any deadly weapon within the limits of said city of Tombstone, without first obtaining a permit in writing for such a purpose (and upon good cause shown by affidavit) from the presiding officer of the Board of Police Commissioners.

Section 2: This prohibition does not extend to persons immediately entering or leaving said city, who in good faith and within reasonable time are proceeding to deposit, or to take from the place of deposit such deadly weapons.

Section 3: All firearms of every description and bowie knives and dirks, are included within the prohibition of this ordinance.

claimed to be acting as a deputy marshall on behalf of his brother Virgil, demanded, "Are you heeled or not?" McLaury denied that he was, though the gun visible at his hip indicated otherwise. Wyatt drew his own gun and beat McLaury with it.

A few hours later, the Earps and their men confronted the Cowboys on Fremont Street, not far from the OK Corral. Virgil was present this time, and upon seeing the Cowboys he shouted, "Throw up your hands, I want your guns!" One or both parties drew their guns and Virgil quickly added, "Hold! I don't mean that!" but his words were followed by a barrage of shots from all sides. As the smoke cleared, Wyatt was unhurt, but Virgil and Morgan were wounded, as was their associate Doc Holliday. Tom McLaury, his brother Frank, and Billy Clanton were all dead or dying.

The legend of the OK Corral is familiar enough, but the gun regulation at its center is not. This is a significant omission, because laws like Tombstone's demonstrate the existence of gun regulation even in places where people might least expect to find it. Some places most associated with guns – Dodge City and Tombstone among them – required people to disarm when arriving in town.[110] Many frontier towns passed "blanket ordinances against the carrying of arms by anyone," and generally prohibited the "carrying of dangerous weapons of any type, concealed or otherwise, by persons other than law enforcement officers."[111] Pointing to these prohibitions, historian Garry Wills concludes that "[t]he West was not settled by the gun but by gun-control laws."[112]

Wills' use of the word "settled" is significant, for guns were far more prevalent, and far less regulated, outside of settlements – continuing the theme, noticeable as far back as the Statute of Northampton, of regulating guns more strictly within city limits. As Winkler describes it: "Guns were widespread on the frontier, but so was gun regulation."[113] He continues, "[a]lmost everyone carried firearms in the untamed wilderness, which was full of dangerous Natives, outlaws, and bears. In the frontier towns, however, where people lived and businesses operated, the law often forbade people from toting their guns around."[114]

Robert Dykstra describes instances of zealous enforcement of urban gun control laws in the West,[115] and Robert Spitzer similarly concludes that "[e]ven in

Section 4: Any person or persons violating the provisions of this ordinance shall be deemed guilty of a misdemeanor, and on conviction thereof shall be fined in a sum not to exceed two hundred and fifty dollars and costs, or imprisonment in the city jail for a period not to exceed five months, or both at the discretion of the court.

Section 5: That this ordinance shall take effect and be in force from and after due publication.

See Paul Lee Johnson, The McLaurys in Tombstone, Arizona: An O.K. Corral Obituary 323 n.18 (2012). Other writers have identified versions of the regulation without the section on affidavits.

[110] Winkler, *supra* note 42, at 13.

[111] Robert R. Dykstra, The Cattle Towns 121 (1968).

[112] Garry Wills, Reagan's America: Innocents at Home 89 (1987).

[113] Winkler, *supra* note 42, at 165 (*citing* Dykstra, *supra* note 111, at 121).

[114] *Id.*

[115] Dykstra, *supra* note 111, at 137 (describing, for example, the nearly one-hundred arrests in 1873 alone in Ellsworth, Texas).

the most violence-prone towns, the western cattle towns, vigilantism and lawlessness were only briefly tolerated .... Prohibitions against carrying guns were strictly enforced, and there were few homicides."[116] David Courtwright concludes that the laws became better enforced in the 1880s and 1890s, because "[a]s the threat of Indians and outlaws receded and the regular police system gradually became more professional and efficient, it was harder to justify carrying personal weapons for self-defense."[117]

In other words, as functioning governance emerged, the need and tolerance for private gun use decreased. This was not solely a frontier phenomenon, but was reflected in law nationwide. Some states made it illegal to fire weapons within the limits of a city or town – a rule that existed in the colonial era,[118] and extended to the antebellum period[119] and after.[120] Some of these laws were extremely specific about their geographic reach. One 1866 Texas statute, for example, provided in part:

> It shall not be lawful for any person to discharge any gun, pistol, or fire arms of any description whatever, on, or across any public square, street, or alley, in any city or town in this State; Provided, this Act shall not be so construed as to apply to the "outer town," or suburbs, of any city or town.[121]

Other laws flatly prohibited the carrying of nearly any weapon within towns, cities, villages, and settlements.[122]

The not-so-wild Western towns are representative of a broader trend that continues today. Indeed, perhaps no characteristic of gun laws in the United States is as longstanding as the stricter regulation of guns in cities than in rural areas. The

[116] SPITZER, *supra* note 90, at 11.

[117] DAVID T. COURTWRIGHT, THE COWBOY SUBCULTURE, *in* GUNS IN AMERICA: A READER 86, 96 (Jan E. Dizard, Robert Merrill Muth, & Stephen P. Andrews, Jr., eds., 1999).

[118] *E.g.*, An Act to Prevent the Firing of Guns Charged with Shot or Ball in the Town of Boston, ch. X, § 2, 1746 Mass. Acts 208; An Act for the More Effectual Preventing Accidents Which May Happen by Fire, and for Suppressing Idleness, Drunkenness, and Other Debaucheries, 1750 Pa. Laws 208.

[119] *E.g.*, An Act Prohibiting the Firing of Guns and Other Fire Arms in the City of New Haven, 1845 Conn. Pub. Acts 10; An Act to Prevent the Discharging of Fire-Arms Within the Towns and Villages, and Other Places Within this State, and for Other Purposes, § 1, 4 Del. Laws 329; An Act to Incorporate the Town of Baltimore, Hickman County, § 10, 1856 Ky. Acts 139.

[120] *E.g.*, An Act to Prevent the Shooting or Firing of Guns or Pistols in the Village of Vineville, in the County of Bibb § 1, 1875 Ga. Laws 189; An Act to Prevent Parties from Shooting Within the Limits of Towns and Private Enclosures, § 1, 1873 Mont. Laws 46; Lincoln, Neb., Gen. Ordinances art. 26, § 1 (1895).

[121] *E.g.*, An Act to Prohibit the Discharging of Fire Arms in Certain Places Therein Named, ch. 170, § 1, 1866 Tex. Gen. Laws 210.

[122] Wyoming, for example, forbade any resident or sojourner bearing "concealed or openly, any fire arm or other deadly weapon, within the limits of any city, town or village." 1876 Wyo. Sess. Laws 352, § 1. Other jurisdictions had similar provisions. *E.g.*, Crimes Against the Public Peace, § 385 & 390, 1901 Ariz. Sess. Laws 1251–52; *id.* § 390; An Act Regulating the Use and Carrying of Deadly Weapons in Idaho Territory, § 1, 1888 Idaho Sess. Laws 23; Act of Jan. 14, 1853, §1, N.M. Laws 67; An Act to Regulate the Keeping and Bearing of Deadly Weapons, § 1, 1871 Tex. Gen. Laws 25.

geographic tailoring of gun regulation has remained largely consistent for more than two centuries. The recent spread of state "preemption" statutes, which limit the ability of municipal governments to pass their own gun control laws, breaks from that tradition and limits the degree of local variation.[123] But it is no accident that the Supreme Court's major gun cases – *Heller* and *McDonald*, addressed in the next two chapters – both involved municipal gun regulation.

RACE, GUNS, AND THE CIVIL WAR

Gun rights and regulation have always been deeply intertwined with America's original sin, slavery, and its legacy of racial oppression.[124] But the relationship between guns and race is more nuanced than it might seem. Guns were used to keep African Americans powerless, but African Americans and their allies also used them in the struggle for freedom and equality. Likewise, some gun regulations, even racially neutral ones, were sometimes used to render African Americans defenseless against public and private harms. But the relevance of this historical fact is a source of deep disagreement – striking down regulations based on their tainted origins could make guns more available to members of "outgroups," but the lack of regulations could contribute to gun violence in those same communities.[125] What cannot be gainsaid is that the histories of guns and race in the United States are inextricable.

Critics of strong gun rights have occasionally suggested that the Second Amendment was ratified at the behest of slaveowners. One recent article argued that "the real reason the Second Amendment was ratified, and why it says 'State' instead of 'Country'" was that the Framers wanted "to preserve the slave patrol militias in the southern states, which was necessary to get Virginia's vote."[126] This

[123] Jon S. Vernick & Lisa M. Hepburn, *State and Federal Gun Law: Trends for 1970–99*, *in* EVALUATING GUN POLICY: EFFECTS ON CRIME AND VIOLENCE 345, 349 (Jens Ludwig & Philip J. Cook, eds., 2003).

[124] See Robert J. Cottrol & Raymond T. Diamond, *The Second Amendment: Toward an Afro-Americanist Reconsideration*, 80 GEO. L.J. 309, 336–38 (1991) (detailing antebellum Southern restrictions on African Americans' use and ownership of guns); *id.* at 344–46 (describing Southern legislative attempts, as part of the "black codes," to disarm newly freed slaves by forbidding them from carrying firearms without a license).

[125] David C. Williams, *Constitutional Tales of Violence: Populists, Outgroups, and the Multicultural Landscape of the Second Amendment*, 74 TUL. L. REV. 387, 390 (1999) ("Outgroup self-arming may in the short term provide a measure of safety, but in the long run, interpreting the Constitution to require decentralized violence will impede the formation of a consensus culture that extends protection to all.").

[126] Thom Hartmann, *The Second Amendment was Ratified to Preserve Slavery*, TRUTHOUT (Jan. 15, 2013), www.truth-out.org/news/item/13890-the-second-amendment-was-ratified-to-preserve-slavery; *see also* Carl T. Bogus, *The Hidden History of the Second Amendment*, 31 U.C. DAVIS L. REV. 309, 318, 321 (1998) (arguing that the Second Amendment "was written to assure the Southern states that Congress would not undermine the slave system by using its newly acquired constitutional authority over the militia to disarm the state militia and thereby destroy the South's principal interest of slave control").

is unlikely.[127] At most, it could be said that the militia was intended to put down rebellions, whether that be a slave revolt in the South or Shays' Rebellion in the North.

But the fact that slave patrols were not the focus of the Amendment does not mean that they were irrelevant. Winkler notes that "[i]n the South, militias were transformed into slave patrols."[128] John Hope Franklin observed that "in most instances there was a substantial connection between the [slave] patrol and the militia, either through the control of one by the other or through identity of personnel."[129] The Fugitive Slave Act arising from the Compromise of 1850 explicitly gave slaveowners the right to organize posses to recapture runaway slaves and obliged law enforcement officers to assist them.[130]

Those patrols are deeply connected to the state-sponsored violence of the Reconstruction era, and are often identified as the ancestors of the Ku Klux Klan.[131] A Mississippi law, for example, required confiscation of black-owned guns – a process enforced by civil and military authorities. A *Harper's Weekly* article from 1866 describes the scene: "The militia of this county have seized every gun and pistol found in the hands of the (so called) freedmen .... They claim that the statute laws of Mississippi do not recognize the negro as having any right to carry arms."[132] White hostility to African American gun ownership may have helped precipitate one of the most egregious examples of Klan violence in history, an outbreak of terror in South Carolina so severe that the President suspended the right to habeas corpus and sent in the military.[133] Klan members defended these and other outrages on the basis that they were simply doing what they had always done – organized themselves into "self-defense" groups,[134] a "peace police" to maintain order.[135] (We discuss the impact of Reconstruction on Second Amendment rights in more detail in Chapter 3.)

[127] Paul Finkelman, *2nd Amendment Passed to Protect Slavery? No!*, THE ROOT (Jan. 21, 2013), www.theroot.com/articles/politics/2013/01/second_amendment_slave_control_not_the_aim/.

[128] WINKLER, *supra* note 42, at 133.

[129] JOHN HOPE FRANKLIN, THE MILITANT SOUTH 1800–1861, at 73 (2002).

[130] Fugitive Slave Act, 9 Stat. 462 (1850) (repealed 1864).

[131] SALLY E. HADDEN, SLAVE PATROLS, LAW AND VIOLENCE IN VIRGINIA AND THE CAROLINAS 3–4; 211–12 (2001).

[132] Laws of Mississippi, 1865 p. 165 [Nov. 29, 1865] *reprinted in* 1 DOCUMENTARY HISTORY OF RECONSTRUCTION 289–90 (Walter L. Fleming, ed., 1906); HARPER'S WEEKLY, Jan. 13, 1866, at 19, col. 2 (cited in *Peruta*, 742 F.3d at 1161–62).

[133] *See* Proceedings in the Ku Klux Trials at Columbia, S.C. in the United States Circuit Court, November Term, 1871, at 151 (Ben Pitman & Louis Freeland Post, eds., 1872); Rep. John Scott, Report of the Joint Select Committee to Inquire into the Condition of Affairs in the Late Insurrectionary States, H.R. Rep. No. 42-41, pt. 1, at 426 (1872) (minority report); *see also* Amanda L. Tyler, *Suspension as an Emergency Power*, 118 YALE L.J. 600, 655–61 (2009).

[134] Proceedings in the Ku Klux Trials at Columbia, S.C. in the United States Circuit Court, November Term, 1871, at 426 (Ben Pitman & Louis Freeland Post, eds., 1872).

[135] Hearing Before the Select Committee To Inquire into the Condition of Affairs in the Late Insurrectionary States (1871) (statement of John B. Gordon), *reprinted in* RECONSTRUCTION (1865–77) at 98, 99, 101 (Richard N. Current, ed., 1965) (discussing the Klan in Georgia).

And yet armed groups also fought for black protection and power. Famous uprisings like those of Denmark Vesey in 1822 and Nat Turner in 1831 did not rely on firearms so much as knives, axes, and repurposed farm tools.[136] But the 1739 Stono Rebellion in the then-colony of South Carolina did.[137] And perhaps the most famous antislavery uprising of all was totally focused on guns, and it was led by a white, wild-eyed zealot who shot into American law and politics like a meteor.

American history has produced few characters quite like John Brown.[138] In 1837, following the murder of abolitionist Elijah Lovejoy by pro-slavery forces, Brown made a public vow: "Here, before God, in the presence of these witnesses, from this time, I consecrate my life to the destruction of slavery!" He was a man who took such things seriously, and he honored his vow to its dramatic and bloody end. Frederick Douglass later wrote, "His zeal in the cause of my race was far greater than mine – it was as the burning sun to my taper light – mine was bounded by time, his stretched away to the boundless shores of eternity. I could live for the slave, but he could die for him."[139] And indeed, wherever John Brown went, death was quick to follow.

In 1855, he set out for Kansas, which had become central to the political (and soon literal) battles over slavery, thanks to the emergence of "popular sovereignty" as a supposed middle road on the slavery question. The Missouri Compromise of 1820 had forbidden slavery in many of the territories soon to be admitted to the United States, including Kansas.[140] But in 1854, Congress passed the Kansas-Nebraska Act, which provided that the people of a territory should be able to decide for themselves whether to permit slavery within their borders.[141]

Eager to pack the polls for the defining moment, abolitionist "free staters" and pro-slavery forces rushed to Kansas, swelling the population with factions who were both called "Jayhawks," after a quarrelsome local bird. What followed is known, thanks to Horace Greeley's turn of phrase, as the era of "bleeding Kansas" – a political conflict whose bitterness demonstrated the difficulty, and eventual futility, of a compromise on slavery.[142]

[136] *See, e.g.*, WINTHROP D. JORDAN, TUMULT AND SILENCE AT SECOND CREEK: AN INQUIRY INTO A CIVIL WAR SLAVE CONSPIRACY (1993).

[137] *See* PETER CHARLES HOFFER, CRY LIBERTY: THE GREAT STONO RIVER SLAVE REBELLION OF 1739, at 83 (2010).

[138] DAVID S. REYNOLDS, JOHN BROWN, ABOLITIONIST: THE MAN WHO KILLED SLAVERY, SPARKED THE CIVIL WAR, AND SEEDED CIVIL RIGHTS ix (2009) ("[John Brown] can be said to have killed slavery ... [and] 'kill' is an apt word for Brown, who went to murderous extremes, unlike other abolitionists, most of whom were pacifists who disavowed violence.").

[139] Frederick Douglass, John Brown. An Address by Frederick Douglass at the Fourteenth Anniversary of Storer College, Harper's Ferry, West Virginia, May 30, 1881 (2010) (ebook).

[140] *See* (Missouri Enabling Acts) Act of Mar. 6, 1820, ch. 22, § 8, 3 Stat. 545–58.

[141] Kansas-Nebraska Act, ch. 59, 10 Stat. 277 (1854).

[142] *See* JAMES A. RAWLEY, RACE & POLITICS: "BLEEDING KANSAS" AND THE COMING OF THE CIVIL WAR vii (1969).

The battle was not solely political, and the blood was not just metaphorical. The abolitionist preacher Henry Ward Beecher reportedly said "You might just as well read the Bible to Buffaloes" as argue scripture to the pro-slavery crowd, but that "they have a supreme respect for the logic that is embodied in Sharp's rifle."[143] Soon thereafter, Kansas's abolitionists started receiving cartons full of Sharp's rifles, known affectionately as "Beecher's Bibles."

Arming slaves and free blacks was another matter entirely. No state specifically guaranteed African Americans a right to keep and bear arms,[144] and many states – especially in the South – forbade blacks from possessing guns and threatened criminal sanctions against those who sold them weapons.[145] The intersection of race, fear, and guns is nothing new, after all; similar laws at the time of the Founding criminalized the sale of guns to Native Americans.[146]

When John Brown arrived, Kansas was not yet "bleeding," having suffered only eight deaths from slavery-related violence in the previous two years.[147] Setting up in the vicinity of Pottawatomie Creek, Brown obtained what he took to be reliable evidence that his family was to be attacked by pro-slavery forces.[148] As is sometimes the case in incidents of armed self-defense, there is reason to believe that Brown exaggerated or over-estimated the threat.[149] In any event, he and seven associates acted first, and on the night of May 24, 1856, took five pro-slavery settlers from their cabins and murdered them with broadswords. After the Massacre at Pottawatomie Creek, bleeding Kansas truly did live up to the name: Twenty-nine people would die in the next four months alone.[150]

Of course, the numbers of Kansans who died during the struggle over slavery would soon be overshadowed by the staggering casualties of the Civil War, which

[143] Kansas Historical Society, *Beecher Bibles* (Jan. 2013), www.kshs.org/kansapedia/beecher-bibles/11977 (quoting Feb. 8, 1856 article from the *New York Tribune*).

[144] *See* Cottrol & Diamond, *supra* note 124, at 335–42.

[145] *Id.* at 336 ("To forestall the possibility that free blacks would rebel either on their own or with slaves, the southern states limited not only the right of slaves, but also the right of free blacks, to bear arms.").

[146] *See, e.g.*, Act XXIII (1642–43), *in* 1 The Statutes at Large: Being a Collection of All the Laws of Virginia from the First Session of the Legislature, in the Year 1619, at 255 (William Waller Hening, ed., New York, R. & W. & G. Bartow, 2nd ed., 1823) (Virginia law banning sale or barter of "powder and shott" with "Indians"); An Act for Regulating the Indian Trade and Making it Safe to the Publick, No. 269, § IV (1707), *in* 2 The Statutes at Large of South Carolina 310 (Thomas Cooper, ed., Columbia, A.S. Johnston, 1837) (banning sale, gift, or other disposition of arms and ammunition to any "Indians" who are "open enemies" of South Carolina).

[147] Dale E. Watts, *How Bloody Was Bleeding Kansas?*, 18(2) Kansas History: A Journal of the Central Plains 116 (1995).

[148] David S. Reynolds, John Brown, Abolitionist: The Man Who Killed Slavery, Sparked the Civil War, and Seeded Civil Rights 95 (2005).

[149] Free-State Leader Charles Robinson would later write that "such threats were as plenty as blue-berries in June, on both sides, all over the Territory, and were regarded as of no more importance than the idle wind, this indictment will hardly justify midnight assassination of all pro-slavery men, whether making threats or not." Charles Robinson, The Kansas Conflict 274 (1898).

[150] Watts, *supra* note 147, at 127–28.

John Brown anticipated and helped incite.[151] Having made his way back East, Brown developed a plan to seize the arsenal at Harper's Ferry, Virginia, and thence to move with a mixed-race militia throughout the South, inducing slaves to desert their plantations and disrupt the region's economy. Bringing bleeding Kansas to the rest of the country in a tangible way, Brown and his co-conspirators were armed in October 1859 with 200 Beecher's Bibles sent by abolitionists. Douglass himself was sympathetic to the cause, but not to the plan, which he actively tried to discourage.[152]

The first victim of Brown's plan – the baggage master of a passing train, who tried to alert others of the raid – was, ironically enough, a free black man. Brown and his men took the arsenal at Harper's Ferry with relative ease, but they could not defend it, and the reinforcements they hoped would emerge from among the local slave population never appeared, leaving them trapped inside. The raid would lead to the deaths of everyone involved, to say nothing of the 600,000 casualties in the war that followed. Brown himself likely would have accepted – even welcomed – all of this death as a necessary corrective for the nation's original sin. But he would not be there to see it. He was captured by a force headed by Lieutenant Colonel Robert E. Lee of the United States Army. And on December 2, 1859, proclaiming that "the crimes of this guilty land will never be purged away but with blood," John Brown was hanged. In the crowd, wearing a borrowed uniform, was a young actor named John Wilkes Booth.

Of course, Brown's raid was only one of the many events that contributed to the Civil War. The Supreme Court itself also played a role. In *Dred Scott v. Sandford*, perhaps the most notorious opinion in Supreme Court history, Chief Justice Roger Taney concluded that those of African descent were not and could never become citizens. Indeed, they "had no rights which the white man was bound to respect."[153] To hold otherwise, the Chief Justice suggested, would mean recognizing that blacks would have a right "to keep and carry arms wherever they went"[154] – a prospect so self-evidently unacceptable to him that it was treated as a basis for the decision.

Dred Scott helped cause the greatest military conflagration the nation has yet seen; a war that claimed roughly as many American lives as all other American wars combined.[155] The four years of the Civil War forced Americans to confront guns,

[151] REYNOLDS, *supra* note 148, at 95–96 ("No single person came closer than Brown to anticipating the war. True, others had predicted war .... But John Brown not only predicted war; he made war.").

[152] For an overview of the historical debate surrounding Douglass's role in Brown's plan, see Theodore Hamm, *When Frederick Douglass Met John Brown*, JACOBIN (Jan. 11, 2017), www.jacobinmag.com/2017/01/harpers-ferry-john-brown-frederick-douglass/. *See also* Steven Lubet, *Execution in Virginia, 1859: The Trials of Green and Copeland*, 91 N.C. L. REV. 1785, 1787 (2013).

[153] Dred Scott v. Sandford, 60 U.S. 393, 407 (1856).

[154] *Id.* at 417.

[155] Civil War Trust, *Civil War Facts*, www.civilwar.org/learn/articles/civil-war-facts (accessed Jan. 5, 2018) ("Roughly 1,264,000 American soldiers have died in the nation's wars – 620,000 in the Civil War and 644,000 in all other conflicts.").

gun violence, and death in ways they had never done before.[156] Walt Whitman, who had written rhapsodically of the "body electric" before the war,[157] served in Civil War hospitals for as long as he could stand it, and soon found himself describing "a heap of feet, legs, arms, and human fragments, cut, bloody, black and blue, swelled and sickening."[158] The experience would haunt him for the rest of his life. A young Union soldier named Oliver Wendell Holmes, Jr. was wounded three times by gunfire, but would later write of how "the generation that carried on the war has been set apart by its experience. Through our great good fortune, in our youth our hearts were touched with fire."[159]

In April 1865, the war was winding down. Less than a week after Robert E. Lee surrendered to Ulysses S. Grant at Appomattox, one of the most famous gunshots in American history was fired at Ford's Theatre in Washington, D.C. The single-shot, six-inch long Derringer that John Wilkes Booth slipped from his pocket was the 1860s version of the concealable weapons that the law had so long regulated, going back to the "Dagges" barred by English monarchs centuries before. The bullet found its mark, and President Lincoln died hours later. About ten days after that, Joseph Johnston surrendered to William Tecumseh Sherman at Bennett Place in Durham, North Carolina, the largest surrender of Confederate troops in the Civil War.

As a constitutional matter, the end of the war brought about revolutionary change. The ratification of the Thirteenth, Fourteenth, and Fifteenth Amendments altered forever the legal relationships between citizens of different races, between them and their government, and between the states and the federal government. But a system of oppression as deeply entrenched as slavery would not go gently. The years following the war saw a spike in racist violence – with implicit and sometimes explicit support from many state and local officials – and the passage of the Black Codes, which denied African Americans even the most basic civil rights, including the right to keep and bear arms. To take just one example, in 1865, Mississippi adopted an "Act to Regulate the Relation of Master and Apprentice Relative to Freedman, Free Negroes, and Mulattoes." The law provided, in relevant part, that "no freedman, free negro or mulatto ... shall keep or carry fire-arms of any kind, or any ammunition, dirk or bowie knife" and that "any freedman, free negro or mulatto found with any such arms or ammunition" could be arrested.[160]

[156] *See generally* Drew Gilpin Faust, This Republic of Suffering: Death and the American Civil War (2009).

[157] Walt Whitman, *I Sing The Body Electric*, *in* Leaves of Grass: The Original 1855 Edition 77–81 (2007).

[158] Randall Fuller, *"Daybreak Gray and Dim": How the Civil War Changed Walt Whitman's Poetry*, 32:1 Humanities, at 20 (Jan./Feb. 2011).

[159] Oliver Wendell Holmes, Jr., Memorial Day Address (May 30, 1884), *reprinted in* The Essential Holmes: Selections from the Letters, Speeches, Judicial Opinions, and Other Writings of Oliver Wendell Holmes, Jr. 86 (Richard A. Posner, ed., 1992).

[160] Laws of Mississippi, 1865 p. 165 [Nov. 29, 1865] *reprinted in* 1 Documentary History of Reconstruction 289–90 (Walter L. Fleming ed., 1906).

In part because of laws like Mississippi's, freedmen could not confidently bear arms in defense of themselves and their communities. But, after the War, the right to keep and bear arms was now officially – if not practically – theirs in a way it had never been before.[161] In January 1866, Union General Daniel Sickles was responsible for overseeing the administration of South Carolina, where the first shots of the Civil War had been fired and where full reconciliation with the Union was, as a practical matter, nowhere on the horizon. To call Sickles a colorful character is something of an understatement. Before the war, he shot and killed his wife's lover (who happened to be Francis Scott Key's son and the District Attorney of the District of Columbia) and evaded jail time through the first successful invocation of the temporary insanity defense in American history.[162] He was wounded by cannon fire at Gettysburg and lost a leg, which he donated to the Army Medical Museum and visited regularly thereafter.

Sickles did not command troops again during the war, but he did eventually serve as Commander of the Department of South Carolina and took significant steps to curb the rampant abuse of freedmen. That abuse included their forcible disarmament, which helped inspire Sickles' famous General Order No 1. It stated in relevant part that "[t]he constitutional rights of all loyal and well-disposed inhabitants to bear arms, will not be infringed," though such a guarantee neither permitted "the unlawful practice of carrying concealed weapons" nor authorized "any person to enter with arms on the premises of another against his consent."[163] Later, Sickles issued Order No. 7, which specified that "[o]rganizations of white or colored persons bearing arms, or intended to be armed, not belonging to the military ... will not be allowed to assemble, parade, patrol, drill, make arrests or exercise any authority."[164] Sickles' actions thus simultaneously recognized the existence of the right to keep and bear arms and the necessity of regulation.

That same year, the Freedmen's Bureau Act of 1866 proclaimed that freedmen should have "full and equal benefit of all laws and proceedings conceding personal liberty, security, and the acquisition, enjoyment, and disposition of estate, real and personal, including the constitutional right to bear arms."[165] These developments fell far short of guaranteeing African Americans the same rights enjoyed by whites. As with every other constitutional right, achieving anything like an equal right to keep and bear arms would take generations' more work.

[161] Akhil Reed Amar, The Bill of Rights: Creation and Reconstruction 266 (1998) ("In short, between 1775 and 1866 the poster boy of arms morphed from the Concord minuteman to the Carolina freedman.").

[162] William Barclay Napton, The Union on Trial: The Political Journals of Judge William Barclay Napton, 1829–83 at 501 n.117 (Christopher Phillips & Jason L. Pendleton, eds., 2005).

[163] Cong. Globe, 39th Cong., 1st Sess. 908 (Feb. 17, 1866) (Rep. William Lawrence) (quoting Sickles' order).

[164] 1 Walter L. Fleming, Documentary History of Reconstruction 211 (1906) (reprinting sections I and III of General Order No. 7).

[165] 14 Stat. 173 §14 (July 16, 1866)

In the United States, the fractures have largely broken along racial lines, but the same logic applies to other "outgroups" whether based on gender, sexual identity, or religion – recall Sir John Knight. Incidents like John Brown's raid and the Klan trials also demonstrate a central tension that still animates the gun debate. Guns in the wrong hands are powerful instruments of violence and oppression. But guns in the right hands can be effective means of self-defense and perhaps even liberation. Accommodating such costs and benefits has always been a central challenge for gun regulation.

THE BEGINNINGS OF MODERN GUN REGULATION

Some of the forms of gun regulation discussed thus far – safe storage for gun powder, race-based restrictions, and the like – seem like anachronisms. Others have stood the test of time with very little change. North Carolina still enforces the Statute of Northampton, basically as it was written in 1328.[166] Still, gun regulations have evolved as the objects of those regulations have changed and become more powerful. Robert Spitzer has shown, for example, that laws banning what are often called "assault weapons" became prevalent in the 1920s and 1930s, precisely at the time that automatic and semi-automatic firing technology became more common.[167]

In 1911, New York adopted the Sullivan Dangerous Weapons Act, named after Tammany Hall politician "Big" Tim Sullivan. The Sullivan Act, which is still on the books, placed a variety of restrictions on firearms, for example prohibiting their gift or sale to anyone under the age of sixteen. (Current federal law imposes a similar restriction on federal firearm licensees, forbidding them to sell rifles to anyone under the age of eighteen, or handguns to anyone under the age of twenty-one.[168]) The most important provision, however, required anyone wishing to own a handgun to first obtain a permit.[169] Those permits, in turn, were to be granted at the discretion

[166] *See, e.g.*, State v. Dawson, 272 N.C. 535, 541–42 (1968) (describing common law offense of "going armed with unusual and dangerous weapons to the terror of the people," and citing the Statute of Northampton and Sir John Knight's case); *see also* Virginia Bridges, *A Durham Man Brought a Semi-Automatic Rifle to a Rumored KKK rally. Did He Break the Law?*, THE HERALD SUN, Sept. 6, 2017, News Section; Dahlia Lithwick & Olivia Li, *Can You Bring a Gun to a Protest?*, SLATE MAGAZINE (Oct. 17, 2017), www.slate.com/articles/news_and_politics/jurisprudence/2017/10/protests_might_be_on_place_you_can't_carry_guns.html ("In North Carolina, officers and prosecutors are finding plenty of modern-day applications for the law, ringing charges for 'going armed to the terror of the public' 344 times last year.").

[167] Robert Spitzer, *America Used to Be Good at Gun Control*, N.Y. TIMES (Oct. 3, 2017), www.nytimes.com/2017/10/03/opinion/automatic-weapons-laws.html.

[168] 18 U.S.C. 922(x).

[169] *See* Sullivan Dangerous Weapons Act, 1911 N.Y. Laws ch. 195, sec. 1, § 1897 (codified as amended at N.Y. Penal Law §§ 265.01(l), 265.20(a)(3)) ("Any person over the age of sixteen years, who shall have in his possession in any city … any pistol, revolver or other firearm of a size that which may be concealed upon the person, without a written license … shall be guilty of a misdemeanor.").

of local police, and a 1913 amendment to the Act specified that one must first show a proper cause for doing so.[170]

The discretionary permitting scheme embodied in the Sullivan Act is emblematic of a regime that preserves local discretion to grant or deny licenses for certain forms of public carrying. This basic model, with analogues reaching back to Edward I's England and Tombstone, Arizona, quickly spread throughout the country. In 1923, the US Revolver Association proposed the first "model" gun regulation: the Revolver Act, which included a permit requirement for concealed carry.[171] The Act had other important provisions as well – some of which are features of modern gun regulation – for example, imposing harsher sentences for crimes committed with handguns and a one-day waiting period for a handgun purchase.

But over the past few decades, most states have loosened their laws, so that "shall issue," or even no licensing requirement at all, is the law of the land in more than forty states. In the remaining states, including highly populated ones such as California and New York, permit requirements are the subject of a great deal of Second Amendment litigation.[172] But *all* states make permits available in one way or another.[173]

The Federal Government Gets Involved

Although the debate over gun rights, gun regulation, and the Second Amendment is national in scope, gun regulation is and has always been primarily a matter of state and local law. The colonial era Militia Act imposed federal rules regarding the ownership and use of arms, but it was not until the 1930s that the federal government really became involved in the regulation of guns for public safety. In part, this reflects the general growth in the scope and power of the federal government – a trend that would continue throughout the twentieth century, particularly with regard to criminal law.[174] But it is also a story of gun-specific historical contingencies

[170] Kachalsky v. Cty. of Westchester, 701 F.3d 81, 85 (2d. Cir. 2012).

[171] The United States Revolver Association Act also contained a "good cause" requirement for the issuance of such a concealed carry license. 35th Conference Handbook of the National Conference on Uniform State Laws and Proceedings of the Annual Meeting 890 (1925). WINKLER, *supra* note 42, at 207 ("Under [the Revolver Act] proposal, civilians would have to obtain a permit to carry a concealed weapon."). The USRA Model Act was soon adopted by the national conference of commissioners on uniform state laws as the Uniform Firearms Act.

[172] *See, e.g.*, Peruta v. Cty. of San Diego, 824 F.3d 919, 927 (9th Cir. 2016) (en banc) (upholding permit requirement); Woollard v. Gallagher, 712 F.3d 865, 868 (4th Cir. 2013) (same); Kachalsky v. Cty. of Westchester, 701 F.3d 81, 85 (2d. Cir. 2012) (same).

[173] Diana Gleason, 2015 *Update: Can I Bring My Gun? A Fifty State Survey of Firearm Laws Impacting Policies Prohibiting Handguns in Public Libraries*, SOCIAL SCIENCE RESEARCH NETWORK (2015), http://papers.ssrn.com/sol3/papers.cfm?abstract_id=2605937 (see figure 1 showing chart of state open- and concealed-carry laws, indicating that permits are available in all states).

[174] Sara Sun Beale, Essay, *The Many Faces of Overcriminalization: From Morals and Mattress Tags to Overfederalization*, 54 AM. U. L. REV. 747, 755 (2005).

and politics, as well as the unintended consequences of another federal intervention into criminal law: Prohibition.

In 1919, the Eighteenth Amendment was ratified, outlawing the manufacture, sale, and transportation of "intoxicating liquors." It would be repealed just a few years later by the Twenty First Amendment (upon whose passage President Roosevelt supposedly said, "America needs a drink") but in the meantime created a black market that facilitated the rise of archetypal gunmen like Al Capone. The conflict between the Irish and Italian mobs in Chicago has been described as "the worst gang war in American history, one that would have a profound effect on gun control legislation and the Second Amendment."[175]

Gangsters lived and died by the gun – most dramatically and most notoriously the Tommy Gun, named after John T. Thompson, who intended it for use in World War I.[176] The gun was not ready for use until 1920, though, and so it became famous for its use on the streets of Chicago rather than in the trenches of Verdun.[177] The violence it facilitated was extraordinary. On Valentine's Day, 1929, Capone and his gang lured seven members and associates of the rival North Side Gang to a warehouse in Chicago with a promise of bootlegged whiskey.[178] Upon arrival, the members of the North Side Gang instead encountered men in police uniforms who made them line up against a wall. Two of the "police officers," who were actually members of Capone's Chicago Outfit, then opened fire with Tommy Guns, spraying seventy bullets into the group.[179] One of them, Frank Gusenberg, was still alive when the real police arrived. Honor among thieves being what it is, when Gusenberg was asked who pulled the trigger, he said, "Nobody shot me." He died hours later of multiple bullet wounds.[180]

Some gangsters and bootleggers embraced the image of the gun-slinging outlaw, and were aided in that regard by a fascinated public and an eager press. John Dillinger was portrayed as a swaggering, colorful rogue, an image which so rankled J. Edgar Hoover that he used it as leverage to help create the Federal Bureau of Investigation. Dillinger's picaresque story would end with a gunshot outside of a Chicago theater – a fittingly dramatic end. But for sheer titillation and press coverage, no one could match Bonnie Parker and Clyde Darrow,

[175] WINKLER, *supra* note 42, at 190.

[176] BILL YENNE, TOMMY GUN: HOW GENERAL THOMPSON'S SUBMACHINE GUN WROTE HISTORY 2 (2009) ("The Thompson submachine gun was born of war, the Great War, and of John Thompson's desire to create something that would break the back of the most insidious of wartime conditions, the meat grinder of the stalemate. Too late for World War I, the Thompson found its way into the hands of guerrillas, soldiers, and thugs, from the Emerald Isle to the dusty, distant corners of China and the muggy jungles of Central America.").

[177] *Id.* at 3.

[178] *Id.* at 74–75.

[179] *Id.* at 75.

[180] *Id.*

whose two-year crime spree from 1932 to 1934 became a myth even as they were living it.[181]

The details were far less romantic. Bonnie and Clyde's life on the road was hard, and their crimes – which included kidnapping, ransom, and murder – were hardly cartoonish bank robberies in which only rich villains paid the price. Fittingly, it all ended in a hail of bullets. Ambushed by a group of lawmen on a rural road in Bienville Parish, Louisiana, Bonnie and Clyde suffered so many bullet wounds that the undertaker had trouble piecing them together for burial. In their bullet-riddled car, police found stolen automatic rifles, sawed-off semi-automatic shotguns, handguns, and several thousand rounds of ammunition.

That same year, Congress passed the first major modern federal gun control law, the National Firearms Act. Just as later federal interventions would target particular types of guns – Saturday Night Specials, for example – the Act focused on the machine-guns and short-barreled shotguns favored by the gangsters of the time. Such guns were not (and still are not) prohibited outright,[182] but were subject to a $200 tax every time one was manufactured, sold, or transferred. Additionally, owners of such weapons had to register with the authorities and be fingerprinted.[183] Four years later, the Federal Firearms Act of 1938 created a more elaborate system of licensing and record-keeping – focusing on gun dealers, rather than purchasers – and also barred violent felons from possessing firearms,[184] a restriction that would be expanded to nonviolent felons in the late 1960s, in response to another wave of violence.[185]

The New Deal and Constitutional Change

These new federal regulations had to answer to the Constitution, not just to political imperatives. The federal government is one of enumerated powers, meaning that, unlike state governments, it has no plenary power to do anything. In order to act, the federal government must do so in furtherance of one of the powers laid out in the Constitution, especially in Articles I and II, which establish the powers of Congress and the President. The scope of the federal government's authority, and how it interacts with that of the states, has been a central obsession of constitutional law since the founding. The fight over the constitutionality of President Obama's health care reform is but one recent example.[186]

[181] *See generally* E. R. MILNER, THE LIVES AND TIMES OF BONNIE & CLYDE 4 (1996).

[182] Under federal law, neither short-barreled shotguns nor machine guns are prohibited. *See* 26 U.S.C. § 5841 (governing the ownership and registration of "firearms") and 26 U.S.C. § 5845(a)–(b) (defining "firearms" to include short-barreled shotguns and machine guns).

[183] WINKLER, *supra* note 42, at 209.

[184] *Id.* at 209.

[185] Federal Gun Control Act of 1968, Pub. L. No. 90-618, 82 Stat. 1213, 1220; Omnibus Crime Control and Safe Streets Act of 1968 Pub. L. No. 90-351 § 1202, 82 Stat. at 236.

[186] *See* National Federation of Independent Business v. Sebelius, 567 U.S. 519 (2012).

In the 1930s, an even more ambitious President pursued a legislative agenda unlike any the nation had seen before. President Franklin Delano Roosevelt's New Deal focused on what historians call "The Three Rs": relief for the poor, recovery of the economy, and reform of the financial system.[187] To achieve those goals, it generated a further alphabet soup of public works projects and agencies – the Tennessee Valley Authority (TVA), the National Labor Relations Board (NLRB), the Works Progress Administration (WPA) and the like – and relied on an expansion of federal authority that would change the face of American law.

Though these initiatives are best known for their economic goals, President Roosevelt believed that crime control, including gun regulation, was part and parcel of the New Deal.[188] Gun violence was close to the President's heart, figuratively and literally. In February 1933, President-Elect Roosevelt gave a speech alongside Chicago Mayor Anton Cermak in Miami's Bayfront Park. At the back of the crowd, Giuseppe Zangara – a poor, immigrant bricklayer suffering from a stomach ailment he blamed on the government – cradled a pistol he had purchased earlier that day at a pawn shop. Zangara, who stood only five feet tall, climbed up on a chair, took aim, and began firing, but the crowd quickly grabbed and disarmed him. The President-Elect was unhurt, but a bullet struck Mayor Cermak, who reportedly said to Roosevelt, "I'm glad it was me instead of you." The mayor died a few weeks later.[189]

The incident helped harden Roosevelt's resolve.[190] But just because there is presidential will does not mean that there is a constitutional way. In the 1930s, the Supreme Court's politically conservative majority repeatedly struck down, on constitutional grounds, many elements of President Roosevelt's New Deal legislation. This was the era of *Lochner v. New York*, which invalidated a New York law regulating bakery conditions on the grounds that it interfered with the freedom of contract,[191] and has come to be reviled as an example of inexcusable interference with economic regulation. Roosevelt's patience wore thin, and in 1937 he responded by proposing a bill that would have granted the President power to appoint an additional Justice to the US Supreme Court, up to a maximum of six, for every member of the court over the age of seventy years and six months. The court-packing plan was unveiled in February of 1937, and met stiff resistance even from Roosevelt's political

[187] Jonathan Peters, *Institutionalizing Press Relations at the Supreme Court: The Origins of the Public Information Office*, 79 Mo. L. Rev. 985, 988 (2014) (citing Rita G. Koman, *Relief, Recovery, Reform: The New Deal Congressional Reaction to the Great Depression*, OAH Mag. of Hist., Summer 1998, at 39).

[188] Mike Lee, Our Lost Constitution: The Willful Subversion of America's Founding Document 163 (2015); Adam Winkler, *Franklin Roosevelt: The Father of Gun Control*, New Republic (Dec. 19, 2012); *see also* Winkler, *supra* note 42, at 197 ("Roosevelt portrayed gun control and crime fighting simply as one more element of the New Deal – indeed, of the new America.").

[189] Frank Freidel, Franklin D. Roosevelt: A Rendezvous with Destiny 88 (1990).

[190] *Id.* at 87–88.

[191] 198 U.S. 45 (1905).

allies.[192] But just a few weeks later, the situation changed markedly when Justice Owen Roberts – theretofore a consistent vote against New Deal legislation – voted to uphold a minimum wage law, generating a 5-4 decision in favor of the kind of laws that Roosevelt supported.[193] Whatever Roberts' motivations for doing so,[194] the "switch in time that saved nine" solidified the constitutional foundations for broad federal power that have, with occasional tremors,[195] remained stable since then.

In the years ahead, this broadened understanding provided a firmer constitutional basis for Congress's power to pass laws, including gun regulations. But that is only half of the constitutional question. In order to assess the constitutionality of a federal government action, one must ask both whether it is properly authorized *and* whether it is otherwise prohibited, for example by a provision of the Bill of Rights.[196] The latter question came before the Supreme Court in *United States v. Miller*, which would be its last real word on the Second Amendment until 2008.

Jack Miller was a member of the bank-robbing O'Malley Gang. In April 1938, he was arrested with an unregistered sawed-off shotgun in his possession, and charged with violating the National Firearms Act. Hauled into district court, Miller argued that the Act violated his Second Amendment rights – an argument that the district judge, himself a supporter of New Deal gun regulation, somewhat surprisingly accepted. This was not particularly unwelcome news for the federal government, however, since Roosevelt's Attorney General Homer Cummings was happy to have a test case for the constitutionality of the Act.[197] Miller's prosecution might even have been engineered for that very purpose.[198]

Miller was apparently not a very good bank robber, and he was an even worse constitutional crusader. He disappeared as soon as he was released from jail, as the district judge had guessed he would. The lawyer who had been appointed to represent him, in turn, had no particular interest in briefing the case, nor in traveling to Washington on his own dime to argue it before the Supreme Court. He wrote "Unable to obtain any money from clients to be present and argue case," and suggested that the Justices decide based solely on the government's briefs.[199]

[192] Curtis Bradley & Neil Siegel, *Historical Gloss, Constitutional Conventions, and the Judicial Separation of Powers*, 105 GEO. L. J. 255, 269 (2017).

[193] West Coast Hotel Co. v. Parrish, 300 U.S. 379 (1937).

[194] *See* BARRY CUSHMAN, RETHINKING THE NEW DEAL COURT: THE STRUCTURE OF A CONSTITUTIONAL REVOLUTION 45 (1998).

[195] *See, e.g.*, United States v. Morrison, 529 U.S. 598 (2000) (striking down portions of the Violence Against Women Act as exceeding Congress's power under the Commerce Clause); United States v. Lopez, 514 U.S. 549 (1995) (same for the Gun Free Schools Zones Act).

[196] For a thoughtful discussion of the distinction between constitutional authorizations and constitutional prohibitions see H. JEFFERSON POWELL, TARGETING AMERICANS: THE CONSTITUTIONALITY OF THE U.S. DRONE WAR 38–42 (2016).

[197] WINKLER, *supra* note 42, at 213–14.

[198] *See* Brian L. Frye, *The Peculiar Story of* United States v. Miller, 3 NYU JOURNAL OF LAW & LIBERTY 48, 50 (2008).

[199] *Id.* at 66–67.

Even if Miller's attorney had made the trip to Washington, the balance of lawyering would have been tilted almost comically in the government's favor. The United States was represented by Solicitor General Robert Jackson, who would go on to serve as a Supreme Court Justice and a prosecutor at Nuremberg. Associate Justice Louis Brandeis, himself one of the nation's greatest lawyers before he became one of its greatest Justices, once said that Jackson should be "Solicitor General for life."[200]

Defending the constitutionality of the Firearms Act against Miller's Second Amendment challenge, Jackson focused on the first clause of the Amendment, arguing that the right was "restricted to the keeping and bearing of arms by the people collectively for their common defense and security." He added that the first clause "indicates that the right ... is not one which may be utilized for private purposes but only one which exists where the arms are borne in the militia or some other military organization provided for by law and intended for the protection of the state."[201]

In doing so, Jackson articulated the militia-based view that was central to the debate about the Amendment's meaning in the decades leading up to *Heller*. On this view, the right extends only to those people, arms, and activities bearing some connection to the militia, and not to "private purposes," including self-defense. It hardly needed to be said that Miller was not a member of a well-regulated militia.

The Court's decision was unanimous, though not exactly its best work. In a relatively brief opinion, Justice McReynolds seemed to embrace Jackson's view: "With obvious purpose to assure the continuation and render possible the effectiveness of such [militia] forces the declaration and guarantee of the Second Amendment were made. It must be interpreted and applied with that end in view."[202] Miller's possession of a sawed-off shotgun did not have any "reasonable relationship to the preservation or efficiency of a well regulated militia," because there was no evidence such a gun would be useful in that context, and thus the Act's regulation of it therefore raised no Second Amendment problems.[203]

The outcome was clear, but its significance was and is contested. Some, especially those who favor a broad reading of the Second Amendment, say that *Miller* should be given relatively little weight, since it was unargued on one side and the opinion is so brief.[204] And even assuming that the holding matters, there is disagreement about what that holding actually *was*: A broad endorsement of the militia-based reading, or a narrow holding about which guns are protected by the Amendment.[205]

[200] E. Barrett Prettyman, Jr., *Robert Jackson: "Solicitor General for Life"*, 17 J. Sup. Ct. Hist. 75 (1992).

[201] *Quoted in* Winkler, *supra* note 42, at 215.

[202] *Miller*, 307 U.S. at 178.

[203] *Id.* at 178.

[204] *Heller*, 554 U.S. at 622–24.

[205] *Compare Heller*, 554 U.S. at 622 (arguing that *Miller*'s holding "is not only consistent with, but positively suggests, that the Second Amendment confers an individual right to keep and bear arms (though only arms that 'have some reasonable relationship to the preservation or efficiency of a well regulated militia')") *with id.* at 637–38 (Stevens, J., dissenting) ("The view of the Amendment we took in *Miller* – that it protects the right to keep and bear arms for certain military purposes, but that it does

As for Miller, the Justices' decision meant nothing. Six weeks before the Supreme Court's decision was published, he and some accomplices robbed a bar in Oklahoma. Hours later, Miller's corpse was found in a dry creek bed nearby, shot four times with a .38. The .45 next to his body had been fired three times.[206]

Federal Gun Regulation in the 1960s

The structure of gun rights and regulation that emerged in the 1930s was shaped by a volatile mix of politics, policy, violence, and uncertainty. The same ingredients led to the next major wave of federal gun regulation in the 1960s. The civil rights movement is a major part of that story, as Chapter 6 explains in more detail, and the Black Panthers' activities in California are particularly important for understanding the changes on the state level. But the chaos and fear of the late 1960s led to a tightening of federal laws as well.

President Kennedy was shot and killed in November 1963; Malcolm X in February 1965. On April 4, 1968, Martin Luther King, Jr. was shot and killed on the balcony of the Lorraine Motel in Memphis. That night, before a largely black audience in Indianapolis, Senator Robert Kennedy publicly spoke of his brother's murder for the first time, and concluded by exhorting Americans to "dedicate ourselves to what the Greeks wrote so many years ago: to tame the savageness of man and to make gentle the life of this world."[207]

Two months later, Kennedy won the California Democratic primary. That night, he gave brief remarks to his supporters at the Ambassador Hotel in Los Angeles, and was making his way through the kitchen when he paused to shake hands with Juan Romero, a busboy. As he did so, a Palestinian activist named Sirhan Sirhan opened fire with a .22, squeezing off five shots before he was wrestled to the ground. Kennedy collapsed, and Romero cradled his head and placed a rosary in his hand. Kennedy asked Romero, "Is everybody okay?" Romero responded, "Yes, everybody's okay." Kennedy turned away and said, "Everything's going to be okay."[208] He died early next the morning.

President Lyndon Johnson used Bobby Kennedy's murder as an occasion to finally win passage of the gun control measures he had been proposing since taking office: "Let us now spell out our grief in constructive action."[209] Moved by the

not curtail the Legislature's power to regulate the nonmilitary use and ownership of weapons – is both the most natural reading of the Amendment's text and the interpretation most faithful to the history of its adoption.").

[206] Frye, *supra* note 198, at 68.

[207] Evan Thomas, *The Worst Week: LBJ. RFK. MLK.* NEWSWEEK, Nov. 19, 2007, at 42.

[208] LARRY TYE, BOBBY KENNEDY: THE MAKING OF A LIBERAL ICON 436 (2016).

[209] Lyndon B. Johnson, Lyndon B. Johnson: 1968–1969 Containing the Public Messages, Speeches, and Statements of the President 695 (Volume 1, U.S. Government Printing Office, 1970).

assassinations, the Panthers, the wave of riots in the summer of 1968, and a stunning increase in the availability of guns,[210] Congress responded.

The Federal Gun Control Act of 1968[211] made an effort to restrict Saturday Night Specials – cheap pistols used disproportionately by criminals – and extended the felon-in-possession ban to cover even nonviolent felons. But perhaps most importantly, it required anyone "engaged in the business" of selling guns to have a federal license and maintain records of all gun sales, including the names and addresses of the purchasers. "Private" transfers were exempt from this requirement. Policing the line between these categories would remain a central challenge for firearms law and policy for decades to come, and it is manifested in modern efforts to close what it sometimes called the "gun show loophole" – an exception for nonlicensed gun dealers supposedly not "engaged in the business" of selling guns, even though many apparently do so in great volume.[212]

Closing the gun show loophole was among the regulatory questions raised in the wake of Sandy Hook, bringing us back to where this book began. Thus far, we've shown that the history of the Second Amendment is a history of accommodating gun rights and regulation. But that tradition, though harmonious in some sense, contains inescapable tensions between emancipation and subjugation, promise and violence, security and fear. It is no option to simply recognize these tensions, for constitutional law sometimes demands a choice between competing narratives. For the Second Amendment, the central question was, as Chapter 2 explains, whether and how the right to keep and bear arms extends beyond the organized militia. Chapter 3 explains the method and substance of the Supreme Court's answer.

[210] The number of imports exploded, from 67,000 in 1955 to over 1 million in 1968. WINKLER, *supra* note 42, at 250.

[211] Pub. L. No. 90-618, 82 Stat. 1213 (codified as amended in scattered sections of 18 and 26 U.S.C.).

[212] *Compare* Andrew Goddard, *A View Through The Gun Show Loophole*, 12 RICH. J.L. & PUB. INT. 357, 358–59 (2009) ("Gun shows have been reported to be involved with the trafficking of approximately twenty-six thousand firearms over a two and a half year period, a figure that represents thirty percent of all guns identified in federal criminal trafficking cases over that period.") (citing Mayors Against Illegal Guns, The movement of Illegal Guns in America 9–10 (2008)) *with* Nicholas Johnson, *Imagining Gun Control in America: Understanding the Remainder Problem*, 43 WAKE FOREST L. REV. 837, 876–77 (2008) (arguing that "people who complain about the gun show loophole can really only be satisfied by a flat ban on private transfers").

2

Militias, Private Purposes, and the Road to *Heller*

As a matter of legal doctrine, the modern Second Amendment was created on June 26, 2008 – the day the Supreme Court held in *District of Columbia v. Heller* that the right to keep and bear arms covers private purposes such as self-defense.[1] At that moment, the Second Amendment became an enforceable personal legal right, one that would be the basis for at least a thousand constitutional challenges over the next decade.[2] But *Heller* also held that the right to keep and bear arms is subject to legal regulation.

Heller is celebrated in some quarters, lamented in others. But, as with the history of gun rights and regulation that helped shape the decision, many people misunderstand what *Heller* was about, what it settled, and what questions it left open. Our object is to understand the Second Amendment as law, so doctrinal questions are our bread and butter. But we do not suppose that *Heller*'s significance can be measured solely by doctrine. Supreme Court decisions have expressive force – they frequently bless one story among competing narratives, even when they do little to change law on the books. *Brown v. Board of Education*, to take just one example, was and is an important statement of constitutional value, whatever its impact on the desegregation of schools.[3]

The same is true of *Heller*. In holding that the right to keep and bear arms includes private purposes like self-defense, the Supreme Court – intentionally or not – endorsed a particular view of guns in the United States. We will show in later chapters that the Court's decision leaves significant leeway for gun regulation, and that few of the gun laws likely to emerge from American gun politics will be anywhere near the constitutional line. But even if not a single law fell in its wake, *Heller*

[1] District of Columbia v. Heller, 554 U.S. 570 (2008).

[2] Eric Ruben & Joseph Blocher, *From Theory to Doctrine: An Empirical Analysis of the Right to Keep and Bear Arms After* Heller, 67 Duke L.J. 1433 (2018).

[3] *See generally* Gerald N. Rosenberg, The Hollow Hope: Can Courts Bring About Social Change? (1991) (arguing that courts have a limited ability to spur political and social reform).

would still be a significant constitutional event. The Supreme Court anointed one constitutional vision of the Second Amendment as definitive. This chapter explains how that happened.

BACKGROUND

D.C.'s Law

Between 1960 and 1969, the homicide rate in the District of Columbia tripled.[4] By 1974, it hit an all-time high, capped off by a triple murder over the Christmas holidays.[5] Embattled residents began to joke that "D.C." stood for "Dodge City."[6] They wanted action, and city officials complied in 1976, passing a law that functionally banned handguns and required guns to be locked or disassembled when not in use.

That the law was passed in the District is significant. As the last chapter showed, the vast majority of gun regulation has always happened at the state and local levels. In part, this is a function of local variation and the fact that gun violence is a persistent urban problem – the District in the 1960s and 1970s was certainly no exception. But the District is not a state, and it is unique as a municipality. Legally, although the city does enjoy some local authority, final control over the District ultimately lies with Congress.[7] And thus it was a subcommittee of the U.S. House of Representatives that held hearings in 1976 about the purposes and justifications underlying the District's proposed Firearms Control Regulations Act.

The basic details and purpose of the Act were captured in a report produced by a committee of D.C.'s governing council.[8] The report declared that the purpose of the law was "to reduce the potentiality for gun-related crimes and gun-related deaths from occurring within the District of Columbia" and to "strengthen the capacity of the District of Columbia government to monitor the traffic in firearms" within the city.[9] The committee noted that firearms accounted for "one out of every 100 deaths"

[4] *See* Paul Duggan, *Crime Data Underscore Limits of D.C. Gun Ban's Effectiveness*, WASH. POST, Nov. 13, 2007, at B1.

[5] *See* Jane Rippleteau, *Three More Slain; District Total 291*, WASH. POST, Dec. 26, 1974, at C10.

[6] *See* Paul Duggan, *Crime Data Underscore Limits of D.C. Gun Ban's Effectiveness*, WASH. POST, Nov. 13, 2007, at B1.

[7] While the 1973 District of Columbia Home Rule Act authorizes a Council for the District of Columbia, any legislation it passes remains subject to Congress' approval. District of Columbia Self-Government and Governmental Reorganization Act, Pub. L. No. 93-198, 87 Stat. 774 (1973) (codified in scattered sections of the D.C. Code). *See also* ADAM WINKLER, GUNFIGHT: THE BATTLE OVER THE RIGHT TO BEAR ARMS IN AMERICA 51 (2011).

[8] The data and justifications are conveyed at greater length in Justice Breyer's dissenting opinion. *Heller*, 554 U.S. at 693–96 (Breyer, J., dissenting).

[9] Firearms Control Regulations Act of 1975 (Council Act No. 1–142): Hearing and Disposition on H. Con. Res. 694 Before the H. Comm. on the District of Columbia, 94th Cong., 2d Sess., 25 (1976) [hereinafter Council Hearing] (reproducing, *inter alia*, the Council Committee Report).

in America.[10] Sixty-nine persons were killed with firearms every day, amounting to "[a]pproximately 25,000 gun-deaths" and 200,000 injuries in addition.[11] "For every intruder stopped by a homeowner with a firearm," the committee reported, "there are 4 gun-related accidents within the home."[12] National trends showed that handguns were used in 54 percent of murders, as well as 60 percent of robberies and 26 percent of assaults.[13] Eighty-seven percent of all murders of law enforcement officers involved a handgun.[14]

Though it cited national statistics, the committee tailored its recommendations to address the District's specific concerns. The District had suffered 285 murders in 1974, 155 of which were committed with handguns.[15] Most crime guns recovered in the city were difficult to track, as less than half a percent of firearms used in crime were registered in the District.[16] The committee concluded that, in the absence of stronger national regulation, local governments [must] "act to protect their citizens, and certainly the District of Columbia as the only totally urban statelike jurisdiction should be strong in its approach."[17] The committee's recommendations "denote[d] a policy decision that handguns ... have no legitimate use in the purely urban environment of the District of Columbia."[18] That said, the committee noted that "[i]t should be apparent that this bill would not cause a confiscation law ... and would take nothing away from sportsmen and collectors."[19]

The final version of the law made it illegal to have an unregistered firearm and simultaneously forbade the registration of new handguns, thus effectively making it illegal to possess a new handgun in the District.[20] Separately, the law required residents to keep their firearms – including long guns like rifles and shotguns – "unloaded and dissembled or bound by a trigger lock or similar device" except when located in a place of business or being used in lawful recreational activities.[21]

[10] *Id.*
[11] *Id.*
[12] *Id.*
[13] *Id.* at 26.
[14] *Id.*
[15] *Id.*
[16] *Id.*
[17] *Id.* at 27.
[18] *Id.* at 31.
[19] *Id.* at 33.
[20] *See* D.C. Code §§ 7–2501.01(12), 7–2502.01(a), 7–2502.02(a)(4) (2001). There was an effort to grandfather weapons in such a way to avoid constitutional problems. *See* Council Hearing, *supra* note 9, at 31, 33. This grandfathering was assumed in subsequent litigation. *See* Parker v. District of Columbia, 311 F. Supp. 2d 103, 103 (D.D.C. 2004) (specifying that registration was not available for a "[p]istol not validly registered to the current registrant in the District prior to September 24, 1976" (internal citation and quotation marks omitted)); Fesjian v. Jefferson, 399 A.2d 861, 864 (D.C. 1979) (rejecting equal protection challenge to rules that made "handguns and new machine guns unregisterable, yet contain a grandfather clause permitting owners of previously registered handguns to retain and re-register their firearms").
[21] *See* D.C. Code § 7–2507.02 (2001).

Although a few localities had adopted handgun bans during roughly the same period,[22] the District's law stood apart in its severity.[23] Such extreme regulations tend to become the focus of political opposition and constitutional challenges, and thus tend to shape constitutional doctrine.[24] The District's regulation did exactly that, galvanizing an organization that, more than any other, has shaped modern American gun law.

The Changing Role of the National Rifle Association

Roughly a century before the District of Columbia adopted its handgun law, a group of Union veterans, disappointed with the poor marksmanship of federal soldiers during the Civil War, founded the National Rifle Association. Its stated goal was to "promote and encourage rifle shooting on a scientific basis," and its major organizational activity was the formation of rifle clubs.[25]

As the nation urbanized and gun regulation gained political salience, the NRA promoted the safe use of guns and helped shape and support restrictions on their use and carry. The NRA's president in the 1930s, Karl Frederick, helped draft the Uniform Firearms Act and later claimed that the NRA "sponsored" it.[26] Almost unimaginably, given the organization's current stance, Frederick once said, "I do not believe in the general promiscuous toting of guns. I think it should be sharply restricted and only under licenses."[27] General Milton Reckord, the Executive Vice President of the organization during the 1930s, said that the NRA was "absolutely favorable to reasonable gun control."[28]

[22] Quilici v. Vill. of Morton Grove, 695 F.2d 261 (7th Cir. 1982), cert. denied, 464 U.S. 863 (1983) (upholding handgun ban in Morton Grove, Illinois).

[23] Outside of Chicago's law – discussed in more detail below, since it was the focus of *McDonald*, the closest analogue was San Francisco's 2005 handgun ban. This ban was enacted through the proposition system as Proposition H – Handgun Ban in San Francisco. The proposition, which passed and became effective in 2006, banned the sale, manufacture, transfer, or distribution of all firearms and ammunition in San Francisco, and limited handgun possession for residents of San Francisco, unless required for "professional purposes" as specified in the proposed ordinance. However, Proposition H was quickly struck down because it was preempted by California law. Fiscal v. City and Cty. of San Francisco, 158 Cal. App. 4th 895 (Cal. Ct. App. 2008).

[24] *Cf.* Griswold v. Connecticut, 381 U.S. 479 (1965) (striking down Connecticut's "Comstock Law" – one of only two remaining in the nation – which criminalized the use of contraceptives).

[25] *See A Brief History of the NRA*, Nat'l Rifle Assoc., https://home.nra.org/about-the-nra/ (last visited Oct. 12, 2017).

[26] Adam Winkler, *The Secret History of Guns*, The Atlantic, Sept. 2011, at 80, 86.

[27] *National Firearms Act: Hearings on H.R. 9066 Before the Committee on Ways and Means*, 73d Cong. 59 (1934) (statement of Karl T. Frederick, President, NRA).

[28] Adam Winkler, Gunfight: The Battle Over the Right to Bear Arms in America 211 (2011). *See also National Firearms Act: Hearings Before a Subcommittee of the Committee on Commerce, United States Senate*, 73d Cong. 2d Sess. 15–18 (1934) (statement of General Reckord, Executive Vice-President, NRA) at 15 ("Yes sir. Now, [regarding the Uniform Firearms Act], we favored licensing the dealer and providing other regulatory measures, which we believed were fair and reasonable

But the country changed, and the NRA did, too. Rising crime rates and a steady decline in the popularity of hunting and recreational gun use (the predominant reasons for private gun ownership until very recently[29]) sapped energy from the NRA's original mission. Self-defense became more prominent in discussions of gun rights and regulation. In keeping with the intensity of this interest, subsequent waves of gun owners and NRA members were less inclined to compromise on gun regulations, and a rift developed within the organization.

The NRA's old guard remained focused on gun safety and shooting sports and was relatively more open to gun regulation. In the 1970s, it was planning to move the organization's headquarters from the outskirts of Washington, D.C. to Colorado.[30] The new leaders, however, were not interested in compromise or in retreating from the corridors of federal power. They were led by a "blue-eyed, bald-headed bulldog of a man" named Harlon Carter,[31] who controlled the NRA's Institute for Legislative Action (NRA-ILA) – the wing of the organization focused on political and legal advocacy. Carter's restive faction was growing in strength when, in November 1976, the old guard tried to re assert control by firing eighty of Carter's allies.

The effort failed. Carter's sympathizers doubled down. And when the District of Columbia passed its gun law that same year, it unwittingly added fuel to the conflagration. Soon after the law was passed, the NRA decided to move the organization's annual meeting from D.C. to Cincinnati. And it was there, on May 21, 1977, that the members of the Carter group executed their takeover. Taking advantage of the NRA's procedural rules, they outmaneuvered and outvoted the old guard. Following an all-night meeting (during which the upstarts coordinated their efforts using walkie-talkies), Carter was named Executive Vice President of the NRA.[32]

The "Cincinnati Coup" produced the modern NRA – a single-issue lobbying juggernaut, opposed to almost every gun regulation. It was this NRA that would play a massive role in the development of gun policy and the modern Second Amendment over the next few decades. Instead of retreating to the mountains of Colorado, the

and proper."); *id.* at 18 ("And I would be very glad, if it appeared advisable, to approve the sale of ammunition only to licensed dealers.").

[29] In a Pew Research study conducted in February 2013, approximately 39 percent of gun owners listed hunting or sport shooting as their primary reason for owning a gun; in 1999, the combined figure was 57 percent. The same study found that 48 percent of gun owners listed protection as their primary reason for ownership in 2013, up from 26 percent in 1999. Pew Res. Ctr., *Why Own a Gun? Protection Is Now Top Reason*, Pew Res. Ctr. (Mar. 12, 2013), www.people-press.org/2013/03/12/why-own-a-gun-protection-is-now-top-reason/; *see also* Kate Masters, *Fear of Other People is Now The Primary Motivation for American Gun Ownership, A Landmark Survey Finds*, The Trace (Sept. 19, 2016), www.thetrace.org/2016/09/harvard-gun-ownership-study-self-defense/; Sabrina Tavernise & Robert Gebeloff, *Share of Homes with Guns Shows 4-Decade Decline*, N.Y. Times, Mar. 9, 2013, at 1, 24 ("According to an analysis of the [2012 General Social Survey], only a quarter of men in 2012 said they hunted, compared with about 40 percent when the question was asked in 1977.").

[30] Osha Gray Davidson, Under Fire: The NRA and the Battle for Gun Control 35 (1998).

[31] Winkler, *supra* note 28, at 65.

[32] *Id.* at 67.

group expanded its headquarters in Fairfax, Virginia. The message was clear: the NRA was going to be a force to be reckoned with in Washington.

The new leadership, starting with Carter and continuing with his "most important successor," Executive Vice President Wayne LaPierre,[33] transformed the NRA from an organization of hunters, sportsmen, and veterans into a feared political and social institution. Part lobbying shop, part think tank, part advocacy group, part industry alliance,[34] the NRA is often called the most powerful interest group in Washington.[35] It rarely loses,[36] despite pushing policies frequently in conflict with popular opinion and sometimes even the preferences of its own membership.[37] When explaining Republican opposition to President Barack Obama's nomination of Judge Merrick Garland to the Supreme Court, Senate Majority Leader Mitch McConnell said, "I can't imagine that a Republican majority in the United States Senate would want to confirm ... a nominee opposed by the National Rifle Association."[38] The *New York Times* editorial board responded by accusing the Senate of "defer[ring]" its constitutional judgment to the NRA.[39]

Alongside this rise to dominance, the NRA's rhetoric has shifted from "favor[ing] ... reasonable gun control," as Reckord said in the 1930s, to near total opposition.[40] Absolutism is common: each gun regulation is the worst,[41] and every debate is the

[33] *Id.* at 69.

[34] Walter Hickey, *How the Gun Industry Funnels Tens of Millions Of Dollars to the NRA*, Bus. Insider (Jan. 16, 2013, 1:25 PM), www.businessinsider.com/gun-industry-funds-nra-2013-1 ("[L]ess than half of the NRA's revenues come from program fees and membership dues. The bulk of the group's money now comes in the form of contributions, grants, royalty income, and advertising, much of it originating from gun industry sources.").

[35] *See, e.g.*, Walter Hickey, *How the NRA Became the Most Powerful Special Interest in Washington*, Bus. Insider (Dec. 18, 2012, 1:43 PM), www.businessinsider.com/nra-lobbying-money-national-rifle-association-washington-2012-12; Joel Achenbach, Scott Higham and Sari Horwitz, *How NRA's True Believers Converted a Marksmanship Group into a Mighty Gun Lobby*, Wash. Post, Jan. 12, 2013, A1.

[36] Mike Weisser, *A Rare Loss for the NRA*, Huffington Post (May 19, 2014, 10:34 AM), www.huffingtonpost.com/mike-weisser/a-rare-loss-for-the-nra_b_5351267.html (last updated July 19, 2014); David Frum, *Why Gun-Rights Backers Win While Other Conservative Causes Lose*, The Atlantic (Apr. 29, 2014), www.theatlantic.com/politics/archive/2014/04/why-gun-rights-supporters-win-when-other-conservative-causes-lose/361396/.

[37] Pew Res. Ctr., *Why Own a Gun? Protection Is Now Top Reason: Section 2: Opinions of Gun Owners, Non-Gun Owners*, Pew Res. Ctr. (Mar. 12, 2013), www.people-press.org/2013/03/12/section-2-opinions-of-gun-owners-non-gun-owners/ ("[P]eople in NRA households overwhelmingly favor making private gun sales and sales at gun shows subject to background checks: 74% favor this proposal while just 26% are opposed.").

[38] Interview by Chris Wallace with Mitch McConnell on Fox News Sunday (Mar. 20, 2016), www.youtube.com/watch?v=ix7lQLplA_E.

[39] The Editorial Board, Opinion, *The Senate Defers to the* N.R.A., N.Y. Times, Mar. 24, 2016, at A26.

[40] *See, e.g.*, Joseph Blocher, *Gun Rights Talk*, 94 B.U. L. Rev. 813, 821–24 (2014).

[41] Davidson, *supra* note 30, at 92 ("Never has an issue been more distorted or downright lied about than the armor-piercing bullet issue. The anti-gun forces will go to any lengths to void your right to keep and bear arms." (quoting an informational mailer sent to NRA members)); *id.* at 110 ("You and I are

last chance to save the right to keep and bear arms.[42] Osha Gray Davidson, in a book-length study of the NRA, provides a few examples of the apocalyptic rhetoric:

> Unless you call, write, help organize and deliver the vote of your Congressman, I guarantee you that strict, total gun control will be imposed on all of America.
>
> ...
>
> [This bill] is the worst gun legislation ever to be seriously considered on Capitol Hill.
>
> It's now or never for our gun rights.
>
> ...
>
> You'd better make your calls now. There won't be time later.
>
> *In the entire history of the NRA Institute, American gun owners have never before been under such constant, vicious attacks from the gun banners to which the truth means nothing.*[43]

The change in rhetoric isn't just stylistic, but reflects a fundamental change in the nature of the NRA's arguments. Gun regulations are depicted not just as bad policy, but as unconstitutional. Adam Winkler notes that in the 1930s, the Second Amendment was largely absent from the NRA's advocacy, and that the NRA's newsletter – which had primarily focused on matters like target shooting – began to regularly cite the Second Amendment in the 1960s.[44] Now, in the NRA's bylaws, "[p]rotect and defend the Constitution of the United States" is listed first among the organization's purposes and objectives.[45]

The NRA's growing reliance on constitutional rhetoric has paralleled an increasingly inflexible opposition to gun regulation. Almost exactly four years after the Cincinnati Coup, John Hinckley – seeking to impress actress Jodie Foster, with whom he was obsessed – shot a .22 caliber revolver six times at President Reagan outside the Hilton Hotel in Washington, D.C. Reagan was wounded in the chest. His press secretary, James Brady, was shot in the head and left partially paralyzed. Brady and his wife Sarah became prominent supporters of gun regulation, and nearly fifteen years after the shooting their efforts eventually helped secure passage of one of the last major federal gun control laws: the Brady Bill, signed during the Clinton administration. Its central mechanism was a system of background checks to ensure

in the middle of the most urgent and critical federal gun battle we have faced in 12 years." (quoting Letter from Nat'l Rifle Ass'n to Nat'l Rifle Ass'n Members (Dec. 8, 1987))).

[42] *Id.* at 66–67.

[43] *Id.* at 150.

[44] Winkler, *supra* note 28, at 95, 212. *But see* Patrick J. Charles, Armed in America: A history of Gun Rights from Colonial Militias to Concealed Carry (2018) (finding earlier evidence of constitutional reasoning by the NRA).

[45] Nat'l Rifle Assoc., Bylaws 1 (2016), www.scribd.com/document/348433530/NRA-2016-Bylaws; *see also* Bruce H. Kobayashi & Joseph E. Olson, In Re 101 California Street: A *Legal and Economic Analysis of Strict Liability for the Manufacture and Sale of* "Assault Weapons", 8 Stan. L. & Pol'y Rev. 41, 41 n.5 (1997) (quoting NRA Bylaws, Art. II(1) (1996)).

that would-be purchasers did not have prior felony convictions, mental illness, or other prohibitors.

Support for the Brady Bill was bipartisan. Former President Reagan himself spoke in favor of the law: "You do know that I'm a member of the NRA, and my position on the right to bear arms is well known[.] But I want you to know something else ... I support the Brady bill, and I urge the Congress to enact it without further delay."[46] Despite this endorsement from one of its most popular members, the NRA was having none of it: The Bill, signed into law by President Bill Clinton, was an affront to the "sovereign American citizen[.]"[47] Government agents, the NRA warned, would soon "go house to house, kicking in the law-abiding gun owners' doors."[48]

D.C.'s gun law coincided with and contributed to the NRA's transformation from a moderate hunting and sportsmanship organization to an entrenched player in D.C. politics, driven by an unwavering devotion to a particular reading of the Second Amendment. In its expanded Fairfax headquarters, the NRA prominently displayed a truncated version of the Amendment: "the right of the people to keep and bear arms shall not be infringed."[49] How to interpret that phrase was the central question in the Supreme Court case that would give new legal life to the Second Amendment.

The Central Question

Amidst the legislative debate over D.C.'s gun law, one consideration was conspicuously absent: the Second Amendment. Although some people raised objections, the record reveals little concern that the law, despite being one of the most stringent in the country, would run afoul of the right to keep and bear arms.[50] In Congress, only a handful of people raised constitutional concerns – among them, a new Congressman from Texas named Ron Paul.[51] Certainly, there was nothing like the insistent invocation of the Second Amendment that accompanies any contemporary gun regulation proposal.

[46] Tom Morganthau, *A Boost for Brady*, NEWSWEEK, Apr. 8, 1991, at 30.

[47] WINKLER, *supra* note 28, at 71.

[48] *Id.* at 71–72.

[49] H. RICHARD UVILLER & WILLIAM G. MERKEL, THE MILITIA AND THE RIGHT TO ARMS, OR, HOW THE SECOND AMENDMENT FELL SILENT 232 n.4 (2002) ("Residents and visitors to Northern Virginia may have noted that, as recently as 1999, the NRA Headquarters building, visible from Interstate 66, proudly displayed the motto 'The Right to Keep and Bear Arms Shall Not Be Infringed,' but failed to quote the Second Amendment's introductory language. The sign has since been removed.").

[50] This is not to say that there was no opposition. WINKLER, *supra* note 28, at 17 ("Douglas Moore, a member of the NRA and the one council member opposed to the ban, warned that the Ku Klux Klan was enjoying a 'resurgence' in the neighboring states of Maryland and Virginia. The ban, he said, 'will make it difficult for the people of this city – the majority of whom are black – to defend themselves.'").

[51] Congressman Ron Paul stated during the committee hearing that the law was "unconstitutional," explaining, "I believe that the second amendment does protect the individual law abiding citizen's right to keep and bear arms, to keep weapons for his protection." Council Hearing, *supra* note 9, at 71 (statement of Ron Paul, Congressman from Texas).

With the benefit of hindsight, it is tempting to marvel at this muted response. But at the time, the vast majority of scholars and lawyers would have reached the same conclusion, and for the same reason: As a matter of constitutional doctrine, the Second Amendment applied only to people, arms, and activities having some connection to a "well-regulated militia."

The central question in *Heller* would be whether this interpretation, or an alternative that included the personal possession of arms for activities like self-defense against crime, better captures the meaning of the Second Amendment. It is important, therefore, to identify the best versions of the arguments on both sides.

Even this descriptive task means stepping into a minefield. The common labels – collective right versus individual right; civic republican right versus Standard Model – all convey something important, but also can mischaracterize what they describe, or fail to distinguish the alternatives. Many who support the militia-focused reading also believe that the right is held by individuals. Many who believe that the right protects armed self-defense also argue that it has an important connection to the militia. Our goal here is to briefly describe and contrast the best versions of each theory.

THE MILITIA-BASED INTERPRETATION

The militia-based reading of the Amendment holds that the right to keep and bear arms is generally limited to people, arms, and activities having some connection to the militia. As a matter of doctrine, this view prevailed for more than two centuries,[52] meaning that most Second Amendment challenges were dismissed on the basis that the person bringing the challenge had no plausible connection to a militia, let alone a well-regulated one.[53] This did not mean that guns were illegal, of course, nor even that they lacked constitutional protection. The vast majority of *state* constitutions include a right to keep and bear arms, and those provisions were often invoked, giving rise to a rich body of doctrine. As Adam Winkler has shown, state courts have long interpreted state constitutional rules to require that a gun regulation be "reasonable" – a standard that gives the government a good deal of latitude, while striking down outlier laws.[54] But these were matters of state law, and the Second Amendment itself did almost no work during this period as a legal matter.

[52] This is primarily a descriptive claim, and some disagree. *See, e.g.*, Don B. Kates, *A Modern Historiography of the Second Amendment*, 56 UCLA L. Rev. 1211, 1211 (2009) [Kates, *A Modern Historiography*] ("The Second Amendment right to arms was uniformly viewed as an individual right from the time it was proposed in the late eighteenth century until legal debate over gun controls began in the twentieth century."). It is, however, difficult to see *Heller* as simply a confirmation of two centuries of settled doctrine – certainly it has brought about a radical change in Second Amendment litigation. Roughly 100 claims have succeeded since 2008, compared to almost none before that. Ruben & Blocher, *supra* note 2.

[53] *See, e.g.*, United States v. Hale, 978 F.2d 1016, 1020 (8th Cir. 1992).

[54] *See* Adam Winkler, *Scrutinizing the Second Amendment*, 105 Mich. L. Rev. 683, 686–87 (2007).

The militia-oriented view dominated not only doctrine, but most commentary and scholarly writing, for most of American history. It was endorsed by leading voices left, right, and center. "I'm not an expert on the Second Amendment," said conservative judicial icon Robert Bork in 1989, "but its intent was to guarantee the right of states to form militia, not for individuals to bear arms."[55] Two years later, he emphasized the point, again in originalist terms: "The National Rifle Association is always arguing that the Second Amendment determines the right to bear arms. But I think it really is people's right to bear arms in a militia. The NRA thinks that it protects their right to have Teflon-coated bullets. But that's not the original understanding."[56] Conservative Chief Justice Warren Burger likewise insisted that individual rights claims under the Second Amendment are "the subject of one of the greatest pieces of fraud – I repeat the word 'fraud' – on the American public by special interest groups that I have ever seen in my lifetime."[57]

Whether the public shared this view is hard to say, as it is difficult to find polling on the question prior to *Heller*.[58] Certainly there have always been people – including judges, lawyers, politicians, and scholars – who have believed that the Second Amendment includes a right to keep arms for private purposes like self-defense. But the most significant obstacle to strict gun regulations was the simple fact that most Americans, in most places, simply did not support it as policy matter.

So if the militia reading of the Amendment does not prohibit stringent regulation of private gun use, what *does* it prevent? The central concern would have to be regulations that would prevent the people of the states from maintaining a well-regulated militia. The Second Amendment right was designed to mitigate the risks of a standing federal army – an astonishing and terrifying institution at the time of ratification – by providing a check on the power Article I gave Congress over military matters. Laws disarming the state militia, or actions similar to those of the British at Concord, would fall within the right's core prohibition. If this worry seems implausibly archaic, consider that the Second Amendment's neighbor, the Third Amendment, prohibits quartering of troops in the home without consent, except in time of war – a real grievance in the late 1700s, although far from a pressing concern today.

Because of the central role it gives to militias and federalism, the militia-based reading is sometimes characterized (occasionally by its supporters, but usually by

[55] Claudia Luther, *Lectures at UCI with Rose Bird: Bork Says State Gun Laws Constitutional*, L.A. TIMES, MAR. 15, 1989, at 5.

[56] Miriam Bensimhorn, *Advocates: Point and Counterpoint, Laurence Tribe and Robert Bork Debate the Framers' Spacious Terms*, LIFE, Fall 1991 (Special Issue), at 96, 98.

[57] *PBS NewsHour: The MacNeil/Lehrer Report* (PBS television broadcast Dec. 16, 1991) (quoting former Chief Justice Warren Burger).

[58] *See* ALEC M. GALLUP AND FRANK NEWPORT, THE GALLUP POLL: PUBLIC Opinion 2008 215 (2009). Polls have long asked general questions about gun rights and regulations, but the specific question of private versus militia right was not posed by most polls until after *Heller*. *See, e.g.*, Pew Res. Ctr., *Public Continues to Oppose Banning Handgun Sales*, PEW RES. CTR. (May 14, 2008), www.people-press .org/2008/05/14/public-continues-to-oppose-banning-handgun-sales/.

its detractors) as a "collective" right, or as one held by states, rather than by individuals. Such a view is rightly criticized, at least inasmuch as it suggests that only states can raise Second Amendment claims.[59] But it is perfectly consistent to say that a structural check on federal power can be enforced by non-state actors – the vast majority of cases claiming Congress has exceeded an enumerated power, after all, are brought by individual plaintiffs.

That said, there are many variations on the militia-based reading of the Amendment. Historian Saul Cornell has argued that the Second Amendment protects a "civic" right.[60] This approach, sometimes called the "sophisticated collective rights view,"[61] casts the right to keep and bear arms in civic republican terms – a right, and sometimes an obligation, to keep and bear arms for the purposes of state militia service, as a check against federal power. Again, this is a right held by individuals, albeit one situated in a broader set of public-regarding interests.

It follows that the hardest question about the meaning of the Second Amendment is not whether it protects a "collective" or "individual" right, but rather what is encompassed by the latter. As Justice Stevens would note in the very first sentence of his opinion in *Heller*: "The question … is not whether the Second Amendment protects a 'collective right' or an 'individual right.' Surely it protects a right that can be enforced by individuals." However, "that the Second Amendment protects an individual right does not tell us anything about the scope of that right."[62]

THE PRIVATE PURPOSES INTERPRETATION

For more than two centuries, the militia-based reading dominated federal legal doctrine. But outside the courtroom, another narrative began to flourish. Even as casebooks and legal reports faithfully noted that the Amendment covers only people, arms, and acts bearing some connection to the well-regulated militia, many people spoke about "Second Amendment" rights in far more individualized terms.

It is well-recognized that changes in constitutional doctrine often begin outside the courts.[63] Statements about the constitution that are far-fetched, aspirational, or just plain false today can become law tomorrow, whether they originate on the right or the left. Those who believed them all along will resist the characterization, but one might say as much about claims that the constitution protects same

[59] Stephen P. Halbrook, That Every Man Be Armed 83–84 (2d ed., 1994).
[60] Saul Cornell, A Well-Regulated Militia: The Founding Fathers and the Origins of Gun Control in America 214 (2006).
[61] *See* Gun Control and the Constitution: Sources and Explorations on the Second Amendment xxxv (Robert J. Cottrol, ed., 1994).
[62] *Heller*, 554 U.S. at 636 (Stevens, J., dissenting).
[63] *See, e.g.*, David D. Cole, Engines of Liberty: The Power of Citizen Activists to Make Constitutional Law (2016); Larry D. Kramer, The People Themselves: Popular Constitutionalism and Judicial Review (2004); Mark Tushnet, Taking the Constitution Away From the Courts (1999).

sex marriage, or that the Affordable Care Act does not fall within the scope of the Commerce Clause power.[64] Both arguments, once "off the wall" as a matter of constitutional doctrine,[65] have now have been recognized by the Supreme Court.[66]

The popular reading of the Second Amendment – ultimately adopted in *Heller* – is that it protects the right to keep and bear arms for some personal purposes, most prominently self-defense against criminals. Some advocates of this view argue that deterrence of tyranny is another such private purpose – to be accomplished not through the organized state militia, but through the "general," "unorganized," or "citizen's" militia. Others speak of gun ownership as a manifestation of liberty itself, and valuable for that reason alone. But even those who favor a broad private purposes reading do not suppose that it covers all private purposes – the crucial point is that it is not *limited* to active militia service.

The private purposes reading, like the militia-based reading, continues to be subject to overstatements by its supporters and distortions by its opponents. Supporters often call it the "individual rights" view. But as noted above, this nomenclature does not distinguish it from the standard militia-based alternative, which is likewise grounded in a right that "can be enforced by individuals."[67] And just as it is misleading to call the militia-based reading a "collective" rights view, so too is it unnecessary for a supporter of the private purposes view to disregard the militia entirely. Indeed, many supporters of the private purposes argument say, as the Court would eventually hold, that individual self-defense is the core of the right to keep and bear arms but that the right was *codified* in order to protect the militia from disarmament.[68]

It is difficult to trace a single starting point for the ascendance of the private purposes reading, especially since its proponents assert that it has always been true. It had undoubtedly gained ground by the 1960s, coinciding with the NRA's increasing emphasis on constitutional argument. As legal scholar Reva Siegel explains, the chaos and fear of the 1960s helped give rise to a "law and order" frame in American social and political life, which in turn helped animate a particular vision of the right to keep and bear arms in American constitutional culture, one that focused less on institutions like the militia and more on the claims of virtuous "law abiding citizens" defending themselves against violent criminals.[69]

[64] Jack M. Balkin, *From Off the Wall to On the Wall: How the Mandate Challenge Went Mainstream*, THE ATLANTIC (June 4, 2012), www.theatlantic.com/national/archive/2012/06/from-off-the-wall-to-on-the-wall-how-the-mandate-challenge-went-mainstream/258040/.

[65] *See* JACK M. BALKIN, LIVING ORIGINALISM 17–18 (2011) (defining "off-the-wall").

[66] Obergefell v. Hodges, 135 S. Ct. 2071 (2015) (holding the Constitution guarantees a right to same sex marriage); Nat'l Fed'n of Indep. Bus. v. Sebelius, 132 S. Ct. 2566, 2593 (2012) (finding that Affordable Care Act did not fall within the Commerce power); *see also id.* at 2649–50 (Scalia, Kennedy, Thomas, Alito, JJ., dissenting) (same).

[67] *Heller*, 554 U.S. at 636 (Stevens, J., dissenting).

[68] *Id.* at 554.

[69] Reva B. Siegel, *Dead or Alive: Originalism as Popular Constitutionalism in* Heller, 122 HARV. L. REV. 191, 239 (2008).

Trends in scholarship followed an analogous path, seemingly influencing the development of constitutional law to a surprising extent. Most modern legal scholarship is published in student-edited law reviews; thousands of articles are published every year in hundreds of journals. In part because law review articles tend to be long and arcane, sometimes with hundreds of footnotes, the vast majority will only ever be read and cited by a handful of people. In fact, although some leading articles might be cited hundreds of times, nearly half of articles are never cited by anyone.[70]

As to substance, it is often said that contemporary law professors give little attention to technical doctrinal developments, especially those originating outside the Supreme Court.[71] Scholarship deemed too "doctrinal" is viewed with disdain in many quarters of the legal academy, while many lawyers and judges seem to regard the whole enterprise as navel-gazing. In Chief Justice John Roberts's assessment, "Pick up a copy of any law review that you see and the first article is likely to be ... the influence of Immanuel Kant on evidentiary approaches in 18th century Bulgaria."[72]

Although some discrete areas of contemporary legal doctrine have been revolutionized by scholarship,[73] few law professors will ever be directly cited by a lawyer or judge, let alone exert noticeable influence on an area of law or even a single case. And that's what makes the role of scholarship in the doctrinal development of the Second Amendment all the more remarkable. In the course of adopting a position elaborated by scholars and advocates for decades, the majority in *Heller* cited more secondary materials, and cited them more often, than all traditional legal sources – constitutional provisions, statutes, cases, and the like – combined.[74] Scholarship shaped the debate and provided materials for the Court's decision long before the case was even filed.

The changing *substance* of Second Amendment scholarship is also notable. As Adam Winkler notes, very few law review articles addressed the Second Amendment until the 1960s. But in 1965, lawyer and future federal judge Robert Sprecher won the American Bar Association's constitutional law prize with an essay in which he argued, "We should find the lost Second Amendment, broaden its scope and determine that it affords the right to arm a state militia and also the right of the individual to keep and bear arms."[75] The NRA's *American Rifleman* began to emphasize the Amendment

[70] *See* Thomas A. Smith, *The Web of Law*, 44 SAN DIEGO L. REV. 309, 336 (2007) (finding that 43 percent of law review articles on LexisNexis have never been cited).

[71] *See* Harry T. Edwards, *The Growing Disjunction Between Legal Education and the Legal Profession*, 91 MICH. L. REV. 34 (1992); Harry T. Edwards, *The Growing Disjunction Between Legal Education and the Legal Profession: A Postscript*, 91 MICH. L. REV. 2191 (1993); David Segal, *What They Don't Teach Law Students: Lawyering*, N.Y. TIMES, Nov. 20, 2011, at A1.

[72] *See* Interview with John G. Roberts, Jr., Chief Justice of the United States, at Fourth Circuit Court of Appeals Annual Conference, approx. 30:40 (June 25, 2011), www.c-span.org/video/?300203-1/conversation-chief-justice-roberts.

[73] For example, Robert Bork's argument that consumer welfare should guide antitrust policy has shaped basic thinking about antitrust's fundamental purpose. *See* Kenneth Hayer, *Consumer Welfare and the Legacy of Robert Bork*, 57 J.L. & ECON. 19 (2014).

[74] *See* Chapter 1, note 4 (citing study by Alyssa Rutsch).

[75] Robert A. Sprecher, *The Lost Amendment*, 51 A.B.A. J. 665, 669 (1965).

throughout the 1960s,[76] and Ronald Reagan himself authored an article arguing that "the Second Amendment is clear, or ought to be. It appears to leave little, if any, leeway for the gun control advocate."[77] These articles generally did not represent traditional voices from within the academy. But in subsequent decades – especially the 1980s and 1990s – law reviews published a wave of pro-gun scholarship, with 125 articles on the Amendment, most of which supported the private purposes reading.[78] Many of these articles were authored by the same handful of people, few of whom were traditional legal academics, and many of whom were paid by one side or the other.[79] Winkler notes that "[m]ost of the early individual-rights scholarship was written by lawyers employed by gun rights organizations .... Seed money from the NRA and others helped transform the once barren field of individual-rights scholarship."[80]

The quality of these articles was uneven at best. But some, whether or not one agrees with their conclusions, were serious pieces of scholarship. In 1983, Don Kates published "Handgun Prohibition and the Original Meaning of the Second Amendment" in the *Michigan Law Review*,[81] representing the first time that an article supporting the private purposes view was published in a major law journal. Kates was not a law professor, but his work was careful and well-supported, and has had a significant impact on Second Amendment debates.[82] (While arguing for an individual purposes interpretation, Kates also acknowledged in the article the constitutionality of many gun regulations, including some regarding public carry.[83]) Six years later, the well-respected liberal constitutional scholar Sanford Levinson joined the fray with his article "The Embarrassing Second Amendment," published in the *Yale Law Journal*.[84] Levinson called out constitutional scholars, especially those who

76 WINKLER, *supra* note 28, at 95.

77 Siegel, *supra* note 69, at 210 (quoting Ronald Reagan, *Ronald Reagan Champions Gun Ownership*, GUNS & AMMO, 34–35, Sept. 1975).

78 WINKLER, *supra* note 28, at 95–96.

79 Kates, *A Modern Historiography*, *supra* note 52, at 1216–17.

80 *See* WINKLER, *supra* note 28, at 97.

81 Don B. Kates, Jr., *Handgun Prohibition and the Original Meaning of the Second Amendment*, 82 MICH. L. REV. 204 (1983) [hereinafter Kates, *Handgun Prohibition*].

82 According to a Westlaw Keycite, Kates' article has been cited in more than twenty cases, including *Heller*, and nearly 300 law review articles.

83 Kates, *Handgun Prohibition*, *supra* note 81. Kates would later reject these limitations, but his initial position is worth noting if only to describe how far the gun rights position has moved. Kates observed that "[l]argely as a result of gun-owner organizations' own legislative proposals, the laws of every state but Vermont prohibit at least the carrying of a concealed handgun off one's own premises." He further noted that "[a] common proposal, already the law in many jurisdictions, is to prohibit even the open carrying of handguns (or all firearms), with limited exceptions for target shooting and the like, without a permit." Some proposals went so far as to "impose a mandatory minimum jail sentence for the unauthorized carrying of a handgun (or any firearm) off the owner's premises." To Kates, "[t]he constitutionality of such legislation under the amendment can be established on the same basis as the unconstitutionality of a ban on possession ... [W]hile the [historical] statutes used 'keep' to refer to a person's having a gun in his home, they used 'bear' only to refer to the bearing of arms while engaged in militia activities." *Id.* at 267.

84 Sanford Levinson, *The Embarrassing Second Amendment*, 99 YALE L.J. 637 (1989).

claimed to be committed to the Bill of Rights, for essentially ignoring the Second Amendment and the strength of the arguments in favor of the private purposes reading.[85] Leading scholars such as Laurence Tribe and Akhil Amar eventually came to agree, albeit on different grounds, that the Second Amendment protects the right to keep and bear arms for private purposes, though both of them stressed that it still permits reasonable regulation.[86]

In 1995, law professor Glenn Harlan Reynolds declared victory for the private purposes reading, dubbing it the "Standard Model,"[87] a label that was celebrated by those who favored it and sometimes used even by those who did not.[88] There was, in fact, much to celebrate, as echoes of the "Standard Model" could soon be heard from the bench. In *Printz v. United States*, NRA lawyer Stephen Halbrook, who had authored many of the articles and books described above, argued that Congress could not compel state and local law enforcement officers to perform the background checks required by the Brady Act. The Supreme Court agreed, holding that the system amounted to unconstitutional "commandeering" of state officials by the federal government.[89]

Technically the case did not involve the Second Amendment, but in his concurring opinion, Justice Clarence Thomas signaled his interest in the private purposes theory and the scholarship that supported it: "Although somewhat overlooked in our jurisprudence, the Amendment has certainly engendered considerable academic, as well as public, debate."[90] He noted the "impressive array of historical evidence" and the "growing body of scholarly commentary [that] indicates that the 'right to keep and bear arms' is, as the Amendment's text suggests, a personal right."[91] Thomas concluded his opinion by speculating that the future may present an opportunity for the Court "to determine whether Justice Story was correct when he wrote that the right to bear arms 'has justly been considered, as the palladium of the liberties of a republic.'"[92]

A few years later, in May 2001, Attorney General John Ashcroft sent a letter to the NRA announcing that the Department of Justice "unequivocally" supported, apparently for the first time, the view that the Amendment protects a non-militia-centered right.[93] After a major court of appeals decision adopted the private purposes reading, Ashcroft issued a memorandum endorsing the "individual" right to keep and bear

[85] *Id.* at 641–42.

[86] LAURENCE H. TRIBE, AMERICAN CONSTITUTIONAL LAW § 5-11, 901–02 n.221 (3rd ed., 2000); Akhil Reed Amar, *The Bill of Rights as a Constitution*, 100 YALE L.J. 1131, 1162–73 (1991).

[87] Glenn Harlan Reynolds, *A Critical Guide to the Second Amendment*, 62 TENN. L. REV. 461, 463–64 (1995).

[88] Kates, *A Modern Historiography*, *supra* note 52, at 1212 n.7 (noting use even by supporters of militia-based interpretation).

[89] A year later, a system of checks on federal government computers – the NICS – was introduced, so the background check system itself is still in place.

[90] Printz v. United States, 521 U.S. 898, 938 n.2 (1997) (Thomas, J., concurring).

[91] *Id.*

[92] *Id.* at 939.

[93] *See* Letter from John D. Ashcroft, Attorney General, to James Jay Baker, Executive Director of the NRA's Institute for Legislative Action (May 17, 2001). Winkler notes that the NRA was one of the

arms, but also insisting that the Justice Department "will continue to defend vigorously the constitutionality, under the Second Amendment, of all existing federal firearms laws."[94]

That court decision – *United States v. Emerson*, decided by the US Court of Appeals for the Fifth Circuit – struck the same balance, adopting the private purposes theory while upholding a federal gun law. Joe Emerson was the subject of a temporary restraining order for having threatened his wife, and was arrested for violating the federal law that barred such persons from possessing a firearm. Emerson argued, among other things, that this restriction implicated his Second Amendment right to bear arms for private purposes. In keeping with Ashcroft's declaration, the Department of Justice conceded that the Second Amendment was implicated, but insisted that the law was constitutional nonetheless.[95] In a divided decision, the Fifth Circuit became the first federal court of appeals to endorse the view as well, finding that Emerson did not have to show a connection to the organized militia in order to claim Second Amendment rights.[96] Nevertheless, the court held that people like Emerson with a history of violence can constitutionally be denied access to guns.[97]

The Ashcroft letter and memorandum and the Fifth Circuit's decision in *Emerson* were important signals that the private purposes view was gaining ground within the law, and not just in scholarship. One small group of committed libertarian lawyers recognized that those developments "all but guaranteed that a Second Amendment case would eventually be brought to the Supreme Court."[98] Within a few years, the Court would get its chance.[99]

THE CHALLENGE

Clark Neily of the Institute for Justice and Robert Levy of the Cato Institute shared what Levy would later describe as "a political philosophy centering on strictly limited government and expansive individual liberties."[100] That philosophy, more than either man's personal predilection for firearms, led them to support the private purposes reading of the Second Amendment and the potential limits it could impose

biggest backers of President Bush's election campaign that year, and had also poured money into Senate races. WINKLER, *supra* note 28, at 46.

[94] US Dept. of Justice, Attorney General John Ashcroft, *Memorandum for all United States' Attorneys from the Attorney General, Re:* United States v. Emerson (Nov. 9, 2001).

[95] *See* United States v. Emerson, 270 F.3d 203, 219–20 (5th Cir. 2001).

[96] *Id.* at 260 ("We hold, consistent with *Miller*, that [the Second Amendment] protects the right of individuals, including those not then actually a member of any militia ... to privately possess and bear their own firearms...").

[97] *Id.* at 261.

[98] WINKLER, *supra* note 28, at 58.

[99] The story of the *Heller* litigation is ably told in Adam Winkler's superb book, *Gunfight*. The following relies heavily on his account, which incorporates interviews with many of the major players in the lawsuit.

[100] WINKLER, *supra* note 28, at 53.

on government authority.[101] In order to get that theory before the Supreme Court, however, they needed a case, and in order to have a case they needed a plaintiff.

In one journalist's description, Dick Heller was not a "tobacco-spitting ... camouflage-wearing caricature" but "an everyman with a spotless background."[102] A special police officer for the Federal Judicial Center (the administrative center of the federal courts), Heller was permitted to carry a handgun while on duty.[103] But Heller, a strong Second Amendment rights supporter whose house had been hit with bullets twice in the 1970s, wanted to keep a handgun at home for self-defense.[104] He also shared Neily and Levy's desire to expand civil liberties more generally. At the urging of a friend, Heller applied for a permit for a pistol, which was summarily denied under the D.C. law.[105] This would prove to be a crucial move in making Heller a legally appropriate plaintiff.

But Heller was not Neily and Levy's first choice to be the face of the litigation. They had originally designated Shelly Parker as lead plaintiff.[106] Parker lived in a high crime area, and her efforts to self-police her community had led to threats from local drug dealers.[107] African American, a long-time District resident, and a neighborhood crusader, she seemed a perfect figurehead for the civil rights framing of their suit.[108] She was joined by a handful of other plaintiffs, including a wealthy Georgetown resident and a gay Cato Institute employee bullied in his youth.[109]

The team now had a theory and a named plaintiff, but still needed a lawyer. To fill that role, Neily and Levy recruited a 37-year-old attorney with libertarian sympathies named Alan Gura. After law school at Georgetown and some time on the Hill, Gura had opened up a private practice in Alexandria, Virginia.[110] He agreed to represent the plaintiffs for what Levy called "subsistence wages"[111] and has been at the vanguard of Second Amendment litigation ever since.

[101] *Id.* at 52–54.

[102] David C. Lipscomb, *'Regular' Guy Takes Aim at the Law: Special Police Officer Helps End Gun Ban in the District*, WASH. TIMES, July 27, 2008, at M12.

[103] *See* Robert A. Levy, *Anatomy of a Lawsuit:* District of Columbia v. Heller, *Engage* 9:3, Oct. 2008, at 28; *About Us: Heller Legal Team*, HELLER FOUNDATION, https://hellerfoundation.org/about/heller-legal-team/ (last visited July 14, 2017).

[104] Levy, *supra* note 103, at 28.

[105] *See* MARCIA COYLE, THE ROBERTS COURT 141–42 (2013).

[106] WINKLER, *supra* note 28, at 60.

[107] *Id.* at 43; Levy, *supra* note 103, at 28; *see also* Mark Obbie, *Dick Heller Transformed Gun-Rights Law – and He's Not Finished*, THE ATLANTIC (Mar. 21, 2016), www.theatlantic.com/politics/archive/2016/03/why-the-man-who-transformed-gun-rights-still-isnt-satisfied/474708/.

[108] WINKLER, *supra* note 28, at 60.

[109] *Id.* at 91; Robert A. Levy, Commentary, *Taking the D.C. Gun Bar to Court*, WASH. TIMES, Feb. 28, 2003, at A21; Elissa Silverman & Allison Klein, *Plaintiffs Reflect on Gun Ruling: Residents Suing D.C. Explain Motivation*, WASH. POST, Mar. 11, 2007, C1.

[110] James Taranto, *The Weekend Interview with Alan Gura: How a Young Lawyer Saved the Second Amendment*, WALL ST. J., July 19, 2008, at A7.

[111] *Id.*

Gura expected support from the Court's four most conservative members, and hoped to win over Justice Kennedy. But he faced opposition from an unexpected quarter: the NRA itself. The organization was so opposed to the lawsuit that it sent two emissaries to argue for dropping it: Charles Cooper, a heavyweight D.C. lawyer, and Nelson Lund, a law professor who held the NRA-funded Patrick Henry Chair at George Mason Law School.[112] Cooper and Lund argued that the votes simply weren't there for the non-militia reading, even though the Court had changed significantly – and become, by nearly any measure, more conservative[113] – since Thomas issued his invitation in *Printz*.

Perhaps the Court was never the main concern, though. Winkler writes that Gura, Neily, and Levy believed the NRA was concerned in part that a Supreme Court victory might undermine the organization's ability to keep its members motivated by fear of confiscatory gun control.[114] Neily and Levy also wondered whether the NRA was upset that the pair were "stepping on some toes" in an area of law and legislation previously dominated by the NRA and its interests.[115] Whatever the reason, the NRA would later try to hijack Gura's suit by filing its own challenge, then petitioning the court to have its suit consolidated with Gura's, with their lawyer Stephen Halbrook at the helm. But the NRA's suit, *Seegars v. Ashcroft*, was dismissed for lack of standing, leaving Gura to carry the mantle.[116]

Trial and Appeal

Although the Supreme Court was the end goal, Gura had to work his way through the lower federal courts. The first stop was the US District Court for the District of Columbia.

Gura's case initially looked to be in peril. Parker was found to have suffered no legally cognizable injury, because she merely desired a gun permit, but had not actually been denied one. She therefore had no legal standing.[117] All the other plaintiffs in the suit were similarly dismissed, except one: Dick Heller, who had sought the permit and had been denied, and thus had standing to sue.[118]

As to the merits of Heller's claim, Judge Emmett Sullivan stitched close to *United States v. Miller*, the Supreme Court's last real statement on the Second Amendment. According to Sullivan, the militia-based reading was the law of the land, notwithstanding "thought-provoking and historically interesting arguments for finding an

[112] WINKLER, *supra* note 28, at 57.

[113] *See* Nate Silver, *Supreme Court May Be Most Conservative in Modern History*, FIVE THIRTY EIGHT (Mar. 29, 2012, 8:06 PM), http://fivethirtyeight.blogs.nytimes.com/2012/03/29/supreme-court-may-be-most-conservative-in-modern-history/.

[114] WINKLER, *supra* note 28, at 58.

[115] Obbie, *supra* note 107.

[116] WINKLER, *supra* note 28, at 60–63, 88–89.

[117] Parker v. District of Columbia, 311 F. Supp. 2d 103, 109 (D.D.C. 2004).

[118] *Parker*, 478 F.3d 370, 378 (D.C. Cir. 2007).

individual right." Judge Sullivan concluded that it would be error "to overlook sixty-five years of unchanged Supreme Court precedent and the deluge of circuit case law rejecting an individual right to bear arms not in conjunction with service in the Militia."[119]

Gura expected this result, and quickly sought review with the US Court of Appeals for the District of Columbia, perhaps the most prominent appellate court besides the Supreme Court itself. In a 2-1 decision, that court became only the second federal court of appeals (along with the Fifth Circuit in *Emerson*) to hold that the Amendment protects an "individual" right to keep and bear arms, and the first to strike down a law on that basis.[120] The majority concluded that although the preservation of the militia was the primary reason for the Amendment's ratification, the right to keep and bear arms also included the right to defend one's home against violent attack. Having done so, it also concluded that D.C.'s handgun ban and safe storage requirements were an unconstitutional violation of that individual right. In dissent, Judge Karen Henderson argued, among other things, that the Second Amendment applied only to the states, and not the District.

It seemed clear, after the D.C. Circuit's decision, that the case would make its way to the Supreme Court, and so it was no surprise when, on November 20, 2007, the Justices granted certiorari. In the meantime, the lineups of plaintiffs and lawyers in the case had shuffled a bit more. Dick Heller was now the lead plaintiff, replacing Parker on the caption on appeal. Meanwhile, the District chose veteran Supreme Court litigator Walter Dellinger to defend the law.[121] Dellinger had been a law professor at Duke Law School (home institution of this book's authors), and subsequently head of the Office of Legal Counsel and Solicitor General in the Clinton Administration, and by the late 2000s was a partner in the Supreme Court practice group of O'Melveny & Myers LLP. (One of the authors of this book was a junior associate at O'Melveny at the time, and assisted the District's briefing in *Heller*.)

The Supreme Court

Since the Court had not squarely confronted a Second Amendment case in eighty years, Gura and Dellinger had to convey an enormous amount of material in their briefs and oral arguments. But they were not alone. Prominent cases often draw what are known as amicus – "friend of court" – briefs from interested parties, some of which can be quite influential.[122] *Heller* saw a record-setting 68 amicus briefs filed

[119] *Parker*, 311 F. Supp. 2d at 109–110.

[120] *Parker*, 478 F.3d at 395.

[121] David Nakamura, *City Picks Head of Team for Supreme Court Case*, WASH. POST, Jan. 4, 2008, B4.

[122] Jonathan Alger & Marvin Krislov, *You've Got to Have Friends: Lessons Learned from the Role of Amici in the University of Michigan Cases*, 30 J.C. & U.L. 503, 507 (2004); *see generally* Allison Orr Larsen & Neal Devins, *The Amicus Machine*, 102 VA. L. REV. 1901 (2016).

by a wide range of advocacy organizations, scholars, and politicians.[123] Halbrook filed one such brief on behalf of 55 Senators and 250 Representatives arguing that D.C.'s law was an unconstitutional infringement of the individual right to keep and bear arms.[124] The fact that a majority of both houses of Congress filed a brief arguing against the constitutionality of a law that they probably could have changed through legislation (given Congress's power over the District[125]) demonstrates that *Heller* was about far more than the D.C. law itself. The most notable signatory on the Halbrook brief was Vice President Dick Cheney, the first vice president to join an amicus that contradicted the position of his own administration.[126]

The Office of the Solicitor General, then led by Paul Clement, represented the United States. Consistent with the earlier Ashcroft letter, Clement's brief – technically filed in support of neither side – argued that the Second Amendment right extends to private purposes, but is nonetheless subject to "reasonable restrictions."[127] Clement requested and received oral argument time, much to the chagrin of more strident gun rights supporters (who thought the administration's position too weak) and Gura, who groused that Clement "advocated for a meaningless individual right."[128]

The common wisdom of modern Supreme Court practice is that briefs are more important than oral arguments, but that oral argument can reveal the Justices' inclinations.[129] Justice Scalia, unsurprisingly, announced at oral argument his view that "The two clauses go together beautifully: Since we need a militia, the right of the people to keep and bear arms shall not be infringed."[130] He was squarely on the side of the private purposes theory. The big question was where the perennial swing vote – Justice Anthony Kennedy – would land. A few minutes into Dellinger's oral argument, the matter was more or less settled. Kennedy suggested that the best way to read the Amendment was as saying "we reaffirm the right to have a militia, we've established it, but in addition, there is a right to bear arms." In his view, the second clause meant "there's a general right to bear arms quite without reference to the militia either way," and that the Amendment must have arisen from "the concern of

[123] Ilya Shapiro, *Friends of the Second Amendment: A Walk Through the Amicus Briefs in* D.C. v. Heller, 20 J. On Firearms & Pub. Pol'y 15, 15 (2008).

[124] Brief for Amici Curiae 55 Members of United States Senate, the President of the United States Senate, and 250 Members of United States House of Representatives in Support of Respondent at 6–9, 36, District of Columbia v. Heller, 554 U.S. 570 (2008) (No. 07-290).

[125] D.C. Code § 1–206.01 (reserving to Congress the power to enact legislation for the District or to amend or repeal any law passed by the Council).

[126] Winkler, *supra* note 28, at 186.

[127] Brief for The United States as Amicus Curiae, at 10, District of Columbia v. Heller, 554 U.S. 570 (2008) (No. 07-290).

[128] Winkler, *supra* note 28, at 183–87.

[129] Eve M. Ringsmuth, Amanda C. Bryan & Timothy R. Johnson, *Voting Fluidity and Oral Argument on the U.S. Supreme Court*, 66 Pol. Res. Q. 429 (2012) (empirical review of justices changing planned votes after oral argument).

[130] Transcript of Oral Argument at 7, District of Columbia v. Heller, 554 U.S. 570 (2008) (No. 07-290).

the remote settler to defend himself and his family against hostile Indian tribes and outlaws, wolves and bears and grizzlies and things like that."[131]

The question from that point was not so much whether the Court would endorse the private purposes view, but whether it would uphold the law nonetheless. Recognizing as much, Dellinger pivoted, arguing that the regulation did not violate the "individual" right, in part because the law should be read to have a self-defense exception. Clement, too, emphasized that the right to keep and bear arms has "always coexisted with the reasonable regulations of firearms."[132] Even Gura noted that the recognition of an individual right would not deprive the District of "a great deal of leeway in regulating firearms."[133] So long as there was an explicit self-defense exception, the District could, he suggested, "require safe storage" of guns, "for example, in a safe."[134] It could require a license, conditioned on "demonstrated competency," require "background checks," and prohibit minors from possessing guns.

As Winkler notes, "None of the justices seemed particularly interested in the only potentially controlling precedent involved in the case, *United States v. Miller*."[135] The decision in *Heller*, it was clear, would be groundbreaking.

[131] *Id.* at 8. As is common, the comment was formed as a question, but seemed to be a statement of Justice Kennedy's thinking.

[132] *Id.* at 39.

[133] *Id.* at 64.

[134] *Id.* at 72.

[135] WINKLER, *supra* note 28, at 261.

3

Understanding *Heller*

On the final day of the 2007–08 Supreme Court term, the day on which the Justices often announce their most significant and divided decisions, Chief Justice Roberts announced, "Justice Scalia also has our opinion this morning in case 07-290, District of Columbia versus Heller." After a slight pause and shuffling of papers, Justice Scalia responded with a perhaps-unintentional pun[1]: "If you can bear with me, I – I can do it."

He continued:

> We hold that the Second Amendment guarantees an individual right to have and use arms for self defense in the home and that the District's handgun ban as well as its requirement that firearms in the home be rendered inoperative, violates that right.
>
> Our opinion is very lengthy examining in detail the text and history of the Second Amendment.
>
> This summary that I'm giving will state little more than the conclusions.
>
> If you want to check their validity against the dissents' contrary claims, you will have to read some 154 pages of opinions.[2]

As promised, Justice Scalia's majority opinion – joined by Chief Justice Roberts and Justices Kennedy, Thomas, and Alito – examined the text and history of the Amendment in detail, taking sixty-four pages to unpack the meaning of the Amendment's twenty-seven words. The other four Justices – Stevens, Ginsburg, Breyer, and Souter – dissented in two separate opinions that added an additional ninety pages. The first dissent, written by Justice Stevens, argued that the right to keep and bear arms is tied to service in the militia and does not cover private

[1] Empirically speaking, Scalia was the Court's funniest Justice. Jay Wexler, *Laugh Track II, Still Laughin'!*, 117 Yale L.J. Pocket Part 130, 130–31 (2007).

[2] Transcript of Opinion Announcement, District of Columbia v. Heller, 554 U.S. 570 (2008) (No. 07-290), available at www.oyez.org/cases/2007/07-290.

purposes such as self-defense. The second, authored by Justice Breyer, argued that D.C.'s regulation was constitutional even if the right to keep and bear arms includes private purposes.

Together, the opinions in *Heller* represent a remarkable depth and diversity of perspectives on the Second Amendment and constitutional law more generally. For that reason, *Heller* is sometimes assigned as the first case in constitutional law courses, even before foundational decisions like *Marbury v. Madison*[3] and *McCulloch v. Maryland*.[4] And yet the opinions in *Heller* are often misunderstood, even by those who celebrate or decry them passionately.

The majority and dissents were in many ways deeply divided about how to approach, let alone answer, the central question described in Chapter 2 – whether the Amendment is confined to the militia. But the Justices were unanimous in concluding that the right to keep and bear arms, whatever it means, does not rule out gun regulation. The majority opinion approved a potentially wide range of gun control, including bans on possession by felons and the mentally ill, "dangerous and unusual" weapons, possession of guns in "sensitive places" like government buildings, and concealed carrying. At a broad level, there can therefore be no doubt that *Heller* permits gun regulation. And yet there are many open questions about the precise scope of that regulation, questions that became all the more pertinent after the Court's decision in *McDonald v. City of Chicago*, which made the Second Amendment applicable to state and local governments.

As a matter of constitutional law, *Heller* ended one major debate about the Second Amendment. The right to keep and bear arms now undoubtedly extends beyond the militia. But in doing so, it opened a new set of issues about exactly what the Second Amendment allows and forbids. To make sense of the case – and through it, the Second Amendment – one must first understand what the opinions do and do not say, what they have in common, and what divides them.

THE OPINIONS

The Majority Opinion

As Justice Scalia announced, his majority opinion is a "very lengthy" piece of work, that focuses closely on "the text and history of the Second Amendment."

The textual structure of the Second Amendment presents an interpretive challenge. Those who favor the militia-based reading emphasize the first part of the Amendment: "A well-regulated Militia, being necessary to the security of a free State."

[3] 5 U.S. (1 Cranch) 137 (1803).

[4] 17 U.S. (4 Wheat.) 316 (1819). *See, e.g.*, Erwin Chemerinsky, Constitutional Law: Principles and Policies 23 (3rd ed., 2009) (presenting *Heller* as second case, after *Marbury*); Ernest A. Young, The Supreme Court and the Constitution 24 (2d ed., 2017) (presenting *Heller* as first case).

Those who prefer the private purposes reading focus on the second part: "[T]he right of the people to keep and bear Arms, shall not be infringed."[5] Despite the depth of the political divide between these readings, neither can ignore the other's favored clause, because making sense of a constitutional text demands a good faith effort to give legal meaning to all of it. As Chief Justice John Marshall put it in *Marbury*, "It cannot be presumed that any clause in the Constitution is intended to be without effect, and therefore such construction is inadmissible unless the words require it."[6]

To unpack the Second Amendment's text therefore requires a prior decision about where in the text to begin. Justice Scalia concluded that the "Second Amendment is naturally divided into two parts: its prefatory clause and its operative clause."[7] The prefatory clause, according to Scalia, was that portion concerning the militia. But "apart from [a] clarifying function, a prefatory clause does not limit or expand the scope of the operative clause."[8] In other words, textual analysis should focus on the second clause.

Justice Scalia began his analysis of that "operative" clause with the phrase "right of the people." This phrase, he concluded, indicates a private right held by individuals, as is the case for similar phrases throughout the Bill of Rights.[9] The phrase "the people" meant the same thing in the Second Amendment as in other parts of the Constitution, like the First Amendment and the Fourth Amendment, which refer "unambiguously" to "individual rights, not 'collective' rights, or rights that may be exercised only through participation in some corporate body."[10] Like these other rights, the Second Amendment right of "the people" should therefore not be confined to some subset, such as those serving in an organized militia.[11] From there, Scalia turned to the phrase "keep and bear Arms." Citing founding era dictionaries and treatises, English and colonial laws, and legal scholarship, he determined that the phrase was not and is not restricted to military uses. It did not have any special technical meaning, but meant simply to have and to carry weapons.[12]

Having concluded that the operative clause unambiguously protects a private right to keep and bear arms independent of militia service, Justice Scalia returned to the "prefatory" clause. The phrase "free State" did not mean the States or the state militias, but rather a "free *polity*."[13] The "well-regulated militia" was not some subset of "the people," like an organized militia, but something far more diffuse and inchoate, a "people's militia" that at the time of ratification would have meant "all

[5] This, recall, is the portion of the Second Amendment formerly displayed in the lobby of the NRA's headquarters in Virginia.
[6] Marbury v. Madison, 1 Cranch 137, 174 (1803).
[7] District of Columbia v. Heller, 554 U.S. 570, 577 (2008).
[8] *Id.* at 578.
[9] *Id.* at 579–81.
[10] *Id.* at 579.
[11] *Id.* at 580–81.
[12] *Id.* at 582–86.
[13] *Id.* at 597.

able bodied men."[14] The notion of that militia being "well regulated" was not an acknowledgment of a plenary power of government over the possession or carrying of weapons, but simply implied the "imposition of proper discipline and training."[15]

In keeping with his statements at oral argument, Justice Scalia found that the two clauses are in harmony: The drafters of the Amendment intended to protect a militia consisting of "the people" by guaranteeing the right of each of them to keep and bear arms. The militia-protective function of the Amendment, he said, explains why the right was included in the Constitution, but does not change the scope of the right, which at its "core" is self-defense.[16]

The text of the Amendment did not create that right, but merely "codified" it. Justice Scalia pointed to the 1689 English Declaration of Rights, which stated that "the Subjects which are Protestants, may have Arms for their Defence suitable to their Conditions, and as allowed by Law," as proof the English were "jealous of their arms" because of the Stuart kings' attempts to disarm the enemies of the crown.[17] A century later, Blackstone and his eighteenth-century contemporaries noted that a right to arms had "become fundamental for English subjects."[18] The colonists' resistance to disarmament was predicated on these ancient understandings of the rights of all English peoples,[19] which are further confirmed by the fact that contemporaneous state constitutional amendments used language similar to the Second Amendment and were clearly understood to include a right to keep and bear arms for purposes other than military service.

The original public understanding of the Amendment remained unaltered in subsequent generations, as evidenced by scholarly and legal commentary on the Second Amendment shortly after ratification, judicial opinions in various jurisdictions, and even records of post-Civil War debates. Scalia concluded that these sources, extending nearly a century after ratification, suggested that the right to keep and bear arms – whether found in state constitutions or in the Second Amendment – comprehended an individual right to keep and bear arms independent of militia service.[20] Justice Scalia argued that these materials were relevant to the original understanding of the Amendment because they helped "to determine the public understanding of a legal text in the period after its enactment or ratification."

"Putting all of these textual elements together," he summarized, "we find that they guarantee the individual right to possess and carry weapons in case of confrontation."[21] As for the Court's own precedents, especially *United States v. Miller*,

[14] *Id.* at 596.
[15] *Id.* at 597.
[16] *Id.* at 630.
[17] *Id.* at 593.
[18] *Id.* at 593.
[19] *Id.* at 594.
[20] *See generally id.* at 605–19.
[21] *Id.* at 592.

the majority certainly could have overruled prior opinions to the extent that they conflicted with this reading. Instead, Justice Scalia concluded that the earlier cases were consistent with the private purposes reading. And to the degree that four generations of judges had misunderstood *Miller* as supporting a militia-based reading, "their erroneous reliance upon an uncontested and virtually unreasoned case cannot nullify the reliance of millions of Americans (as our historical analysis has shown) upon the true meaning of the right to keep and bear arms."[22]

Having thus defined the right to keep and bear arms, Justice Scalia evaluated the District's regulation in light of it. Though he did not technically apply any of the familiar standards of constitutional scrutiny (strict scrutiny, intermediate scrutiny, or rational basis review[23]), he concluded that the law would fail any that might plausibly be applied.[24] The majority therefore struck down the two major provisions of the D.C. law: the handgun ban and the requirement that any gun not in use must be unloaded and disassembled or have a trigger lock in place.[25] The first provision was unconstitutional because handguns fell within the category of arms in "common use at the time" and had become "the quintessential self-defense weapon."[26] As to the latter, Justice Scalia refused to read into the law a self-defense exception (despite the District's insistence that it contained one), noting that none was explicitly included and citing an earlier D.C. case to that effect.[27]

He emphasized, however, that recognizing an individual right to keep and bear arms does not rule out all gun regulation. In a passage that has been central to post-*Heller* Second Amendment litigation and debate, he explained:

> Like most rights, the right secured by the Second Amendment is not unlimited ... For example, the majority of the 19th-century courts to consider the question held that prohibitions on carrying concealed weapons were lawful under the Second Amendment or state analogues. Although we do not undertake an exhaustive historical analysis today of the full scope of the Second Amendment, nothing in our opinion should be taken to cast doubt on longstanding prohibitions on the possession of firearms by felons and the mentally ill, or laws forbidding the carrying of firearms in sensitive places such as schools and government buildings, or laws imposing conditions and qualifications on the commercial sale of arms.[28]

[22] *Id.* at 624 n.24.

[23] Chapter 4 explains these in more detail.

[24] Justice Scalia conceded that the law would survive rational basis review, but denied that such a standard would ever be applicable. *Id.* at 626 n.27. For a thoughtful analysis of what this could mean not just for the Second Amendment, but for constitutional law more generally, see H. Jefferson Powell, *Reasoning about the Irrational: The Roberts Court and the Future of Constitutional Law*, 86 Wash. L. Rev. 217 (2011).

[25] *Heller*, 554 U.S. at 635.

[26] *Id.* at 629.

[27] *Id.* at 630.

[28] *Id.* at 626–27 (internal citations omitted).

These "presumptively lawful regulations," he noted, were merely "examples" and not intended to be "exhaustive."[29] He went on to emphasize "another important limitation": that the weapons protected by the Second Amendment are those "in common use at the time," a category linked to traditional prohibitions on carrying "dangerous and unusual weapons."[30]

The "historical justifications" for these exceptions were left for "future evaluation," with the proviso that the Amendment "surely elevates above all other interests the right of law-abiding responsible citizens to use arms in defense of hearth and home."[31] Justice Scalia noted that while optimal gun regulation is still a matter of political debate, "[W]hat is not debatable is that it is not the role of this Court to pronounce the Second Amendment extinct."[32]

Justice Stevens' Dissent

Justice Stevens opened his dissent by reframing the disagreement, saying that it was about the *scope* of the Second Amendment, not about whether it protects an "individual" right. In Stevens' view, a conclusion that the right can be asserted by an individual says little about its scope.[33] On the latter question, Justice Stevens' conclusion was straightforward:

> The Second Amendment was adopted to protect the right of the people of each of the several States to maintain a well-regulated militia. It was a response to concerns raised during the ratification of the Constitution that the power of Congress to disarm the state militias and create a national standing army posed an intolerable threat to the sovereignty of the several States. Neither the text of the Amendment nor the arguments advanced by its proponents evidenced the slightest interest in limiting any legislature's authority to regulate private civilian uses of firearms. Specifically, there is no indication that the Framers of the Amendment intended to enshrine the common-law right of self-defense in the Constitution.[34]

As this explanation suggests, Justice Stevens' substantive disagreement with the majority was made starker by the fact that he, too, relied on history as an interpretive guide.

Justice Stevens took issue with the majority's "novel" approach to the Amendment's two clauses.[35] He argued that the majority erred in its insistence that the operative clause is unambiguous and that the preamble's reference to the militia should

[29] *Id.* at 627 n.26.
[30] *Id.* at 627.
[31] *Id.* at 635.
[32] *Id.* at 636.
[33] *Id.* at 636 (Stevens, J., dissenting).
[34] *Id.* at 637 (Stevens, J., dissenting).
[35] *Id.* at 643 (Stevens, J., dissenting).

therefore be disregarded. Instead, the two clauses should be read in sequence, with the language of the first clause helping to establish the meaning of the second. This was the way a typical reader in the eighteenth century would have read the Amendment, he emphasized.[36] Read this way, he said, the phrase "right to keep and bear arms" was used in a military sense and was intended to preserve the militia.[37] Stevens contrasted the explicit purpose of preserving the militia in the preamble with the lack of any mention of self-defense.[38]

Justice Stevens emphasized his agreement with the majority that the Amendment was written to protect and assure the continuation of an effective militia but disagreed that it *also* included private purposes. First, he rejected as flawed the majority's comparison of "the people" in the First and Fourth Amendments.[39] The First Amendment's Assembly Clause, for example, clearly contemplated individual rights that were only effective when exercised collectively.[40] The Fourth Amendment could be read as more individual, but, unlike the First Amendment, was phrased as a "right *against* governmental interference" rather than an "affirmative right *to* engage in protected conduct," and therefore was even less illuminating.[41]

To determine the original meaning of "to keep and bear arms," Stevens pointed to evidence showing that the phrase "bear arms," which derives from the Latin *arma ferre* ("to carry war equipment"), was overwhelmingly used in a military context at the time of the framing of the Constitution.[42] Even the state constitutional provisions identified by Justice Scalia actually "embedded the phrase within a group of principles that are distinctly military in meaning."[43] Indeed, several states proposed language that would have more clearly protected a right to bear arms disconnected from militia service, but James Madison rejected these proposals.[44] If Justice Scalia was serious about recovering what the words meant in 1791, Stevens suggested, he would prioritize how that generation most often used the term, not how it occasionally used it. Turning Justice Scalia's own words against him: "The Court does not appear to grasp the distinction between how a word *can be* used and how it *ordinarily* is used."[45]

[36] *Id.* at 643 (Stevens, J., dissenting).

[37] *Id.* at 647 (Stevens, J., dissenting).

[38] *See id.* at 647–48 (Stevens, J., dissenting) ("The absence of any reference to civilian uses of weapons tailors the text of the Amendment to the purpose identified in its preamble.").

[39] *Id.* at 644–46 (Stevens, J., dissenting).

[40] *Id.* at 645 (Stevens, J., dissenting).

[41] *Id.* at 645–46 (Stevens, J., dissenting).

[42] *Id.* at 646–47 (Stevens, J., dissenting).

[43] *Id.* at 657 (Stevens, J., dissenting) (noting that both Virginia and New York's proposals stated that people "have a right to keep and bear arms; that a well-regulated militia ... is the proper, natural, and safe defense of a free state").

[44] *See* Chapter 1 notes 85–86 and accompanying text.

[45] *Heller*, 554 U.S. at 554 U.S. at 649 n.11 (quoting Smith v. United States, 508 U.S. 223, 242 (1993) (Scalia, J., dissenting) (some internal quotation marks, footnotes, and citations omitted)); *see also* Akhil Reed Amar, Heller, *HLR, and Holistic Legal Reasoning*, 122 HARV. L. REV. 145, 173 (2008).

As for the later-in-time sources cited in the majority opinion, Justice Stevens said that they amounted to "post enactment legislative history" that "shed only indirect light on the question before us, and in any event offer little support for the Court's conclusion."[46] He chastised the majority for citing commentary out of context or without sufficient analysis, arguing for example that Justice Joseph Story's commentaries on the Constitution, written in the early nineteenth century, actually supported the militia-based meaning of the Second Amendment.[47]

Having surveyed the historical material, Justice Stevens found scant support for the private purposes reading. He insisted that the right to self-defense came not from the Second Amendment, nor the Constitution as a whole, but from common law.[48] And even if the arguments for and against a private purposes reading "were evenly balanced, respect for the well-settled views of all of our predecessors on this Court, and for the rule of law itself, would prevent most jurists from endorsing such a dramatic upheaval in the law."[49] Those well-settled views were captured in *United States v. Miller*, which Justice Stevens read as holding that the Second Amendment "protects the right to keep and bear arms for certain military purposes, but that it does not curtail the Legislature's power to regulate the nonmilitary use and ownership of weapons."[50]

JUSTICE BREYER'S DISSENT

Justice Breyer wrote a separate dissent, joined by the same Justices who had signed on with Stevens, but addressing a different issue: Assuming that the Second Amendment protects a right to keep and bear arms for private purposes, how is one to evaluate the constitutionality of a gun regulation?[51]

Breyer criticized the majority for essentially avoiding this question, and for failing to specify a means to evaluate the District's law and others like it.[52] Advocating deference to the political branches – an approach he has taken in other areas of constitutional law – he argued that an individual right to keep and bear arms must be subject to regulation reflecting the balance of public and private interests:

> I here assume that one objective (but, as the majority concedes not the primary objective) of those who wrote the Second Amendment was to help assure citizens that they would have arms available for purposes of self-defense. Even so, a legislature could reasonably conclude that the law will advance goals of great public importance, namely, saving lives, preventing injury, and reducing crime. The law is tailored to the urban crime problem in that it is local in scope and thus affects

[46] *Heller*, 554 U.S. at 663 n.28 (Stevens, J., dissenting).
[47] *Id.* at 667–68 (Stevens, J., dissenting).
[48] *Id.* at 637 (Stevens, J., dissenting).
[49] *Id.* at 639 (Stevens, J., dissenting) (internal citation omitted).
[50] *Id.* at 637 (Stevens, J., dissenting).
[51] *Id.* at 683 (Breyer, J., dissenting).
[52] *Id.* at 687–88 (Breyer, J., dissenting).

> only a geographic area both limited in size and entirely urban; the law concerns handguns, which are specially linked to urban gun deaths and injuries, and which are the overwhelmingly favorite weapon of armed criminals; and at the same time, the law imposes a burden upon gun owners that seems proportionately no greater than restrictions in existence at the time the Second Amendment was adopted. In these circumstances, the District's law falls within the zone that the Second Amendment leaves open to regulation by legislatures.[53]

The fulcrum of Justice Breyer's approach would therefore operate as a kind of interest-balancing, "with the interests protected by the Second Amendment on one side and the governmental public-safety concerns on the other."[54] The issue for a judge, then, would be to see "whether the regulation at issue impermissibly burdens the former in the course of advancing the latter."[55]

Although Justice Breyer's dissent focused on the purposes and effects of the District's regulation, he drew support from colonial-era gun regulations and First Amendment jurisprudence. First, Justice Breyer noted that colonial gunpowder storage laws "would have *burdened* armed self-defense, even if they did not completely *prohibit* it."[56] Like the majority, Breyer cited these colonial laws for the proposition that the right to bear arms is not absolute, though he drew a different conclusion from that fact: "This historical evidence demonstrates that a self-defense assumption is the *beginning*, rather than the *end*, of any constitutional inquiry. That the District law impacts self-defense merely raises *questions* about the law's constitutionality."[57] Second, analogizing to the Court's First Amendment cases, Justice Breyer suggested that, when weighing interests, a court need only determine whether the legislature "has drawn reasonable inferences based upon substantial evidence."[58] Put differently, when supported by "substantial evidence," gun regulation in the name of public safety "represents the kind of empirically based judgment that legislatures, not courts, are best suited to make."[59]

In contrast to Justice Scalia's originalist analysis, which was replete with citations to historical sources, Justice Breyer's opinion was full of contemporary statistics on gun violence and the effectiveness of various means to combat it. But Breyer also questioned the majority's reading of history, saying "insofar as we look at history to discover how we can constitutionally regulate a right to self-defense, we must look not to what 18th-century legislatures actually *did* enact, but to what they would have thought they *could* enact."[60]

[53] *Id.* at 682 (Breyer J., dissenting) (internal citation omitted).
[54] *Id.* at 689 (Breyer, J., dissenting).
[55] *Id.* at 689 (Breyer, J., dissenting).
[56] *Id.* at 687 (Breyer, J., dissenting).
[57] *Id.* at 687 (Breyer, J., dissenting).
[58] *Id.* at 704 (Breyer, J., dissenting).
[59] *Id.* at 704–05 (Breyer, J., dissenting).
[60] *Id.* at 718 (Breyer, J., dissenting).

Justice Breyer also decried the majority's decision as judicial overreach. The decision threatened "to limit the ability of more knowledgeable, democratically elected officials to deal with gun-related problems."[61] He criticized the majority for depriving the District of the tools to combat these problems, asserting that "[i]t fails to list even one seemingly adequate replacement for the law it strikes down."[62] In Breyer's view, this conflicted with the principle that "[d]ifferent localities may seek to solve similar problems in different ways, and a 'city must be allowed a reasonable opportunity to experiment with solutions to admittedly serious problems.'"[63]

Although Breyer explored the conflicting evidence about whether particular forms of gun regulation are effective, he reached no firm conclusions about the effectiveness of gun control as a whole – only that the matter was a close enough question that it should be left to the political branches.[64]

CRITICISM AND COMMON GROUND

Most gun rights supporters were jubilant after *Heller*. Articles with triumphant headlines like "Praise the Lord and pass the ammunition!"[65] splashed across opinion pages and zipped around the internet.[66] Some commentators compared *Heller* to civil rights watersheds like *Brown v. Board of Education*.[67] In the academy, many scholars subscribing to a history-centric method of interpreting constitutional text – the "originalist" school – were equally cheerful. Professor Randy Barnett called *Heller* "the finest example of what is now called 'original public meaning' jurisprudence ever adopted by the Supreme Court."[68] Justice Scalia had shown that originalism could generate more than spectacular dissents; it could coax from the "dead" constitution new life for the right to keep and bear arms.

Not everyone celebrated. Gun regulation advocates, unsurprisingly, worried about the implications. Senator Diane Feinstein declared that Americans would

[61] *Id.* at 719 (Breyer, J., dissenting).

[62] *Id.* at 719 (Breyer, J., dissenting).

[63] *Id.* at 705 (Breyer, J., dissenting) (quoting Renton v. Playtime Theatres, Inc., 475 U.S. 41, 52 (1986)).

[64] *Id.* at 705, 719 (Breyer, J., dissenting).

[65] *Praise the Lord and Pass the Ammunition! Supreme Court Strikes Down DC Gun Ban*, LIBERTY COUNSEL (June 26, 2008), www.lc.org/newsroom/details/praise-the-lord-and-pass-the-ammunition-supreme-court-strikes-down-d-c-gun-ban-1.

[66] Kay Bailey Hutchison & Stephen Halbrook, *Citizens' Rights Reloaded*, WASH. TIMES, June 29, 2008, at B01.

[67] Nicholas J. Johnson, *Rights Versus Duties, History Department Lawyering, and the Incoherence of Justice Stevens's* Heller *Dissent*, 39 FORDHAM URB. L.J. 1503, 1505 n.7 (2012) (concluding that *Brown v. Board*, 347 U.S. 483 (1954), *Lawrence v. Texas*, 539 U.S. 558 (2003), and *Loving v. Virginia*, 388 U.S. 1 (1967), "fit comfortably in the same basket as *Heller*").

[68] Randy Barnett, *News Flash: The Constitution Means What It Says*, WALL ST. J. VIA THE CATO INST. (June 27, 2008), www.cato.org/publications/commentary/news-flash-constitution-means-what-it-says.

be "less safe" because of *Heller*.[69] The District's Mayor, Adrian Fenty, lamented that "more handguns in the District of Columbia will only lead to more handgun violence."[70]

But those on the political left were not the only ones concerned. Some on the right thought *Heller* opened the door to too much regulation. Law professor Nelson Lund, one of the intellectual architects of the private purposes view, criticized *Heller*'s "casual and sweeping" dictum concerning felons, the mentally ill, and "sensitive places."[71] Others thought the opinion went too far, and accused the majority of exhibiting the same hubris and guile that had so aggravated conservatives during the liberal Warren Court years. Judge Richard Posner saw in *Heller* not principled reason-giving but "faux originalism"; a historical "snow job[]."[72] Judge J. Harvie Wilkinson III wrote that the unsupported caveats and limitations in the holding showed a Court determined to "recognize a right to bear arms without having to deal with any of the more unpleasant consequences of such a right."[73] He went so far as to compare *Heller* to *Roe v. Wade* – the *bête noire* of many constitutional conservatives.

Commentary noted that the Justices, like the public as a whole, were deeply divided.[74] There is much truth in that perception. Within the political sphere, *Heller* was rightly taken as the highest court in the land blessing a certain vision of the Second Amendment – one that has been held by gun rights supporters for several decades – over another. It is also undeniable that, when it comes to the Supreme Court of the United States, there's no rule so inflexible as the Rule of Five. Five Justices make the law, so *Heller*'s five Justice majority opinion controls. But too much attention to the divisions can shroud what actually united the Court.

First, every member of the Court concluded that the Amendment protects an "individual" right, inasmuch as that means a right that can be enforced by individuals and not only, say, by states. This is obviously central to the majority's reading, but it was also endorsed by the dissents. The very first lines of Justice Stevens' opinion clarified as much: "The question presented by this case is not whether the Second Amendment protects a 'collective right' or an 'individual

[69] *Gun Ruling To Spark Legal Battles Nationwide*, NBC NEWS (June 26, 2008), www.nbcnews.com/id/25390404/ns/us_news-crime_and_courts/t/gun-ruling-spark-legal-battles-nationwide/#.WSyyBFKZOu4.

[70] *Id.*

[71] Nelson Lund, *The Second Amendment,* Heller, *and Originalist Jurisprudence*, 56 UCLA L. REV. 1343, 1357–58 (2009).

[72] Richard Posner, *In Defense of Looseness*, NEW REPUBLIC (Aug. 27, 2008), https://newrepublic.com/article/62124/defense-looseness.

[73] J. Harvie Wilkinson III, *Of Guns, Abortions, and the Unraveling Rule of Law*, 95 VA. L. REV. 253, 273 (2009).

[74] Richard C. Boldt, *Decisional Minimalism and the Judicial Evaluation of Gun Regulations*, 71 MD. L. REV. 1177, 1177 (2012); Tom Ramstack, *Court's '08 Term Exposed Division*, WASH. TIMES, June 28, 2008, at A01.

right.' Surely it protects a right that can be enforced by individuals."[75] And Justice Breyer went out of his way to emphasize that the Second Amendment "protects an 'individual' right – *i.e.*, one that is separately possessed, and may be separately enforced, by each person on whom it is conferred."[76] It follows that the battle line between the "individual" and "collective" readings – labels which, as explained in Chapter 2, were never particularly accurate – was not central to the case.

Second, every opinion noted that the right to keep and bear arms is not absolute, but can be subject to government regulation. For the majority, this meant long-standing restrictions such as "prohibitions on the possession of firearms by felons and the mentally ill, or laws forbidding the carrying of firearms in sensitive places such as schools and government buildings, or laws imposing conditions and qualifications on the commercial sale of arms."[77] The dissents instead emphasized the balance between the government's interest in public safety and the burden placed on Second Amendment rights.[78] The majority and the dissents agreed that there are numerous regulations that are constitutional but disagreed on the reasoning that supported that conclusion – whether to reason from history or from contemporary interest-balancing, or whether some history itself incorporates interest-balancing (a topic we take up in subsequent chapters).

Third, every member of the Court agreed that the Amendment was adopted, in the words of *United States v. Miller*, "[w]ith obvious purpose to assure the continuation and render possible the effectiveness of [militia] forces," and that it "must be interpreted and applied with that end in view."[79] There are, to be sure, serious divisions about the purpose of the right to keep and bear arms – the centrality of self-defense in the Second Amendment, for example, or even what self-defense means (a question addressed in more detail in Chapter 6). But the Justices were united in saying that the militia were central to the Amendment's ratification, and that this historical fact matters for contemporary legal analysis. *How* it matters is a more difficult and disputed question.

Fourth and finally, the Justices agreed that there is a right to self-defense, even though they strongly disagreed about its relationship to the Second Amendment. The District affirmatively argued that its safe storage law – which had never been enforced against a person using a gun in self-defense – had a self-defense

[75] *Heller*, 554 U.S. at 636 (Stevens, J., dissenting).

[76] *Id.* at 682 (Breyer, J., dissenting).

[77] *Id.* at 626–27.

[78] *Id.* at 689–90 (Breyer, J., dissenting).

[79] *Id.* at 628; *id.* at 661–62 (Stevens, J., dissenting) (quoting United States v. Miller, 307 U.S. 174, 178 (1939)); *id.* at 651 (Stevens, J., dissenting) ("When each word in the text is given full effect, the Amendment is most naturally read to secure to the people a right to use and possess arms in conjunction with service in a well-regulated militia."); *id.* at 681 (Breyer, J., dissenting) (noting that the Second Amendment protects militia-related interests).

exception.[80] These kinds of exceptions are presumed to exist for most laws, from speed limits to trespass. The dissenters agreed, emphasizing the majority's own assumption that an exception would have applied to colonial-era gun laws,[81] but they insisted that this self-defense right was subsidiary to the Amendment's primary militia-protecting purpose.[82] The majority, by contrast, concluded that D.C.'s law could not be read to have such an exception,[83] and that although "self-defense had little to do with the right's *codification*; it was the *central component* of the right itself."[84]

In sum, every member of the Court agreed on the importance of self-defense, that the right to keep and bear arms can be enforced by individuals, that it bears some connection to the militia, and that it has limits. These points of agreement provide a surprisingly broad foundation on which to construct Second Amendment doctrine, but they are not determinative. Going forward, *Heller* leaves open a great many difficult questions, and there are significant – even bitter – disagreements about the scope and strength of the right to keep and bear arms and how to decide Second Amendment cases.

THE SCOPE OF GUN REGULATION AFTER *HELLER*

As a matter of constitutional law, *Heller* ended one debate about the Second Amendment's meaning. The right to keep and bear arms, the Supreme Court held, includes some private purposes, such as self-defense. But as a matter of practical and legal impact, knowing that the right to keep and bear arms includes an individual right to have weapons for private purposes does not take us very far. When someone claims this right, what is a court to do? What kinds of gun regulation does the Amendment permit and prohibit?

These, of course, are fundamental questions about how best to accommodate gun rights and gun regulation – the same kinds of questions that, as Chapter 1 describes, have been central to the story of guns in America from the very beginning. All of the opinions in *Heller*, albeit in different ways, recognized the fundamentality of rights and of regulation. Making room for both requires drawing lines between state and private action, between governmental and private interests, and between political choice and constitutional mandates.

For constitutional scholars and lawyers, this is an extraordinary challenge and opportunity – akin to the landscape that Holmes, Brandeis, and others faced when

80 *See* Brief for Petitioners at 56, *Heller*, 554 U.S. 570 (No. 07-290) (arguing that a self-defense exception is fairly implied in the trigger lock requirement); Brief for the United States as Amicus Curiae at 30–31, *Heller*, 554 U.S. 570 (No. 07-290) (same).

81 *Heller*, 554 U.S. at 686–87 (Stevens, J., dissenting); *id.* at 692–93 (Breyer, J., dissenting).

82 *Id.* at 681 (Stevens, J., dissenting).

83 *Id.* at 630.

84 *Id.* at 599.

they began settling First Amendment doctrine. Indeed, the majority opinion consciously compared *Heller* to exactly such a moment: "Because this case represents this Court's first in-depth examination of the Second Amendment, one should not expect it to clarify the entire field, any more than *Reynolds v. United States*, our first in-depth Free Exercise Clause case, left that area in a state of utter certainty."[85] There would be plenty of opportunity in the coming years, Justice Scalia assured, to work out the details.[86]

Those details have been the subject of more than 1,000 cases since *Heller*. Chapter 4 will describe in more depth the approaches that courts have taken in those cases, but it is also worth sketching here the significant challenges, contradictions, and questions they face even with regard to some of the basic building blocks of the Second Amendment: "the people," "keep and bear," and "Arms."

"the people"

Heller holds that the right to keep and bear arms is held by "the people." But it offers conflicting accounts of who falls within that category. In the space of two paragraphs, *Heller* identifies "the people" as "all Americans,"[87] "all members of the political community"[88]; and all persons "who have ... developed sufficient connection with this country to be considered part of that [national] community."[89] Elsewhere, *Heller* appears to equate "the people" with "citizens,"[90] "law-abiding citizens,"[91] "law-abiding, responsible citizens,"[92] and "all citizens capable of military service."[93] As Justice Stevens remarked in his dissent: "when it finally drills down on the substantive meaning of the Second Amendment, the [majority] limits the protected class to 'law-abiding, responsible citizens.'"[94]

Who can claim to be a member of "the people" is further complicated by the majority's holding that some individuals are either categorically or presumptively without Second Amendment rights. The "presumptively lawful regulatory measures" *Heller* describes include "longstanding" prohibitions of firearm possession by "felons and the mentally ill."[95] But as Justice Stevens pointed out, even felons are

85 *Id.* at 635 (internal citation omitted).

86 *Id.*

87 *Id.* at 581.

88 *Id.* at 580.

89 *Id.* at 580 (citing United States v. Verdugo-Urquidez, 494 U.S. 259, 265 (1990) (internal quotation marks omitted)).

90 *Id.* at 584, 593.

91 *Id.* at 625.

92 *Id.* at 635.

93 *Id.* at 627. For a discussion, see Pratheepan Gulasekaram, *"The People" of the Second Amendment: Citizenship and the Right to Bear Arms*, 85 N.Y.U. L. Rev. 1521 (2010) (noting this multiplicity of usage).

94 *Id.* at 644 (Stevens, J., dissenting).

95 *Id.* at 626.

"members of the political community" who have recognized rights under other amendments, such as the First.[96] Nor did the Court say anything about state and federal regulations that deny guns to those convicted of domestic violence misdemeanors and those subject to certain types of restraining orders.[97]

These are not the only categories of "the people" whose rights might be in doubt. Minors have many of the same constitutional rights as adults, including rights to speech, but one might ask if they qualify under *Heller* as "responsible citizens" or "citizens capable of military service" so as to possess a right to keep and bear arms. Similar arguments could also be made with respect to those who face physical challenges with regard to using firearms safely, such as the blind.[98] Federal law (and the law of some states) also forbids certain categories of aliens, including undocumented aliens, from possessing firearms.[99] Conversely, corporations count as "the people" for purposes of the First Amendment right to freedom of expression and Fourth Amendment right against unreasonable searches, but the Court did not say whether they could claim Second Amendment rights as well.[100]

Finally, *Heller* says that the "central component" of the Second Amendment is individual self-defense.[101] All people – including criminals, children, the mentally and physically infirm, and aliens – have an interest in self-defense. In fact, although the Court has never so ruled, some Justices have suggested that to deny someone an opportunity to assert self-defense in a criminal trial would be a violation of due process.[102] Do the Second Amendment's exceptions override that right?

"keep and bear"

Heller holds that the terms "keep and bear" are to be understood in their ordinary sense, a meaning that has not changed since the founding generation.[103] The word bear, the majority held, means "wear, bear, or carry ... upon the person or in the clothing or in a pocket, for the purpose ... of being armed and ready for offensive or defensive action in a case of conflict with another person.'"[104] The word "keep"

[96] *Id.* at 644 (Stevens, J., dissenting).

[97] *See, e.g.*, 18 U.S.C. § 922.

[98] See Eugene Volokh, *Implementing the Right to Keep and Bear Arms for Self-Defense: An Analytical Framework and a Research Agenda*, 56 UCLA L. Rev. 1443, 1498–503 (2009).

[99] 18 U.S.C. § 922(g)(5); 18 Pa.C.S.A. § 6105(c)(5); Va. Code Ann. § 18.2-308.2:01.

[100] *See* Darrell A.H. Miller, *Guns, Inc.*: Citizens United, McDonald, *and the Future of Corporate Constitutional Rights*, 86 N.Y.U. L. Rev. 887, 910–11 (2011); *see generally* Adam Winkler, We the Corporations: How American Businesses Won Their Civil Rights (2018).

[101] *Heller*, 554 U.S. at 599.

[102] *See* Gilmore v. Taylor, 508 U.S. 333, 359 (1993) (Blackmun, J., dissenting) ("It is easy to see in the context of self-defense how the omission of an affirmative-defense instruction fundamentally denies the defendant due process.").

[103] *Heller*, 554 U.S. at 584 ("At the time of the founding, as now, to 'bear' meant to 'carry.'").

[104] *Id.* at 584 (quoting Muscarello v. United States, 524 U.S. 125 (1998)).

means to "have."[105] Therefore the phrase "keep and bear arms" means to "have and carry weapons."

But *Heller* also insisted that "the right [is] not a right to keep and carry any weapon whatsoever in any manner whatsoever and for whatever purpose."[106] It is clear that some forms of gun-related activity – armed robbery of a bank, for example – are entirely outside the scope of the Amendment, while others – possessing a handgun in the home for self-defense – fall squarely within it.[107] The Court suggested that the right is limited to keeping and bearing arms for "traditionally lawful purposes."[108] But the Court did not specify what those traditionally lawful purposes are, nor how to identify them. It seems unlikely that lawful purposes are completely determined by present law. After all, *Heller* itself was a constitutional challenge to the lawfulness of a firearm regulation. But neither can today's regulatory environment be irrelevant to the question of lawfulness.

Heller also said that guns may be prohibited in "sensitive places such as schools and government buildings."[109] Justice Breyer professed puzzlement: "Why these?" he asked. "Is it that similar restrictions existed in the late-18th century? The majority fails to cite any colonial analogues." And even if one could find an analogue, "why should these colonial laws count, while the Boston loaded-gun restriction ... apparently does not count?"[110] Certainly the Court did not seem to limit its category of "sensitive places" to schools and government buildings. But, Justice Breyer wrote, the Court did not offer anything other than "inconclusive historical research [and] judicial *ipse dixit*" for the rationale behind these exceptions.[111] There are many places one might consider "sensitive" that do not fall neatly within the category of schools and government buildings: the cabin of an airplane, for example, or a church, hospital, or polling station.

It also appears that particular ways of carrying weapons are categorically or presumptively outside the scope of the Second Amendment. *Heller* does not explicitly state that the right to keep or bear arms extends to public carrying, though lower courts have held or assumed that it does.[112] But *Heller* cited nineteenth-century laws banning the "carrying [of] concealed weapons," and noted that these categorical prohibitions "were lawful under the Second Amendment or state analogues."[113] *Heller* suggests, then, that a blanket prohibition on carrying concealed weapons would be constitutional, or at least presumptively so. But must a city or state permit

[105] *Id.* at 582.
[106] *Id.* at 626.
[107] See Joseph Blocher, *Good Cause Requirements for Carrying Guns in Public*, 127 Harv. L. Rev. F. 218 (2014).
[108] *Heller*, 554 U.S. at 577.
[109] *Id.* at 626.
[110] *Id.* at 721 (Breyer, J., dissenting).
[111] *Id.* at 722 (Breyer, J., dissenting).
[112] *But see* United States v. Masciandaro, 638 F.3d 458 (4th Cir. 2011), Chapter 4.
[113] *Heller*, 554 U.S. at 626.

concealed carry if it bans open carry?[114] And even if the Second Amendment right extends outside the home, does it necessarily do so with the same strength?[115]

"Arms"

The meaning of the word "Arms," according to *Heller*, is "no different" today than it was in 1791.[116] "Arms," according to *Heller*, means "weapons."[117] But, again, the rest of the opinion complicates that verbal continuity.

Clearly, not all weapons are either covered or protected by the Second Amendment. The Second Amendment does not cover "dangerous and unusual"[118] weapons, but does protect weapons in "common use." (There is some confusion about the standard, since common law sources referred to both "dangerous *and* unusual" and "dangerous *or* unusual," and *Heller* cites both formulations.[119]) The Court, however, did not explain what makes a weapon dangerous and unusual as compared to a presumptively protected weapon in "common use."[120]

Heller appeared to elaborate "common use" in two slightly different ways. One was loosely historical, extending protection to weapons in "common use at the time." That "time" was not limited to 1791, as that would be "bordering on the frivolous."[121] It might instead mean "lineal descendants" of those weapons that existed in 1791, as both Chief Justice Roberts and the D.C. Circuit suggested.[122] If there is some kind of historical analogue for the modern weapon, at some unspecified level of abstraction, then the Second Amendment is implicated.[123] How one determines whether a contemporary firearm is a lineal descendant of an arm in common use in the eighteenth century, however, is hard to say.

But there's another, slightly different formulation. On the facts of *Heller*, short-barreled shotguns are categorically excluded as "dangerous and unusual" because they

[114] *See generally* Peruta v. County of San Diego, 824 F.3d 919 (9th Cir. 2016) (en banc); Jonathan Meltzer, Note, *Open Carry for All:* Heller *and our Nineteenth-Century Second Amendment*, 123 YALE L.J. 1486 (2014).

[115] See Darrell A. H. Miller, *Guns as Smut: Defending the Home-Bound Second Amendment*, 109 COLUM. L. REV. 1278 (2009).

[116] *Heller*, 554 U.S. at 581.

[117] *Id.* at 581, 647 (Stevens, J., dissenting) (citation omitted).

[118] Volokh, *supra* note 98, at 1478–79.

[119] *Compare Heller*, 554 U.S. at 623, *with id.* at 627.

[120] For a broader debate about how the two standards interact, see the majority and dissent in Kolbe v. Hogan, 849 F.3d 114 (4th Cir. 2017) (en banc).

[121] *Heller*, 554 U.S. at 582.

[122] Heller v. District of Columbia *(Heller II)*, 670 F.3d 1244, 1275 (D.C. Cir. 2011) (Kavanaugh, J., dissenting) (quoting Transcript of Oral Argument at 77, *Heller*, 554 U.S. 570 (No. 07-290) (question of Roberts, C.J.)); *see also Parker*, 478 F.3d at 398 (referring to "lineal descendant[s]" of firearms), *aff'd sub nom. Heller*, 554 U.S. 570.

[123] *See* Darrell A. H. Miller, *Text, History, and Tradition: What the Seventh Amendment Can Teach Us About the Second*, 122 YALE L.J. 852, 917; Volokh, *supra* note 98, at 1477–78 (discussing but rejecting this test).

are not weapons "typically possessed by law-abiding citizens for lawful purposes."[124] By contrast, handguns like the one at issue in *Heller* are protected because they are the type of gun "overwhelmingly chosen by American society for [the] lawful purpose" of defending the home.[125] This suggests that the "lineal descendant" inquiry may not be necessary or sufficient for constitutional protection, and that something like a barrel-count of weapons in current circulation is the deciding factor.[126]

As Eugene Volokh has noted, to identify constitutionally relevant "arms" in this fashion raises serious problems, not the least of which is the metric one uses to determine "common use." One can come to quite a range of conclusions, depending on whether one calculates common use by absolute numbers, by absolute dollars, or by the percentage of the market for firearms, or for handguns, or for all self-defense technology.[127] Furthermore, law-abiding people choose weapons from among the weapons that are lawful to possess, leading to the seemingly circular result that what is protected by the Constitution depends on what has been regulated by the government.[128]

Heller also seems to suggest that the fact that other weapons may be commercially available and equally suitable for self-defense in the home has little bearing on whether an arm is protected, so long as that arm is otherwise in common use. "It is no answer to say," the majority reasoned, "that it is permissible to ban the possession of handguns so long as the possession of other firearms (i.e., long guns) is allowed. It is enough to note ... that the American people have considered the handgun to be the quintessential self-defense weapon."[129] But why is that "enough"? In other areas of constitutional law, the availability of adequate alternative means to exercise a right – speech, for example – is frequently relevant to the constitutionality of particular regulation.[130]

Finally, one needs some sense of the level of generality to assess whether an arm in common use has been "completely prohibited." It is not obvious what should

[124] *Heller*, 554 U.S. at 625.

[125] *Id.* at 628.

[126] In fact, "following *Heller*, almost every federal court to have considered 'whether a weapon is popular enough to be considered in common use has relied on statistical data of some form, creating a consensus that common use is an objective and largely statistical inquiry.'" *Kolbe*, 849 F.3d at 153 (Traxler, J., dissenting) (quoting Hollis v. Lynch, 827 F.3d 436, 449 (5th Cir. 2016)).

[127] *See* Volokh, *supra* note 98, at 1480 (discussing the empirical and definitional challenges of counting weapons for a "common use" test).

[128] This is, it should be noted, not a complication limited to the Second Amendment. Other fundamental rights under Due Process depend in part on what kind of legal practices already exist. *See* Washington v. Glucksberg, 521 U.S. 702, 721 (1997) ("Our Nation's history, legal traditions, and practices thus provide the crucial guideposts for responsible decisionmaking ... that direct and restrain our exposition of the Due Process Clause.") (internal quotation marks omitted) (citation omitted).

[129] *Heller*, 554 U.S. at 629.

[130] Joseph Blocher & Darrell A.H. Miller, *Lethality, Public Carry, and Adequate Alternatives*, 53 HARV. J. ON LEGIS. 279, 282 (2016).

count as the "denominator" for complete as opposed to partial prohibition.[131] Not every weapon can be a class unto itself.

Our point is not that *Heller* was wrong to leave these hard questions unanswered. Instead, we want to emphasize that they are *hard* questions, without obvious answers, and that the post-*Heller* Second Amendment forces us to face them. Two years after *Heller*, the Supreme Court had an opportunity to clarify some of these issues; instead, it magnified the importance of those questions by expanding dramatically the range of laws subject to the Second Amendment.

MCDONALD: THE SECOND AMENDMENT LEAVES WASHINGTON

Just hours after Justice Scalia delivered his magnum opus in the Supreme Court building in Washington, D.C., a 74-year-old man named Otis McDonald sued the City of Chicago for the right to own a pistol.

Otis McDonald was a fighter.[132] Born in the Deep South in 1933, he fled the dead-end life of a Louisiana sharecropper at seventeen and, after a stint in the Army, joined the Great Migration of African Americans heading North. With a few dollars borrowed from his mother, he moved to Chicago, eventually settling on the far South Side. He bought a house in the Morgan Park neighborhood, and raised a family with his wife Laura. He began work as a janitor at the University of Chicago, and eventually achieved the position of maintenance engineer. And, although he had left school at fourteen, he obtained an associate's degree before retiring in the late 1990s.[133]

McDonald's neighborhood did not prosper as much as he did. Once-tranquil nights became punctuated by the thrum of loud music and gunfire.[134] Trim single-family bungalows decayed into drug dens.[135] McDonald's own house was broken into, and he received personal threats for standing up to gang members.[136] McDonald was a hunter and owned two shotguns, but he was concerned they wouldn't be enough to protect him and his family.[137] He wanted to legally own a pistol,[138] which Chicago's gun regulation – a near-replica of D.C.'s – prevented.[139]

[131] In this way, the problem is almost identical to Fifth Amendment takings jurisprudence.

[132] Dahleen Glanton, *Otis McDonald, 1933–2014: Fought Chicago's Gun Ban*, CHICAGO TRIB. (Apr. 6, 2014), http://articles.chicagotribune.com/2014-04-06/news/ct-otis-mcdonald-obituary-met-20140406_1_gun-ban-illinois-state-rifle-association-gun-rights; Mary Katherine Ham, *Meet Otis McDonald: The Man Behind the SCOTUS Gun Case*, WEEKLY STD. (Mar. 2, 2010), www.weeklystandard.com/meet-otis-mcdonald-the-man-behind-the-scotus-chicago-gun-case/article/422191.

[133] *Id.*

[134] Ham, *supra* note 132.

[135] Colleen Mastony, *The Public Face of Gun Rights*, CHI. TRIB., JAN. 30, 2010, at 1.1.

[136] *Id.*; Ham *supra* note 134.

[137] Mastony, *supra* note 135.

[138] Ham, *supra* note 134.

[139] Veronica Rose, *Summary of the Recent* McDonald v. Chicago *Gun Case*, Conn. Gen Assemb. 2010–314, 2010 Sess., at 4 (2010).

The similarity of the two city ordinances might have made his case look easy or insignificant. Surely if a handgun ban is unconstitutional in D.C., the same should be true in Chicago. But as a practical and constitutional matter, the stakes were higher and more complex, because the Bill of Rights does not automatically apply to non-federal law. And despite high profile federal laws like the National Firearms Act of 1934 and the Gun Control Act of 1968, most firearm regulation has always been a state and local matter. McDonald's case had the potential to affect every level of government, from the largest state legislature to the smallest county fair. It also raised a technical, historically fraught, but extremely pertinent question of constitutional law: When and why does the Bill of Rights apply to states and localities?[140]

Incorporating Constitutional Rights

For most of the United States' early history, states and localities could operate heedless of the Bill of Rights. In the 1833 case *Barron v. Baltimore*,[141] the Supreme Court held that the federal Bill of Rights applied only to the national government. As Chief Justice John Marshall wrote, "[t]hese amendments contain no expression indicating an intention to apply them to the state governments. This court cannot so apply them."[142] In theory, then, nothing in the federal constitution prevented states and their subdivisions from establishing churches, compelling persons to incriminate themselves, seizing property without just compensation, or imposing cruel and unusual punishments.[143] They faced constraints, to be sure, including *state* constitutional provisions,[144] but where those protections failed, litigants could not count on a federal backstop.

In the aftermath of the Civil War, the nation experienced something akin to a second Founding era[145] – a "New Birth of Freedom"[146] in which a new generation of framers, including Lyman Trumbull, John Bingham, and Charles Sumner, codified a broader set of foundational legal protections. As a matter of statutory law, the post-Civil War Reconstruction period promised federal protection of basic civil rights for African Americans. The Civil Rights Act of 1866 granted birthright citizenship to all

[140] As far as the federal Constitution is concerned, cities are essentially creatures of state law. *See* Hunter v. City of Pittsburgh, 207 U.S. 161, 178 (1907) ("Municipal corporations are political subdivisions of the state, created as convenient agencies for exercising such of the governmental powers of the state as may be [e]ntrusted to them.").

[141] Barron v. Baltimore, 32 U.S. 243 (1833).

[142] *Id.* at 250.

[143] *See* G. Alan Tarr, *The Past and Future of the New Judicial Federalism*, 24 PUBLIUS 63, 65 (1994) ("The federal Constitution offered few protections against state violations of rights because prior to incorporation, the U.S. Bill of Rights only restricted the federal government.").

[144] *See* Joseph Blocher, *Reverse Incorporation of State Constitutional Law*, 84 S. CAL. L. REV. 323, 329–33 (2011).

[145] Jeffrey Rosen & Tom Donnelly, *America's Unfinished Second Founding*, ATLANTIC (Oct. 19, 2015), www.theatlantic.com/politics/archive/2015/10/americas-unfinished-second-founding/411079/.

[146] Abraham Lincoln, *Gettysburg Address*, Nov. 19, 1863.

those born in the United States, as well as essential legal protections that came with that citizenship. A companion measure, the Second Freedmen's Bureau Bill, stated that all "negroes, mulattoes, freedmen, refugees, or any other persons" should have the "full and equal benefit of all laws and proceedings for the security of person and estate, including the constitutional right of bearing arms."[147]

The Reconstruction Congress attempted to further secure freedmen's rights in 1868 through the Fourteenth Amendment, embedding many of the protections – and even the some of the language – of the Civil Rights Act of 1866 into the Constitution. Section 1 of the Fourteenth Amendment reads in part: "No state shall make or enforce any law which shall abridge the privileges or immunities of citizens of the United States; nor shall any state deprive any person of life, liberty, or property, without due process of law; nor deny to any person within its jurisdiction the equal protection of the laws."[148]

But the Supreme Court maintained the *Barron* barrier between state law and the Bill of Rights even as Southern vigilante groups – sometimes alone, sometimes in concert with government officials – acted to thwart the freedmen's gains. The interaction between state law, racist violence, and the federal constitution was on full display in the facts and holding of the Supreme Court's 1875 case *United States v. Cruikshank*.[149] The case arose out of what was perhaps the worst single episode of racial violence in the Reconstruction era[150] – an incident known as the Colfax Massacre.[151] *Cruikshank* represented one of the Court's first real engagements with the Second Amendment, and confirmed, almost in passing, that the Amendment had no real practical impact.

The story of *Cruikshank* is harrowing. In 1872, a black militia in Grant Parish, Louisiana, tried to stop a white supremacist group from establishing control over the government of Colfax. The political battle soon became a physical one, and the black militia eventually holed up in the county courthouse, besieged by a white mob. The black defenders were outnumbered roughly three to one, and heavily outgunned – the white mob, led by a self-proclaimed sheriff named Christopher Columbus Nash, even had a cannon. On the evening of Easter Sunday, Nash and his co-conspirators set fire to the courthouse and forced the defenders out under a white flag of surrender.

The surrender was not honored. An 1875 congressional report stated that at least 105 perished in the ensuing massacre.[152] A 1950 state historical marker put the

[147] Second Freedmen's Bureau Bill, § 7 (Dec. 4, 1865) *reprinted in* THE AMERICAN NATION, PRIMARY SOURCES (Bruce Frohnen, ed., 2008).

[148] U.S. CONST, amend. XIV § 1.

[149] United States v. Cruikshank, 92 U.S. 542 (1875).

[150] ERIC FONER, RECONSTRUCTION: AMERICA'S UNFINISHED REVOLUTION, 1863–1877, at 437 (1988).

[151] *See generally* CHARLES LANE, THE DAY FREEDOM DIED: THE COLFAX MASSACRE, THE SUPREME COURT, AND THE BETRAYAL OF RECONSTRUCTION (2009).

[152] *Id.* at 265.

figure at 150. (That same marker described the event as a "riot" that marked the end of "carpetbag misrule."[153]) Members of the black militia who fled were chased down and slaughtered. Those who hid in the smoldering courthouse were dragged out and met the same fate. Roughly fifty men were taken prisoner, and nearly all were summarily executed later that night. Levi Nelson was among the captives. He was shot by Bill Cruikshank, another leader of the mob, but survived and managed to crawl away.

Nelson would later be the star witness in a federal prosecution of the leaders of the Colfax Massacre. Having rounded up dozens of members of the white mob, the US Attorney in New Orleans convicted three of them – including Cruikshank – for violating the Enforcement Act of 1870, a federal law passed pursuant to the newly ratified Fourteenth Amendment. Under the terms of the Act, Cruikshank was convicted for conspiracy to violate freedmen's civil rights, including their "right to keep and bear arms for a lawful purpose." But the convictions were dismissed on appeal, and the men released while the federal government appealed to the Supreme Court, which held that the Act could not be applied to private conspiracies like the one Cruikshank had helped lead.[154] The Court found that the Act only applied where constitutional rights were at issue, and that none were threatened in this particular circumstance because the Bill of Rights did not apply to the states, let alone individuals like Cruikshank: "The second amendment declares that it shall not be infringed; but this ... means no more than it shall not be infringed by Congress."[155] The Amendment, the Court held, "has no other effect than to restrict the powers of the national government."[156]

As it often does in federalism cases, the Court suggested that the states themselves could do the job.[157] But Louisiana never prosecuted any of the perpetrators of the massacre, and the decision in *Cruikshank* helped embolden white supremacists throughout the South. As historian Eric Foner later noted, "[a]mong blacks in Louisiana, the incident was long remembered as proof that in any large confrontation, they stood at a fatal disadvantage."[158] Even as the case was winding its way up to the Supreme Court, Nash founded a chapter of the White League – a paramilitary-style organization similar in style to the old slave patrols, which acted as the "military arm of the Democratic party," suppressing Republican votes and helping to tilt the balance of power against freedmen throughout the South.[159]

[153] Richard Rubin, *The Colfax Riot*, ATLANTIC, July/Aug. 2003, at 155, 155.

[154] *Cruikshank*, 92 U.S. 542 (1875).

[155] *Id.* at 553.

[156] *Id.*

[157] *See, e.g.*, United States v. Morrison, 529 U.S. 598, 627 (2000) ("[U]nder our federal system [the Petitioner's] remedy must be provided by the Commonwealth of Virginia, and not by the United States.").

[158] FONER, *supra* note 150, at 437.

[159] GEORGE C. RABLE, BUT THERE WAS NO PEACE: THE ROLE OF VIOLENCE IN THE POLITICS OF RECONSTRUCTION 132 (1984).

The Supreme Court would address the Second Amendment claims of another armed and un-sanctioned "militia" a decade later in *Presser v. Illinois*. Herman Presser had been indicted and later convicted on the grounds that he "did unlawfully belong to, and did parade and drill in the city of Chicago with an unauthorized body of men with arms."[160] According to the Court's description of the scene, Presser, bearing a cavalry sword, "marched at the head" of a troop of around four hundred men armed with rifles. They paraded down the streets of Chicago, although "the company had no license from the governor of Illinois to drill or parade as part of the militia of the state" and despite the fact that Presser's band "was not a part of the regular organized militia of the state, nor a part of troops of the United States, and had no organization under the militia law of the United States."[161]

Presser's "company" was part of the Lehr und Wehr Verein (Instruct and Defend Association), a socialist-affiliated group dedicated to defending workers against private security forces like the Pinkertons. Presser argued that his activity fell within the scope of his Second Amendment rights, but the Court – as it had in *Cruikshank* just a few years earlier – held that the Amendment only protected against regulation by the federal government. "We think it clear," wrote the Court, that laws that prohibit "men to associate together as military organization, or to drill or parade with arms in cities and towns" without authorization, "do not infringe the right of the people to keep and bear arms." But "a conclusive answer to the contention that this amendment prohibits the legislation in question lies in the fact that the amendment is a limitation only upon the power of congress and the national government, and not upon that of the state."[162]

Cruikshank and *Presser* were not the Supreme Court's only references to the Second Amendment.[163] But they represented the Court's closest analysis of the Second Amendment until *Miller*. They did not provide much guidance on the proper scope of gun rights and regulation, because they rested on the simple proposition that the Bill of Rights, including the right to keep and bear arms, only applied to federal law and federal officers.

Barron was the law for nearly a century. Only in the middle of the twentieth century did the barrier between the Bill of Rights and the states truly crack, as federal constitutional guarantees gradually came to be applied to state and local governments. The mechanisms of that transformation are the subject of intense debate. Many scholars argue that the states should be bound to the federal constitution by the Privilege, Immunities, and Clause of the Fourteenth Amendment, which provides

[160] Presser v. Illinois, 116 U.S. 252, 253 (1886).

[161] *Id.* at 254.

[162] *Id.* at 264–65.

[163] *See, e.g.*, Eugene Volokh, *Supreme Court Cases on the Right to Keep and Bear Arms*, www2.law.ucla.edu/volokh/beararms/sct.htm (accessed Nov. 28, 2017); *see also* David B. Kopel, *The Supreme Court's Thirty-Five Other Gun Cases: What the Supreme Court has said about the Second Amendment*, 18 St. Louis U. Pub. L. Rev. 99 (1999).

that "No State shall make or enforce any law which shall abridge the privileges or immunities of citizens of the United States." But that clause was, in the words of one scholar, "strangl[ed] ... in its crib" by the Supreme Court's widely criticized 1873 decision in the *Slaughterhouse Cases*.[164]

Instead, the Court has pursued a course of "selective incorporation" through the Due Process Clause. Under this approach, only those federal rights that are "fundamental" are applicable against the states.[165] Unsurprisingly, most rights in the Bill of Rights meet this standard. By the time *Heller* was decided, only a handful did not, such as the Third Amendment's guarantee against quartering of troops in the home (a right that few courts have even addressed), the Seventh Amendment's right to a jury in civil cases, the Fifth Amendment's requirement of a grand jury indictment before criminal prosecution, and, of course, the Second Amendment's right to keep and bear arms.[166] The status of the latter was the essential question in *McDonald*.

McDonald's *Holding*

Justice Samuel Alito wrote the plurality opinion,[167] which began by recounting the Court's existing precedents, including its rejection of Second Amendment claims in *Cruikshank* and *Presser*. Those cases, he noted, predated not only *Heller*, but also the development of the Court's selective incorporation jurisprudence. Applying the same test that had been used to incorporate most of the rest of Bill of Rights, Alito concluded that the right to keep and bear arms must apply to the states because it is "deeply rooted in this Nation's history and tradition."[168] He pointed to the historical pedigree of the right, from Blackstone and colonial-era state constitutions on through its inclusion in the Freedmen's Bureau Bill and the Civil Rights Act of 1866. Since it is the Due Process Clause of the Fourteenth Amendment that provides the basis for incorporation, it was particularly significant that the right was discussed in connection with the Amendment's ratification after the Civil War.

Justice Thomas agreed with the result, but would have grounded incorporation in the Privileges or Immunities Clause, which had long ago been interred by the

[164] Akhil R. Amar, *The Bill of Rights and the Fourteenth Amendment*, 101 YALE L.J. 1193, 1259 (1992).

[165] *See* Palko v. Connecticut, 302 U.S. 319, 324–25 (1937) (Those rights that "have been found to be implicit in the concept of ordered liberty" may be incorporated against the states because they enforce "principle[s] of justice so rooted in the traditions and conscience of our people as to be ranked as fundamental" (alteration added, internal quotation marks and citation omitted)).

[166] The status of the "excessive fines" and "excessive bail" provisions of the Eighth Amendment are somewhat more ambiguous, but the Court has unquestionably incorporated other parts of that Amendment.

[167] No single opinion garnered the support of five justices. Justice Alito's opinion was joined in full by Chief Justice Roberts and Justices Scalia and Kennedy. Justice Thomas joined portions of Alito's opinion and offered an opinion concurring in part and concurring in the judgment. Justice Scalia wrote an additional concurring opinion. Justice Stevens dissented, and Justice Breyer wrote a dissenting opinion joined by Justices Ginsburg and Sotomayor.

[168] McDonald v. City of Chicago, 561 U.S. 742, 806 (2010).

Slaughterhouse Cases. Justice Thomas was convinced by the arguments – to which Alan Gura had overwhelmingly devoted his brief, much to the consternation of the NRA[169] – that the *Slaughterhouse Cases* were wrongly decided on originalist grounds. Justice Scalia, Thomas' originalist companion on the Court, appeared to agree in theory, but preferred to stick with the tried-and-true method of selective incorporation. At oral argument, he derided Gura's argument as "the darling of the professoriate," and said that "even I have acquiesced" in the Due Process route to incorporation.[170] (It is true, in any event, that an interesting combination of liberal and libertarian members of "the professoriate" had argued for the Privileges or Immunities Clause, apparently united in the belief that the *Slaughterhouse Cases* were wrongly decided and also in the hope that the Clause might provide the basis for protecting unenumerated rights going forward.[171]) Justice Thomas provided the fifth vote for incorporation, meaning that – whatever one's preferred grounds for the result – the right to keep and bear arms would apply against state and local governments. But, as in *Heller*, the Justices divided 5-4, this time with Justice Sonia Sotomayor taking the place of Justice Souter in dissent.

Justice Stevens, writing his last opinion as an active member of the Court (he retired that summer and soon wrote a book, one chapter of which was devoted to the Second Amendment[172]), argued that the majority had taken the wrong route. Like Justice Thomas, he thought it inappropriate to use Due Process doctrine as a means of incorporation, because the Due Process Clause provides "its own bottom."[173] Following the test articulated by Justice Cardozo in *Palko v. Connecticut*, the Court should simply ask whether a particular right is "implicit in the concept of ordered liberty."[174] Justice Stevens concluded that the right to have a handgun was not. In reaching that conclusion, he made clear his discomfort with the kind of history-based approach that both he and Justice Scalia had employed in *Heller*. History, Justice Stevens wrote, was relevant but not determinative, and could very easily be used to disguise subjective judgments. It is hard not to read the opinion as one last critique of originalism.[175]

[169] Brannon P. Denning & Glenn H. Reynolds, *Five Takes on* McDonald v. City of Chicago, 26 J.L. & POL. 273, 289 (2011) (remarking that Gura's strategy "so alarmed the National Rifle Association" that it filed briefs urging conventional use of selective incorporation and asking for oral argument time).

[170] Transcript of Oral Argument at 7, *McDonald*, 561 U.S. 742 (No. 98-1521).

[171] *See, e.g.*, Randy Barnett, *Foreword: What's So Wicked About* Lochner?, 1 N.Y.U. J.L. & LIBERTY 325 (2005) (arguing for the reversal of the *Slaughterhouse Cases*); J. M. Balkin, *Constitutional Interpretation and the Problem of History*, 63 N.Y.U. L. REV. 911, 934 (1988) (arguing that the *Slaughterhouse Cases* represented a "misreading" of the Privileges or Immunities Clause which "profoundly influence[d] its future development"); Brief of Constitutional Law Professors as *Amici Curiae* in Support of Petitioners, *McDonald*, 561 U.S. 742 (No. 98-1521) (brief on the issue co authored by Barnett and Balkin).

[172] JOHN PAUL STEVENS, FIVE CHIEFS: A SUPREME COURT MEMOIR (2011).

[173] *McDonald*, 561 U.S. at 866 (Stevens, J., dissenting).

[174] *Id.* at 871 (Stevens, J., dissenting).

[175] Justice Scalia responded in a separate concurrence. *Id.* at 791 (Scalia, J., concurring).

Justice Breyer wrote the lead dissent on the merits, which opened by noting that "[s]ince *Heller*, historians, scholars, and judges have continued to express the view that the Court's historical account was flawed," suggesting that the case should be reconsidered.[176] Even on its own terms, though, he rejected the majority's conclusion that *Heller*'s right is fundamental in the relevant sense. It is, Breyer suggested, difficult to find a right to be "deeply rooted" in American history and tradition when it was not clearly recognized by the Supreme Court until 2008.[177]

McDonald completed the transformation that *Heller* had begun. As a matter of constitutional doctrine, the dominant understanding of the Second Amendment changed from a federalism provision designed to protect states from the federal government to a private-purposes right that federal judges could use to strike down state laws. By incorporating the right to keep and bear arms, *McDonald* made *Heller* applicable to state and local laws, which constitute the vast majority of gun regulation in the United States. In other words, it did not change *Heller*'s basic holding, but vastly expanded its reach. Indeed, Justice Alito cited *Heller*'s paragraph of exceptions, and added that "[s]tate and local experimentation with reasonable firearms regulations will continue."[178]

As in *Heller*, then, the Justices in *McDonald* agreed that the Second Amendment permits some types of firearms regulation. But *McDonald* also highlighted deep disagreement about the boundaries of permissible restriction, and – equally fundamentally – how to define those boundaries. Justice Alito pointed to *Heller* as "expressly reject[ing] the argument that the scope of the Second Amendment right should be determined by judicial interest balancing."[179] Instead, as Justice Scalia had done in *Heller*, Justice Alito appeared to endorse a historical-categorical approach to evaluating Second Amendment claims. Even so, he went on to "repeat th[e] assurances" that incorporation would not imperil the longstanding regulatory measures like felon-in-possession bans that *Heller* had guaranteed were lawful.[180]

In dissent, Justice Breyer argued that the "determination whether a gun regulation is constitutional would thus almost always require the weighing of the constitutional right to bear arms against the 'primary concern of every government – a concern for the safety and indeed the lives of its citizens.'"[181] This, he concluded, was a reason not to incorporate the right at all, though the underlying point echoes his argument in *Heller* – namely, that the constitutionality of gun regulation cannot be determined by categorical analysis alone.

[176] *Id.* at 914 (Breyer, J., dissenting).
[177] *Id.* at 899 (Breyer, J., dissenting).
[178] *Id.* at 785 (quoting Brief for State of Texas et al. as *Amici Curiae* at 23, *McDonald*, 561 U.S. 742 (No. 98-1521)).
[179] *Id.* at 785.
[180] *Id.* at 786.
[181] *Id.* at 922–23 (Breyer, J., dissenting) (internal citation omitted).

This debate has been at the heart of the more than 1,000 Second Amendment cases decided since *Heller*, the vast majority of which involve the kinds of state and local regulation that *McDonald* made relevant.[182] Chapter 4 explores the jurisprudential undercurrents and their doctrinal manifestations in more detail.

HELLER IN LAW AND POLITICS

Justice Scalia understood, as well as any Justice ever has, the many roles and audiences of constitutional rhetoric. His published opinions often seemed crafted for public consumption, and indeed he frequently said that he was writing for law students and future generations.[183] *Heller* itself should be understood with that in mind.

As a matter of legal doctrine, *Heller* was a watershed moment, and established – for the first time clearly – that the Second Amendment includes certain private purposes. And yet *Heller* leaves many open questions. This was inevitable, and perhaps even a virtue. Had the Justices attempted to establish a single over-arching test for future Second Amendment challenges, they might have been criticized even more harshly for judicial activism. The Court faced an enormously difficult set of questions, with a wide range of possible answers. That simple point is worth emphasizing, because debates over the Second Amendment are often characterized as binary: Individual rights versus collective rights; gun rights versus gun regulations; gun nuts on one side versus gun grabbers on the other. The reality is far more complicated, as this chapter has tried to show.

Since *Heller*, the doctrinal challenges have revolved around two categories of jurisprudential questions, as Chapter 4 explains in more detail: What kind of arms, people and activities fall within the scope of the Amendment (the question of "coverage"), and how much are they protected when they do (the question of "protection").

The coverage and protection debates are rooted in *Heller* and *McDonald*. The majorities in these cases favored a bright-line approach to coverage, with boundaries set according to the private purposes reading, and suggested that protection was essentially a binary question. The matters the Second Amendment covers are immune to regulation; those that fall outside of it raise no problems. The dissenters, by contrast, would have pegged coverage to the militia and militia-related activities. But even if the right covers private purposes, the dissenters argued, the inquiry doesn't end there. To find Second Amendment coverage is not to say that its protection is perfect – even activities covered by the right are subject to some regulation.

[182] *Protecting Strong Gun Laws: Supreme Court Leaves Lower Court Victories Untouched*, Law Center to Prevent Gun Violence (Aug. 2, 2016), http://smartgunlaws.org/protecting-strong-gun-laws-the-supreme-court-leaves-lower-court-victories-untouched/ (accessed Jan. 15, 2018).

[183] Adam J. White, *Antonin Scalia, Legal Educator*, Nat'l Affairs, Fall 2017, at 145, 145.

On one point, though, there was unanimous assent: The Second Amendment is not absolute. In fact, *Heller* itself included a list of exceptions broad enough to accommodate the vast majority of gun regulations that are politically imaginable in the United States: felon-in-possession bans, concealed carry bans, bans on dangerous and unusual weapons, restrictions on carrying guns in sensitive places, and the like. As a result, *Heller*'s practical impact on the scope of gun regulation has been, and likely will continue to be, somewhat muted.

But it would be a mistake to think that *Heller* was anything but a landmark decision. Even from a strictly legal point of view, *Heller* and its implementation raise the kinds of fundamental methodological challenges and opportunities that rarely appear in constitutional law. We are witnessing, in real time, the formation of a constitutional right.

And *Heller*'s significance goes beyond the courtroom. As Chapter 2 described, the debate between the militia-based and private purposes is about identity and meaning as well as legal doctrine. A year before he became a Supreme Court Justice, then-Judge Scalia bemoaned "a perhaps inevitable but nonetheless distressing tendency to equate the existence of a right with the nonexistence of a responsibility" – that having a legal right to engage in a behavior means it is "proper and perhaps even good" to do so.[184]

Twenty years later, in a speech to a hunting organization, Justice Scalia described some of the lenses through which people view guns. "I grew up at a time when people were not afraid of people with firearms," he said, remarking that he was rifle team member at the military school he attended. "I used to travel on the subway from Queens to Manhattan with a rifle," he said. "Could you imagine doing that today in New York City?" He acknowledged the obstacle to recovering that vision: "The attitude of people associating guns with nothing but crime, that is what has to be changed."[185]

Two years after giving that speech, Justice Scalia helped provide momentum for the change. His opinion for the majority in *Heller* made it easier to associate the private use of guns with the Constitution, rather than with crime.[186] The Supreme Court's valorization of this vision is immensely significant. But the Court also left open a wide range of *legal* questions that *Heller* – for all its power as a symbol – did not answer. The following chapter begins to address those questions.

[184] Antonin Scalia, *Law, Liberty and Civic Responsibility*, *in* RIGHTS, CITIZENSHIP AND RESPONSIBILITIES 3 (Bradford P. Wilson, ed., 1985); *see also* JAMES E. FLEMING & LINDA C. MCCLAIN, ORDERED LIBERTY: RIGHTS, RESPONSIBILITIES, AND VIRTUES 5 (2013) (describing, without endorsing, the view that "legal rights equal moral rightness"); Mary Ann Glendon, *Introduction: Forgotten Questions*, *in* SEEDBEDS OF VIRTUE 1 (Mary Ann Glendon & David Blankenhorn, eds., 1995).

[185] *Young Scalia Carried Rifle While Riding N.Y. Subway*, A.P. *via* DESERET NEWS, Feb. 27, 2006, at A05.

[186] Robin West, *Rights, Harms, and Duties: A Response to Justice for Hedgehogs*, 90 B.U. L. REV. 819, 826 (2010) ("This person [with a gun] is not a redneck gun-toting potentially dangerous renegade; he is now a constitutional icon – a rights-bearing hero bucking the tide of an intrusive and potentially totalitarian nightmare state.").

4

Heller's Aftermath: "A Vast *Terra Incognita*"

Sean Masciandaro owned and operated Raging Reptiles,[1] a small business that consisted of Masciandaro, his collection of snakes and lizards (including a blue-tongued skink named Semper Fi[2]), and long drives to educational events up and down the East Coast.[3]

Most of the week he spent on the road, driving and sleeping in his car – a Toyota hatchback loaded with his animals, his laptop computer, and several hundred dollars in cash.[4] He also traveled armed, with a "machete-type" knife tucked under his seat and a loaded 9mm semi-automatic pistol locked in a case inside a messenger bag.[5]

On June 5, 2008, just a few weeks before the Supreme Court handed down its decision in *District of Columbia v. Heller*, Masciandaro was driving with his girlfriend through Virginia. Exhausted from the journey, he pulled into a gravel parking lot on a little finger of land called Daingerfield Island just off the George Washington Memorial Parkway, less than an hour from his home. Reclining their seats, the two soon fell asleep. At 10 in the morning, Masciandaro awoke to a tapping on his window.

National Park Officer Ken Fornshill was on patrol when he observed the hatchback parked illegally on the lot. After waking Masciandaro, he requested identification. Masciandaro reached back to collect his wallet from the messenger bag,[6] when

[1] Robert Barnes, *Cases Lining Up to Ask Supreme Court to Clarify Second Amendment Rights*, WASH. POST (Aug. 14, 2011), www.washingtonpost.com/politics/cases-lining-up-to-ask-supreme-court-to-clarify-second-amendment-rights/2011/08/11/gIQAioihFJ_story.html?utm_term=.c3a535735ba7.

[2] Raging Reptiles Home Page, RAGING REPTILES, www.ragingreptiles.com/home (accessed Jan. 15, 2018).

[3] Raging Reptiles FAQs, RAGING REPTILES, www.ragingreptiles.com/faqs (accessed Jan. 15, 2018).

[4] Brief of the Appellant at 6, 8, United States v. Masciandaro, 638 F.3d 458 (4th Cir. 2011) (No. 09-4839).

[5] *Id.* at 7; United States v. Masciandaro, 639 F. 3d 458, 460 (4th Cir. 2011).

[6] Brief of the Appellant, *supra* note 4, at 7.

Fornshill saw the knife under the seat. He asked Masciandaro and his girlfriend to step out of the car and then asked Masciandaro whether the vehicle contained any other weapons. Masciandaro then told him about the gun.[7]

At the time, National Park Service regulations made it illegal to "[c]arry or possess a loaded weapon in a motor vehicle" while on National Park Service land.[8] Masciandaro was arrested, tried before a federal magistrate judge, convicted of the parking and weapons violations and, at the government's urging, given a modest $200 fine.[9] He nonetheless appealed his conviction, claiming that the Park Service regulation violated his Second Amendment right to keep and bear arms.[10]

The appeal, *United States v. Masciandaro*, ended up before a three-judge panel of the United States Court of Appeals for the Fourth Circuit. One panel member, Patrick Michael Duffy, was a federal trial court judge sitting by designation on the Court of Appeals, a routine practice in the federal system. The other two – Judge Paul Niemeyer and Judge J. Harvie Wilkinson III – were well-respected fixtures of the appellate judiciary and both generally regarded as conservative. Masciandaro's constitutional challenge was the immediate issue before the three judges. But, more fundamentally, the case was about how courts should go about deciding Second Amendment challenges after *Heller*.

Heller had resolved a profound dispute over the Second Amendment's meaning, holding that individuals have a right to keep and bear arms for private purposes and rejecting the notion that participation in an organized militia was necessary to claim that right. But, as Chapter 3 showed, that holding opened a host of other questions. Who can assert that right? What kind of weapons? Under what circumstances? What kind of reasons can limit the right, if any? *Heller* didn't purport to decide all those questions, stating that "there will be time enough" to resolve them later.[11]

Masciandaro's case was just one of the more than 1,000 Second Amendment challenges that inundated the courts in the decade after *Heller*.[12] Initially, judges rested on *Heller*'s list of excluded people, arms, and activities. *Heller*, after all, made clear that it "did not cast doubt on such longstanding regulatory measures as 'prohibitions on the possession of firearms by felons and the mentally ill,' 'laws forbidding the

[7] *Id.*

[8] 36 CFR § 2.4(b) (2009). The regulation was changed before Masciandaro's trial to allow guns on National Park Service land if allowed under state law where the land is located. Masciandaro's argument to reject his conviction based on the change was unsuccessful. United States v. Masciandaro, 638 F.3d 458, 462–65 (4th Cir. 2011).

[9] Brief of the Appellant, *supra* note 4, at 4.

[10] *Masciandaro*, 638 F.3d at 459–60.

[11] District of Columbia v. Heller, 554 U.S. 570, 635 (2008).

[12] *See* Eric Ruben & Joseph Blocher, *From Theory to Doctrine: An Empirical Analysis of the Right to Keep and Bear Arms After* Heller, 67 DUKE L. J. 1433 (2018); *see also Protecting Strong Gun Laws: Supreme Court Leaves Lower Court Victories Untouched*, LAW CTR. TO PREVENT GUN VIOLENCE (Aug. 2, 2016), http://smartgunlaws.org/protecting-strong-gun-laws-the-supreme-court-leaves-lower-court-victories-untouched/ (accessed Jan. 15, 2018).

carrying of firearms in sensitive places such as schools and government buildings, or laws imposing conditions and qualifications on the commercial sale of arms.'"[13] *McDonald v. City of Chicago* reiterated these assurances, insisting that *Heller* "does not imperil every law regulating firearms."[14] These brief passages were often sufficient to resolve the claims of the least sympathetic Second Amendment litigants – the hundreds of felons wanting to avoid conviction for violating the federal law that prohibits felons from possessing firearms.[15] In those cases, judges generally invoked *Heller* and moved on.[16]

But not all challenges fit so neatly within *Heller*'s exceptions. The exceptions don't say what to do with domestic battery misdemeanants caught with rifles[17] or juveniles sporting handguns.[18] They don't address firearms with obliterated serial numbers[19] or public spaces that are neither schools nor government buildings, as in Masciandaro's case. As Judge Wilkinson recognized in *Masciadaro, Heller* had opened a "vast *terra incognita*,"[20] and gave judges the job of mapping it.

THE COVERAGE AND PROTECTION OF THE SECOND AMENDMENT

To navigate the post-*Heller* terrain, judges must do more than determine what the Second Amendment means in some abstract sense. Constitutional rights must not only be defined but also be implemented. To do this, as Richard Fallon has observed, judges "frequently must function as practical lawyers and ... craft doctrines and

[13] McDonald v. City of Chicago, 561 U.S. 742, 786 (2010). Some courts rejected characterizing these exceptions as dicta. *E.g., United States v. Barton*, 633 F.3d 168, 171–72 (3d Cir. 2011); *United States v. Rozier*, 598 F.3d 768, 771 n.6 (11th Cir. 2010). Larson suggested the dicta were binding. See Carlton F. W. Larson, *Four Exceptions in Search of a Theory:* District of Columbia v. Heller *and Judicial Ipse Dixit*, 60 HASTINGS L.J. 1371, 1372 (2009) ("For all practical purposes, these [exceptions] have been decided ... in favor of constitutionality.").

[14] McDonald v. City of Chicago, 561 U.S. 742, 786 (2010).

[15] 18 U.S.C. § 922(g).

[16] As one court observed: "Where a challenged statute apparently falls into one of the categories signaled by the Supreme Court as constitutional, courts have relied on the 'presumptively lawful' language to uphold laws in relatively summary fashion." Hall v. Garcia, No. C 10-03799 RS, 2011 WL 995933, *2 (N.D. Cal. Mar. 17, 2011) (upholding state restrictions on firearms near schools); *see also* United States v. Vongxay, 594 F.3d 1111, 1115 (9th Cir. 2010) (concluding that *Heller*'s exceptions are not dicta and instead constitute a binding determination that "felons are categorically different" from rights-bearing individuals); United States v. White, 593 F.3d 1199, 1206 (11th Cir. 2010) (concluding that a statute prohibiting a person convicted of a misdemeanor crime of domestic violence from possessing a firearm or ammunition falls within *Heller*'s "presumptively lawful" category); United States v. Roy, 742 F. Supp. 2d 150, 152 (D. Me. 2010) (citing language from *Heller* and *McDonald* to uphold firearm restrictions imposed on a person involuntarily committed for mental illness); Epps v. State, 55 So. 3d 710, 711 (Fla. Dist. Ct. App. 2011) (dismissing a challenge to a state felon-in-possession conviction based on exclusionary dicta).

[17] *See, e.g.*, United States v. Chester, 628 F.3d 673 (4th Cir. 2010); United States v. Elkins, 780 F. Supp. 2d 473 (W.D. Va. 2011); United States v. White, 593 F.3d 1199, 1206 (11th Cir. 2010).

[18] *See, e.g.*, United States v. Rene E., 583 F.3d 8 (1st Cir. 2009).

[19] United States v. Marzzarella, 614 F.3d 85 (3rd Cir. 2010).

[20] *Masciandaro*, 638 F.3d at 475.

tests" that are influenced, but not "perfectly determined," by the meaning of the Constitution.[21] Judges "have an obligation to produce clear, workable law"[22] that faithfully and effectively translates the relevant constitutional provision into rules applicable to specific cases and controversies. This difficult task is made even more challenging by the institutional constraints on the judiciary. Judges are passive. They don't choose the litigants or the lawyers. Their decisions rely on the limited factual record before them.

Masciandaro argued that the Second Amendment gave him a right to take a loaded pistol into the park, despite a federal regulation prohibiting that very thing. *Heller* did not supply a clear answer, because *Heller* only concerned a man who wanted to keep a pistol in his house. A threshold question, then, was whether the right to keep and bear arms extends beyond the home.

The United States took the position that nothing in *Heller* addressed the Second Amendment outside the home, and therefore there was no constitutional problem with the prohibition on loaded weapons in cars in national parks.[23] But even if the court should find that restrictions on guns outside the home raised a Second Amendment issue, the United States continued, a national park was a "sensitive place" like a school or a government building, which can presumably bar firearms.[24]

Masciandaro's lawyers, of course, took the opposite position. They argued that the Second Amendment clearly covers the carrying of weapons outside the home, including in vehicles, because "[t]he phrase 'bear arms' means carrying weapons and 'being armed and ready for offensive or defensive action in a case of conflict with another person.'"[25] Further, they argued, the George Washington Memorial Parkway was not a "sensitive place."[26]

To resolve these questions, the judges in *Masciandaro* had to consider whether their answer should take the form of a rule or a standard. Roughly speaking, rules are rigid and correspond to bright lines; standards are flexible and operate more like guiding principles. "Always offer a guest a drink" is a rule. "Always treat guests with respect" is a standard. Rules tend to limit the facts that a decision maker can

[21] Richard H. Fallon, Implementing the Constitution 4 (2001). Fallon was referring to the Justices of the Supreme Court in particular, but the point applies to the judiciary more generally. *See also* Lawrence B. Solum, *Originalism and Constitutional Construction*, 82 Fordham L. Rev. 453, 453 (2013) (arguing that "constitutional construction is ubiquitous in constitutional practice"); *see generally* Keith Whittington, Constitutional Construction: Divided Powers and Constitutional Meaning (1999).

[22] Fallon, *supra* note 21, at 4–5.

[23] Brief of the United States at 22, United States v. Masciandaro, 638 F.3d 458 (4th Cir. 2011) (No. 09-4839).

[24] *Id.* at 28–29.

[25] Brief of the Appellant, *supra* note 4, at 23.

[26] *Id.* at 24–29.

consider, while standards expand them.[27] Rules are expected to be clear, while standards anticipate disagreement at the margins.[28] Rules reduce judicial discretion; standards enlarge it.[29]

That the court was working with a written constitutional provision – the Second Amendment – did not dictate one approach or the other. Constitutional history, social practice, precedent, and any number of other sources, including text, can supply the raw material for fashioning either a rule or a standard.[30] The Fourth Amendment prohibits "unreasonable" searches and seizures, and the Eighth Amendment outlaws "cruel and unusual" punishment, neither of which lends itself to a bright-line rule. Conversely, some rules can emerge from doctrinal development even in the absence of a clear textual command – the First Amendment's prohibition on viewpoint discrimination, for example.[31]

Neither would the ideological inclinations of the judges necessarily tip the matter in one direction with regard to the form of doctrinal output. Rules are often associated with conservatives – one of Justice Scalia's best-known articles is "The Rule of Law as a Law of Rules."[32] But rules need not have a liberal or conservative bent. Justice Black's free speech absolutism was strongly rule-like and applied to all laws regardless of ideology.[33] Justice Thurgood Marshall, a lion of the left, wrote one of the most rule-like Fifth Amendment opinions of all time, holding that a harmless (and probably beneficial) cable box atop an apartment building was a taking of property without just compensation.[34]

Finally, rules and standards are in some sense mutually defining. Elements of one make the other intelligible. A rule that applies only once and a standard that guides no subsequent decision are effectively indistinguishable. If the *Masciandaro* court

[27] Frederick Schauer, Playing by the Rules: A Philosophical Examination of Rule-Based Decision-Making in Law and in Life 231–32 (Tony Honoré & Joseph Raz, eds., 1991); *see generally* Pierre Schlag, *Rules and Standards*, 33 UCLA L. Rev. 379 (1985).

[28] *See* Jamal Greene, *Rule Originalism*, 116 Colum. L. Rev. 1639, 1652 (2016). Greene offers the following definition: "A constitutional rule is a constitutional norm whose scope of application is not expected to be subject to reasonable disagreement. A constitutional standard is a constitutional norm whose scope of application is inherently unclear at the margins, such that reasonable disagreement is anticipated." *Id.*

[29] *See* Louis Kaplow, *Rules Versus Standards: An Economic Analysis*, 42 Duke L.J. 557, 609 (1992) ("Rules may be preferred to standards in order to limit discretion, thereby minimizing abuses of power.").

[30] *See* Chapter 5.

[31] Police Dep't v. Mosley, 408 U.S. 92, 95 (1972) (holding that the "government has no power to restrict expression because of its message, its ideas, its subject matter, or its content").

[32] Antonin Scalia, *The Rule of Law as a Law of Rules*, 56 U. Chi. L. Rev. 1175 (1989).

[33] Barenblatt v. United States, 360 U.S. 109, 143–44 (1959) (Black, J., dissenting); *see also* Konigsberg v. State Bar of Cal., 366 U.S. 36, 61–65 (1961) (Black, J., dissenting) ("[T]he very object of adopting [the Bill of Rights] was to put the freedoms protected there completely out of the area of any congressional control that may be attempted through the exercise of precisely those powers that are now being used to 'balance' the Bill of Rights out of existence.").

[34] Loretto v. Teleprompter Manhattan CATV Corp., 458 U.S. 419, 421–22 (1982).

had treated *Heller* as strictly limited to its facts – an individual resident in the District of Columbia who wanted a particular pistol in his specific home – then *Heller* would fail both as a rule and as a standard. Rules must be abstract enough to apply to new facts, and standards must be definite enough to have clear applications.[35]

Masciandaro's suit was about these fundamental questions of jurisprudence as much it was about the incidents of parks, hatchbacks, and pistols. But Masciandaro's case raised these questions in a new context: the post-*Heller* Second Amendment. Rarely does a case present such a clear window into the evolution of doctrine.

In constitutional litigation, the choice between rules and standards often manifests as a doctrinal choice between coverage and protection. Coverage is a rule-like inquiry about the applicability of a constitutional provision; protection is a standard-like analysis of whether the provision, if applicable, prohibits a certain government action.

Coverage issues are not unique to the Second Amendment. All constitutional rights have boundaries – borders beyond which their dictates do not apply. Those limits tend to be rule-like.[36] Their identification and application can be quite complicated, even counterintuitive, but once marked they help sort constitutional from non-constitutional arguments.

The First Amendment provides many examples. It takes speech, sometimes a lot of it, to defraud someone out of her money. But judges do not recognize speech intended to defraud as "speech" in a First Amendment sense.[37] Similarly, true threats, obscenity, child pornography, and some other types of communication fall outside the boundaries of the First Amendment – the First Amendment doesn't "cover" these categories of expression.[38] It's not that these uncovered forms of speech can be regulated because other considerations (functioning markets, public morals,

[35] *See* Kathleen M. Sullivan, *The Justices of Rules and Standards*, 106 HARV. L. REV. 22, 61–62 (1992) ("These distinctions between rules and standards, categorization and balancing, mark a continuum, not a divide. A rule may be corrupted by exceptions to the point where it resembles a standard; likewise, a standard may attach such fixed weights to the multiple factors it considers that it resembles a rule. All kinds of hybrid combinations are possible. A strict rule may have a standard-like exception, and a standard's application may be confined to areas demarcated by a rule.").

[36] Frederick Schauer, *The Boundaries of the First Amendment: A Preliminary Exploration of Constitutional Salience*, 117 HARV. L. REV. 1765, 1769–70 (2004).

[37] U.S. S.E.C. v. Pirate Inv'r LLC, 580 F.3d 233, 255 (4th Cir. 2009) (prosecution of securities fraud is not a First Amendment violation); Illinois, ex rel. Madigan v. Telemarketing Assocs., Inc., 538 U.S. 600, 601 (2003) ("The First Amendment ... does not shield fraud."); Commodity Trend Serv., Inc. v. Commodity Futures Trading Comm'n, 233 F.3d 981, 992 (7th Cir. 2000) ("Laws directly punishing fraudulent speech survive constitutional scrutiny even where applied to pure, fully protected speech."). *But see* Wendy Gerwick Couture, *The Collision Between the First Amendment and Securities Fraud*, 65 ALA. L. REV. 903, 905–06 (2014) (questioning this conclusion).

[38] *See generally* Chaplinsky v. State of New Hampshire, 315 U.S. 568, 571–72 (1942) ("There are certain well-defined and narrowly limited classes of speech, the prevention and punishment of which have never been thought to raise any Constitutional problem. These include the lewd and obscene, the profane, the libelous, and the insulting or 'fighting' words.").

child safety) outweigh the individual's interest in the expression in particular cases.[39] It's that the First Amendment doesn't even "show up" in those cases.[40]

The government in *Masciandaro* urged the court to decide the case using a coverage rule. Guns in national parks did not raise a Second Amendment issue because guns carried outside the home are not covered by the Second Amendment; or, more narrowly, because parks are "sensitive places" in which the government may ban firearms.

The basic structure of this argument follows *Heller* itself. The *Heller* Court held that some kinds of Second Amendment questions could be resolved through coverage rules. *Heller* suggested that felons and the mentally ill were categorically excluded from Second Amendment coverage, for example.[41] "Dangerous and unusual weapons," although "arms" in the vernacular, were not covered by "the right to keep and bear Arms."[42] The government could ban firearms in schools and government buildings because they are "sensitive places" where the Second Amendment does not reach.[43] The government's position was fairly simple, and depended only on facts relevant to defining homes and sensitive places. If the facts showed that the gun was taken outside the former, or inside the latter, the Second Amendment did not protect Masciandaro.

But the clarity of *Heller*'s rule-like approach was complicated by *Heller*'s own terms, as is often the case when attempting to specify a coverage rule. First, *Heller* defined the coverage rules at a fairly high level of abstraction, meaning an unknown number of facts may be relevant to their application in particular cases. The consequence of being found to be a "sensitive place" might be clear – no Second Amendment coverage – but the facts relevant to make a place sensitive were not. Consider the model sensitive place – a school. Perhaps the presence of children makes a school sensitive. But perhaps it is an educational purpose that makes a school sensitive, even when no children are present. Second, *Heller* described these categories as presumptive, suggesting that there could be some criteria for their rebuttal. Perhaps some sensitive places – empty schools or schools with adult students – can be carved out from the carve-outs. Third, *Heller* indicated that these examples were non-exhaustive, suggesting that some facts could create other exclusions.[44] For example, one court found the Second Amendment did not cover a firearm in an airplane, although airplanes are not enumerated in *Heller*'s list of sensitive places.[45]

[39] It could have been that at one time this kind of balancing took place. But, after repeated balancing, it becomes apparent that the costs of a certain category of speech – child pornography, for example – are never outweighed by the benefits. *See generally* Joseph Blocher, *Categoricalism and Balancing in First and Second Amendment Analysis*, 84 N.Y.U. L. Rev. 375 (2009); *see also* Sullivan, *supra* note 35, at 62.

[40] Schauer, *supra* note 36, at 1769.

[41] *Heller*, 554 U.S. at 626.

[42] *Id.* at 627.

[43] *Id.* at 626.

[44] *Id.* at 627 n.26 ("We identify these presumptively lawful regulatory measures only as examples; our list does not purport to be exhaustive.").

[45] United States v. Davis, No. 05-50726, 304 Fed. Appx. 473 (9th Cir. Nov. 21, 2008).

Faced with a dilemma regarding coverage, the *Masciandaro* court fragmented and no majority emerged for any of the possible rule-like resolutions of the case. One possible answer would have been to say that Masciandaro was covered by the Second Amendment because his car was analogous to his home. (Another court later followed that line of reasoning in a case where a man had a firearm in a tent.[46]) But Judge Niemeyer did not take that route.[47] Instead, he rejected the government's characterization of the right as limited to the home (however defined) as implausibly narrow. *Heller*, Niemeyer said, was not about self-defense in the home, but simply about self-defense. Self-defense is the primary interest of the Second Amendment, and "self-defense has to take place wherever [a] person happens to be."[48]

Neither were national parks a kind of sensitive place categorically excluded from Second Amendment coverage, according to Niemeyer. Here, he appeared skeptical that *Heller*'s "sensitive place" language clearly created a categorical rule. Instead, he suggested that sensitive places might simply be *presumed* to fall outside Second Amendment coverage; facts could potentially rebut that presumption. On this view, to conclude a place was sensitive would only lessen the burden on the government to show its reasons for the regulation, but not eliminate the need for such a showing.[49] Judge Niemeyer did not resolve the question one way or the other, since he concluded that the law was constitutional on either understanding of "sensitive place" – whether as a categorical exclusion from the Second Amendment, or just as a factor that changes the Second Amendment analysis.

Judges Wilkinson and Duffy took a different approach. Wilkinson, a former law professor critical of *Heller* in his scholarly writing,[50] wrote that the case "[u]nderscores the dilemma faced by lower courts in the post-*Heller* world." That dilemma: "[H]ow far to push *Heller* beyond its core holding."[51] *Heller* did not send any clear signal about a right to carry firearms off of one's property. There "may or may not be a Second Amendment right in some places beyond the home, but we have no idea what those places are."[52]

To Wilkinson, reference to the "central component"[53] of the Second Amendment – self-defense – was no help, because the need for self-defense can arise anywhere. If self-defense is the sole metric for coverage of the Second Amendment, Wilkinson

[46] Morris v. U.S. Army Corps of Engineers, 990 F. Supp. 2d 1082 (D. Idaho, 2014).

[47] *Masciandaro*, 638 F.3d at 467 (Niemeyer, J.).

[48] *Id.* at 467–68 (Niemeyer, J.) (quoting Eugene Volokh, *Implementing the Right to Keep and Bear Arms for Self-Defense: An Analytical Framework and a Research Agenda*, 56 U.C.L.A. L. Rev. 1443, 1515–18 (2009)).

[49] *Masciandaro*, 638 F.3d at 472 (Niemeyer, J.).

[50] J. Harvie Wilkinson III, *Of Guns, Abortions, and the Unraveling Rule of Law*, 95 Va. L. Rev. 253, 254 (2009) ("*Heller* represents a triumph for conservative lawyers. But it also represents a failure – the Court's failure to adhere to a conservative judicial methodology in reaching its decision.").

[51] *Masciandaro*, 638 F.3d at 475 (Wilkinson, J.).

[52] *Id.*

[53] District of Columbia v. Heller, 554 U.S. 570, 599 (2008).

worried, then the Second Amendment "portend[s] all sorts of litigation over schools, airports, parks, public thoroughfares, and various additional government facilities."[54] The courts should enter this uncharted territory "only upon necessity and only then by small degree."[55]

The judges could not agree whether Masciandaro's acts were covered by the Second Amendment, but they did agree that the regulation was constitutional either way. This second question – whether the government has demonstrated the necessity of the regulation – is the essence of the protection inquiry,[56] and on this point the judges were unanimous. Even assuming Masciandaro's case fell within the Second Amendment's coverage, the Amendment did not prevent the government from banning loaded guns in the park.

Matters of protection are more contextual than matters of coverage, and therefore leave more room for the evaluation of facts. Consequently, they tend to be more standard-like than rule-like. There is no general rubric for setting the level of protection of a constitutional right, although some factors are widely recognized as relevant. As Chapter 7 discusses in more detail, courts tend to protect rights more stringently when the political process cannot be trusted (as is the case for the rights of "discrete and insular minorities,"[57] for example), where the right is fundamental, or where the burden on the individual claimant is particularly high. Based on those and other factors, courts calibrate constitutional protection through a variety of legal tools. They can, for example, place the burden on either the government or the challenger,[58] require the government to show a particularly important interest, or require a certain level of "fit" between the challenged law and the government interest the law is meant to serve.

For more than fifty years, courts have often used what are usually called "levels of scrutiny" to define the strength of constitutional protection.[59] These levels are conventionally divided into three tiers.[60] The lowest level of protection is rational

[54] *Masciandaro*, 638 F.3d at 475 (Wilkinson, J.).

[55] *Id.*

[56] Schauer, *supra* note 36, at 1769–70.

[57] United States v. Carolene Products, Inc., 304 U.S. 144, 152 n.4 (1938).

[58] Rational basis scrutiny places the burden on the challenger; intermediate and strict scrutiny on the government. Washington v. Glucksberg, 521 U.S. 702, 771 n.11 (1997).

[59] *See* Erwin Chemerinsky, *The Supreme Court and the Fourteenth Amendment: The Unfulfilled Promise*, 25 Loy. L.A. L. Rev. 1143, 1153–55 (1992).

[60] There is plenty of academic commentary suggesting that, in practice, the three-tiered structure of constitutional scrutiny – rational basis, intermediate scrutiny, and strict scrutiny – has weakened, if not completely disintegrated. *See, e.g.*, Jack M. Balkin, Plessy, Brown, *and* Grutter: *A Play in Three Acts*, 26 Cardozo L. Rev. 1689, 1727 (2005) (suggesting the "doctrinal structure is coming apart"); Pamela S. Karlan, *Foreword: Loving* Lawrence, 102 Mich. L. Rev. 1447, 1450 (2004) (noting the sexual orientation cases have undermined tiers-of-scrutiny analysis); R. Randall Kelso, *Standards of Review Under the Equal Protection Clause and Related Constitutional Doctrines Protecting Individual Rights: The 'Base Plus Six' Model and Modern Supreme Court Practice*, 4 U. Pa. J. Const. L. 225 (2002) (arguing that there are actually seven standards of review).

basis review, which requires only that a law be rationally related to a legitimate government purpose, even if the purpose or relationship hadn't actually been considered prior to enactment.[61] The highest form of protection is strict scrutiny, which requires that the challenged regulation be "narrowly tailored to promote a compelling governmental interest."[62] Frequently, regulations fail strict scrutiny – so often, in fact, that the test is sometimes described as "strict in theory, fatal in fact,"[63] though that is not entirely accurate.[64] Between these two poles falls intermediate scrutiny. Although courts articulate this standard in various ways, intermediate scrutiny generally requires the government's interest to be more than legitimate, but not necessarily compelling. Usually it must be significant or important. With respect to fit, the regulation need not be narrowly tailored to advance that interest, but must at least be reasonably tailored – a higher degree of fit than rational basis review.[65]

Although they disagreed on coverage, all three judges agreed that Masciandaro's Second Amendment claim must fail as a matter of protection. Masciandaro's loaded pistol in the park was not protected by the Second Amendment, even if it fell within the Amendment's ambit.

In setting the optimal level of protection, the *Masciandaro* court held that the proper standard – the level of scrutiny or degree of protection – depended on how close the regulation came to the "core" of the Second Amendment right as defined in *Heller*. Courts often use spatial metaphors like cores and peripheries when trying to draw distinctions between various levels of protection.[66] *Heller* suggested that self-defense in the home was the "core" of the right to keep and bear arms – regulations burdening that core, *Masciandaro* held, must satisfy strict scrutiny.[67] But, "as we move outside the home, firearm rights have always been more limited, because public safety interests often outweigh interest in individual self-defense."[68]

Because self-defense outside the home is at the periphery of the right, the judges applied intermediate scrutiny. Daingerfield Island is a recreational spot visited by thousands of people, including children. The government's interest in keeping the public parks safe was substantial and even compelling. As to the impact on the

61 Heller v. Doe by Doe, 509 U.S. 312, 320 (1993).

62 *See* Lorillard Tobacco Co. v. Reilly, 533 U.S. 525, 582 (2001).

63 Gerald Gunther, *Foreword: In Search of Evolving Doctrine on a Changing Court: A Model for a Newer Equal Protection*, 86 HARV. L. REV. 1, 8 (1972).

64 *See* Williams-Yulee v. Fla. Bar, 135 S. Ct. 1656, 1668–69, 1673 (2015) (upholding nonsolicitation rule in judicial campaigns under First Amendment strict scrutiny); Holder v. Humanitarian Law Project, 561 U.S. 1, 40 (2010) (applying strict scrutiny but upholding material-support-for-terrorism statute against First Amendment challenge). *See generally* Adam Winkler, *Fatal in Theory and Strict in Fact: An Empirical Analysis of Strict Scrutiny in the Federal Courts*, 59 VAND. L. REV. 793 (2006).

65 *See Marzzarella*, 614 F.3d at 97–98 (discussing these factors).

66 *Cf.* H. L. A. Hart, *Positivism and the Separation of Law and Morals*, 71 HARV. L. REV. 593, 607 (1958) ("There must be a core of settled meaning, but there will be, as well, a penumbra of debatable cases in which words are neither obviously applicable nor obviously ruled out.").

67 *Masciandaro*, 638 F.3d at 470 (Niemeyer, J.).

68 *Id.*

claimant, the regulation only kept Masciandaro from possessing a *loaded* firearm in his car. He could have other weapons, or he could have the firearm unloaded. As a result, the regulation was "reasonably adapted" to a substantial governmental interest.[69]

THE TWO-PART TEST: VARIATIONS AND CRITICISMS

The *Masciandaro* court took an approach that has come to be called the "two-part test" for Second Amendment cases. That test maps directly onto the two jurisprudential divisions described above – between rules and standards, coverage and protection. The first question is rule-like and concerns coverage: Is this a Second Amendment case at all? The second question is standard-like and concerns protection: When and how are these restrictions on Second Amendment rights justified?

Heller did not need to fully elaborate Second Amendment doctrine to resolve the case before it. But lower courts do not have that luxury. They face questions that could come out differently depending on the Amendment's breadth of coverage or the level of protection it affords. The constitutionality of banning guns near post offices might depend on whether a post office is a "sensitive place."[70] A ban on "assault weapons" might survive intermediate scrutiny but fail strict scrutiny.[71]

In the decade since *Heller*, the federal courts of appeals have widely adopted the two-part approach used in *Masciandaro*.[72] (*Masciandaro* accepted the test, but did not create it.[73]) Judges use various tools to map out the first, rule-like coverage questions. Almost all begin with the specific categories identified in *Heller*. Where those run out, they rely on some mix of precedent, history, and tradition, or even abstract moral claims rooted in the concept of self-defense. If the challenge fails this coverage question, then the case is over. If not, or if the coverage question proves too difficult or divisive, the court moves to the second, more standard-like protection question: Whether the regulation satisfies the applicable type of means-end tailoring. Frequently, although not universally, that second step utilizes intermediate scrutiny, requiring the government to show that the regulation reasonably advances some important or legitimate government interest.[74] In the vast majority of cases, the

[69] *Id.* at 470, 473–74.

[70] *See* Bonidy v. U.S. Postal Service, 790 F.3d 1121 (10th Cir. 2015).

[71] *See* Kolbe v. Hogan, 849 F.3d 114 (4th Cir. 2017) (en banc).

[72] *See* Nat'l Rifle Ass'n of Am., Inc. v. Bureau of Alcohol, Tobacco, Firearms, & Explosives, 700 F.3d 185, 194 (5th Cir. 2012) ("A two-step inquiry has emerged as the prevailing approach."); *see also* N.Y. State Rifle & Pistol Ass'n, Inc. v. Cuomo, 804 F.3d 242, 254 (2d Cir. 2015), *cert. denied sub nom.* Shew v. Malloy, 136 S. Ct. 2486, 195 L. Ed. 2d 822 (2016) (noting two-part test had been largely adopted by Third, Fourth, Fifth, Sixth, Seventh, Ninth, Tenth, Eleventh, and D.C. Circuits).

[73] That honor may go to the Third Circuit in United States v. Marzzarella, 614 F.3d 85, 89 (3d Cir. 2010).

[74] *See* Nelson Lund, *Promise and Perils in the Nascent Jurisprudence of the Second Amendment*, 14 Geo. J.L. & Pub. Pol'y 207, 216 (2016) (noting that courts have tended to use intermediate scrutiny for Second Amendment cases dealing with regulations that do not severely restrict core rights).

government has prevailed.[75] However, the precise level of deference, the evidence supplied for coverage or protection, and even the portions of *Heller* cited to support these opinions, have diverged – sometimes significantly.

In many cases, the difficulty of addressing coverage in a rule-like fashion causes the two-step inquiry to collapse into a single step that looks much like intermediate scrutiny. In *United States v. Chester*,[76] for instance, the court could not decide whether domestic battery misdemeanants were, like felons, excluded from Second Amendment coverage.[77] It therefore assumed that they were covered, and moved on to the second part of the test. Concluding that misdemeanants were "not within the core right identified in *Heller*,"[78] it held that "intermediate scrutiny" applied to individuals like Chester, and remanded for further litigation.[79] Other courts have avoided difficult coverage questions, including whether the Second Amendment extends to public carrying, in a similar fashion.[80]

Even within the second step, there is variation with regard to what burden the government must meet. Some courts state that the regulation must be "*substantially* related to an *important* government objective";[81] others say that the regulation needs to be "*reasonably* adapted to a *substantial* governmental interest."[82] Some courts separately evaluate whether there are less restrictive or less burdensome methods of advancing the stated goal;[83] some courts require that the regulation go no further than necessary to advance the goal[84]; and some require no such inquiry at all.[85] Second, even when courts agree on how to formulate the test, they diverge on how

[75] *See* Eric Ruben & Joseph Blocher, *From Theory to Doctrine: An Empirical Analysis of the Right to Keep and Bear Arms After* Heller, 67 DUKE L.J. 1433 (2018).

[76] 628 F.3d 673 (4th Cir. 2010).

[77] *Chester*, 628 F.3d at 680–81.

[78] *Id.* at 683.

[79] *Id.* at 683.

[80] *See, e.g.*, Kolbe v. O'Malley, 42 F. Supp. 3d 768, 789 (D. Md. 2014), *aff'd in part, vacated in part, remanded sub nom.* Kolbe v. Hogan, 813 F.3d 160 (4th Cir. 2016), *on reh'g en banc*, 849 F.3d 114 (4th Cir. 2017), and *aff'd sub nom.* Kolbe v. Hogan, 849 F.3d 114 (4th Cir. 2017) (assuming without deciding that a firearms regulation placed "some burden" on the Second Amendment right in order to move on to the means-end scrutiny analysis); Woollard v. Gallagher, 712 F.3d 865, 875 (4th Cir. 2013) ("[W]e are not obliged to impart a definitive ruling at the first step of the [two-part] inquiry ... [W]e and other courts of appeals have sometimes deemed it prudent to instead resolve post-*Heller* challenges to firearm prohibitions at the second step...").

[81] *See Chester*, 628 F.3d at 683 (citing *Marzzarella*, 614 F.3d at 97 and United States v. Skoien, 614 F.3d 638, 641 (7th Cir. 2010)) (emphasis added).

[82] *Masciandaro*, 638 F.3d at 471 (Niemeyer, J.) (emphasis added); *see also* Nat'l Rifle Ass'n of Am., Inc., 700 F.3d at 194 (seeking "reasonable fit between the law and an important government objective").

[83] *See Heller II*, 670 F.3d at 1257 ("[A] regulation that imposes a substantial burden upon the core right of self-defense protected by the Second Amendment must have a strong justification, whereas a regulation that imposes a less substantial burden should be proportionately easier to justify.").

[84] *See* Peruta v. Cty. of San Diego, 742 F.3d 1144, 1177 (9th Cir. 2014), *rev'd en banc*, 824 F.3d 919 (9th Cir. 2016) (arguing that a gun regulation must "not burden 'substantially more' of the Second Amendment right than was necessary to advance its aim of public safety" (quoting Turner Broadcasting System, Inc. v. FCC (*Turner I*), 512 U.S. 622, 662 (1994))).

[85] *See* Woollard v. Gallagher, 712 F.3d 865, 878–79 (4th Cir. 2013).

to assess what counts as a "reasonable" adaptation. These questions often amount to disputes over how much constitutionally covered behavior is being swept up in the regulation.[86]

Intermediate scrutiny also depends on some assessment of the importance of a government objective. Other areas of constitutional litigation proceed with a modicum of agreement about legitimate versus illegitimate government interests. In Fourteenth Amendment litigation, subordinating classifications based on racial and gender animus illegitimate. The same is true of efforts to discriminate on the basis of viewpoint in First Amendment litigation.[87] But Second Amendment litigation still suffers from lingering disagreement on how to distinguish a government evil from a government function. Laws that protect police from firearms can also protect tyrants from firearms. Laws denying guns to minors and undocumented immigrants also deprive them of an effective means of self-protection. Between the clear evil of universal citizen disarmament and modest regulation to prevent crime or accident there's a huge gulf of opinion as to where the government should be able to act. There is also a clear lack of trust, as some insist that any regulation, no matter how modest, will inevitably slide toward confiscation. The purposes of the Second Amendment are a topic we take up in Chapter 6, but the lack of agreement complicates discussions about the strength of government interests and the over- or under-inclusiveness of laws designed to accomplish those interests.

Further muddying the waters, some judges have expressed dissatisfaction with the two-part test, often because they think it is unwieldy or unprincipled. One appellate panel called it a "quagmire."[88] Another seemed skeptical that it "resolve[s] any concrete dispute."[89] Yet another judge wrote that she was "bound" to apply the "existing analytical frameworks" but acknowledged that "it is possible that an entirely new test [for the Second Amendment] will develop."[90] Some judges have simply adopted a wait and see approach, as Judge Wilkinson advocated in *Masciandaro*.[91]

More radically, some judges have entirely rejected the second step of the two-part test. They read *Heller* and *McDonald* as casting doubt on the legitimacy of any test that smacks of balancing government interests against rights, and their position is not without support. During *Heller*'s oral argument, Chief Justice Roberts remarked

86 *See* United States v. Chester, 847 F. Supp. 2d 902, 911 (S.D.W. Va. 2012), *aff'd*, 514 F. App'x 393 (4th Cir. 2013) (describing the defendant as "swept up with others in a reasonably tailored ban on firearm possession in order to achieve a weighty objective ... Congress is not obligated to legislate with perfect precision").

87 *See generally* Joseph Blocher, *Viewpoint Neutrality and Government Speech*, 52 B.C. L. Rev. 695 (2011).

88 *Skoien*, 614 F.3d at 642.

89 Friedman v. City of Highland Park, 784 F.3d 406, 410 (7th Cir. 2015).

90 United States v. Oppedisano, No. 09-CR-0305 JS, 2010 WL 4961663, at *2 n.2 (E.D.N.Y. Nov. 30, 2010).

91 *Masciandaro*, 638 F.3d at 475–76 (Wilkinson, J.).

that the tiers of scrutiny do not appear in the Constitution but had "just kind of developed over the years as sort of baggage" that the First Amendment picked up.[92] That same kind of dubiousness was prominent in the colloquy between Justice Breyer and Justice Scalia in their *Heller* opinions.

In his *Heller* dissent, Breyer argued that "[t]he ultimate question" should be "whether the statute imposes burdens that, when viewed in light of the statute's legitimate objectives, are disproportionate."[93] This formulation did not explicitly track any of the traditional tiers of scrutiny, but the basic structure was similar. Even without adopting terms like intermediate or strict scrutiny, Breyer's "disproportionate burden" approach would have accomplished much the same thing. Justice Scalia rejected Justice Breyer's approach, however, saying "[w]e know of no other enumerated constitutional right whose core protection has been subjected to a freestanding 'interest-balancing' approach."[94] He wrote that the Second Amendment "is the very *product* of an interest balancing" that occurred at the Founding.[95] (In any event, Justice Scalia waved off the question of protection by suggesting the District's regulation was so draconian that it would fail any level of heightened scrutiny.[96])

Justice Alito reiterated and seemed to amplify that skepticism in *McDonald*: "[W]e expressly reject the argument that the scope of the Second Amendment right should be determined by judicial interest balancing."[97] But it remains unclear whether Alito's barb was directed at "unguided" interest balancing of the kind arguably proposed in Breyer's dissent, or more generally at the balancing required by the conventional tiers of scrutiny.

For judges inclined toward a more rule-like approach to the Second Amendment, the Chief Justice's question, magnified by this disagreement between Justices Scalia, Alito, and Breyer, is proof the Court has rejected all standard-like balancing of interests by judges, and that *any* test to the contrary is lawless Third Branch tinkering.[98] These judges would instead look to text, history, and tradition for answers, generally aiming to argue from analogy to history or longstanding

[92] Transcript of Oral Argument at 44, District of Columbia v. Heller, 554 U.S. 570 (2008) (No. 07-290).

[93] *Heller*, 554 U.S. at 693 (Breyer, J., dissenting).

[94] *Heller*, 554 U.S. at 634.

[95] *Id.* at 635. In *Heller*, Justice Scalia hedged as to whether traditional standards of scrutiny analysis would suffice. *Id.* at 628–29 & n.27, 634. Justice Alito in *McDonald* appears much more resolute. 561 U.S. at 785–86.

[96] *Heller*, 554 U.S. at 628–29. Justice Scalia wrote that rational basis review was no different than any other review for arbitrary or irrational regulation, and did not think it applied at all. *Heller*, 554 U.S. at 628 n.7.

[97] *McDonald*, 561 U.S. at 785 (referring to the Court's decision in *Heller*).

[98] *See* Tyler v. Hillsdale County Sheriff's Department, 837 F.3d 678, 702–07 (6th Cir. 2016) (Batchelder, J., concurring in most of the judgment); Houston v. City of New Orleans, 675 F.3d 441, 448 (5th Cir. 2012) (Elrod, J., dissenting), *opinion withdrawn and superseded on reh'g by* 682 F.3d 361 (5th Cir. 2012); *Heller II*, 670 F.3d at 1273 n.5, 1280–81 (Kavanaugh, J., dissenting); Gowder v. City of Chicago, 923 F. Supp. 2d 1110, 1124–25 (N.D. Ill. 2012).

practices to fashion legal decisions.[99] This historical approach need not rule out all modern firearm regulation. For example, these judges may concede that there were no basketball arenas at state universities until the early twentieth century, but conclude that longstanding regulations on carrying firearms into fairs or other places of amusement or education are sufficiently analogous to support bans on guns at university sporting events. Nevertheless, if their preferred approach were to prevail, it would certainly represent a significant break with past methods of implementing most constitutional rights.

To be sure, judges who reject the second part of the two-part test remain a distinct minority. It is possible that the Second Amendment will shed the "baggage" of First Amendment doctrine, and entirely new tests will arise. But even if it does not, the atmosphere of skepticism hovering over the tiers of scrutiny could nudge the developing doctrine. It may result in a Second Amendment doctrine that adopts rule-like bright lines, categorical exclusions, and absolute prohibitions, rather than standard-like levels of scrutiny, interest balancing, and evaluation of effects. Regardless, it is almost certain that tests designed to address these two issues – coverage and protection – will break down and blend over time, as they have in other areas of constitutional law.[100] Rules will beget exceptions; standards will calcify into rules. Some of the most important issues in current Second Amendment doctrine involve precisely that evolution.

BEYOND THE TWO-PART TEST

In 1997, 41-year-old Daniel Binderup had a consensual affair with a 17-year-old employee of the bakery he owned. His wife forgave him, he moved on to a job as a plumber, and he had no other run-ins with the law. But he had committed a crime. Under Pennsylvania law, consensual sexual intercourse between a middle-aged man and a 17-year-old woman constituted corruption of a minor – officially a misdemeanor offense, but one that could be punished by up to five years in prison.[101] Binderup pled guilty in Pennsylvania state court and received a $300 fine and three years of probation.

Twenty years later, Binderup wanted to purchase firearms for protection of his home and family. But under the terms of federal law, he risked committing a federal crime if he attempted to do so.[102] Although he had not committed a felony under Pennsylvania state law, the federal prohibition uses its own definition, and

[99] *See generally* Darrell A. H. Miller, *Text, History, and Tradition: What the Seventh Amendment Can Teach Us About the Second*, 122 Yale L.J. 852, 895–96 (2013).

[100] *See* Joseph Blocher, *Categoricalism and Balancing in First and Second Amendment Analysis*, 84 N.Y.U. L. Rev. 375, 381–98 (2009).

[101] Binderup v. Holder, No. 13-CV-06750, 2014 WL 4764424, *26 (E.D. Pa. Sept. 25, 2014), *aff'd sub nom.* Binderup v. Attorney Gen. United States of Am., 836 F.3d 336 (3d Cir. 2016).

[102] *Id.* at *4.

forbids anyone guilty of a crime punishable by more than a year in prison – the traditional common-law definition of a felony – from owning a firearm. Binderup sued the Justice Department, claiming, among other things, that the potential criminal liability of his possessing a firearm based on a decades-old conviction violated the Second Amendment. He didn't claim that every convicted criminal who wanted a firearm should have Second Amendment rights to possess one, only that the prohibition was unconstitutional in his particular case. His suit was, in the lingo of constitutional litigation, an "as-applied" challenge rather than a "facial" challenge.

Heller purported to leave undisturbed constitutional bans on guns in the hands of felons. That formulation was just about as rule-like as one could imagine. The only constitutional question appeared a formal one: was the conviction a felony? If yes, the person was not covered by the Second Amendment. Binderup and nonviolent felons like Martha Stewart may be lumped in with mass murderers, but that's just the nature of rules – they are always under- or over-inclusive.[103]

Binderup wanted a case-specific exception to that rule. Such efforts tend to blur the distinction between rules and standards, because they carve out exceptions to exceptions, making rules turn more closely on the facts of each individual case. In a deeply fractured *en banc* opinion, the US Court of Appeals for the Third Circuit accepted Binderup's invitation and broke open the felon-in-possession rule, permitting as-applied challenges to the federal statute. What had previously operated as a rule-like matter of coverage would now look more like a standard-like matter of protection.

According to the plurality, a person like Binderup could overcome the categorical exclusion if he first identified the "traditional justifications" for excluding the group from Second Amendment coverage, and then "present[ed] facts" that distinguished him from that group.[104] The *Binderup* court defined the traditional justification for the felon prohibition as a historical desire to deny guns to the "unvirtuous," rather than simply preventing those likely to commit a violent crime from owning a gun. Persons convicted of serious offenses lacked virtue, whether the crime was violent or not.[105]

Defining the exclusion in this way opened the door for Binderup to demonstrate that his conviction – while traditionally disqualifying – was not serious enough to permanently exclude him from the scope of the Second Amendment. The court acknowledged that, unlike well-established First Amendment exceptions for obscenity and fighting words, there are "no fixed criteria for determining whether crimes

[103] *See* Kevin C. Marshall, *Why Can't Martha Stewart Have a Gun?*, 32 Harv. J.L. & Pub. Pol'y 695 (2009). Stewart was convicted of obstruction of justice and making false statements in connection with a tip she received about stock in her portfolio.

[104] Binderup v. Attorney Gen. United States of Am., 836 F.3d 336, 347 (3rd Cir. 2016).

[105] *Id.* at 348.

are serious enough to destroy Second Amendment rights."[106] Those categories may change over time based on legislative and political notions of virtuous conduct.[107]

Nevertheless, the court tallied up specific facts of Binderup's case to show his conviction was not serious in the relevant sense. First, the state law he'd violated, while permitting more than a year of prison as punishment, was denominated a misdemeanor, indicating that Pennsylvania did not think it as serious as other crimes.[108] Second, the crime did not involve violence. While nonviolent crimes could still be serious, the lack of violence was relevant to the seriousness of Binderup's specific case. Third, he faced only a fine and probation, again calling into question the seriousness of his crime, as judged by the state of Pennsylvania. Finally, the Court noted a lack of consensus among the states regarding crimes like Binderup's. Some states treat sex with a 17-year-old employee by a middle-aged employer as serious; many others do not.[109]

Having transformed the rule-like part of the two-part test into something resembling a multi-factor balancing test, the court then moved on to the second, ostensibly more fact-sensitive protection question. Had the government shown that the regulation reasonably fit an important government objective? The plurality found that the government had not. It had provided no evidence that nonviolent criminals like Binderup were likely to commit crimes with guns, nor that banning them for life from possessing weapons would lead to more responsible use of firearms.[110] The prohibition thus violated the Second Amendment as applied to Binderup.

Binderup was not an aberration. In other areas of Second Amendment litigation, seemingly clear lines of coverage are starting to fray, largely as a result of as-applied challenges. In the Sixth Circuit, a person who had once been involuntarily committed to a mental institution successfully argued that the federal prohibition on possession by such persons was unconstitutional as applied to him.[111] Until it was reversed, a panel of the Ninth Circuit suggested the categorical exclusion of concealed carry from constitutional protection must gave way to something more fact-specific and contextual.[112] Other categorical rules are likely to become more hazy and indistinct at their margins. Blanket prohibitions on guns in schools, for instance, may be subject to specific fact-dependent challenges by, for instance, teachers who reasonably fear attack. This dynamic isn't unique to the Second Amendment. It's almost a given that any rule will eventually generate exceptions, simply because no human-made rule can anticipate all present or future contingencies.

[106] *Id.* at 351.
[107] *Id.*
[108] *Id.*
[109] *Id.* at 353.
[110] *Id.* at 355–56.
[111] *See Tyler*, 837 F.3d 678.
[112] *See* Peruta v. Cty. of San Diego, 742 F.3d 1144 (9th Cir. 2014), *rev'd en banc* 824 F.3d 919 (9th Cir. 2016).

How the two-part test that has percolated in the lower courts will develop over time is hard to predict. It may be confirmed by the Supreme Court, modified or ignored. Whatever test the high court comes to endorse will depend on the methodological commitments of the Justices, the benefits of clarity, the costs of over- and under-breadth, the trustworthiness of the political process, the contested nature of empirical data, the staffing of the courts, and other factors.[113] Whatever questions the Court answers will inevitably raise others.

The two-part test currently employed by the courts is a framework for addressing coverage and protection questions. It manages some of the rough outlines of *Heller* and attempts to apply them in a way that makes sense for busy judges with a full docket. But the two-part test is only a decision-making structure. It does not specify the various analytical tools or evidence judges can, should, or must use to decide Second Amendment questions. It does not neatly encapsulate all the various formulations of the right in *Heller* or the values the Second Amendment is supposed to advance. Those topics are the subject of the following chapters.

[113] *See generally* Kathleen M. Sullivan, *Post-Liberal Judging: The Roles of Categorization and Balancing*, 63 U. Colo. L. Rev. 293 (1992) (exploring whether the choice between rules and standards makes a difference in terms of outcomes); *see also* Frederick Schauer, *Rules and the Rule of Law*, 14 Harv. J.L. & Pub. Pol'y 645, 679–91 (1991) (discussing advantages and disadvantages of rule-based decision making).

5

The Constitutional Grammar of the Second Amendment

Prior to *Heller*, the gun debate was something of a babel. From the guardians of the English common law, to the Framers and ratifiers of the Second Amendment, to the Americans who debated its meaning in the generations that followed, everyone had a voice, and they spoke in innumerable tongues: personal preferences, political first principles, identity politics, historicism, utilitarianism, Kantianism, welfare economics, and the like. Each of those languages helped, in its own way, to shape the debate about gun rights and regulations, eventually leading to *Heller* itself.

After *Heller*, people continue to discuss the right to keep and bear arms in the vernacular of their choosing. But now, when it comes to making constitutional *doctrine*, some languages and speakers command more attention than others. The litigants who bring Second Amendment challenges, the lawyers who make Second Amendment arguments, the judges who render Second Amendment decisions, and the scholars who provide the materials for those decisions[1] now enjoy a privileged role. To be sure, politicians, philosophers, economists, and others still have much to say about the right to keep and bear arms, and their voices continue to be important. But now that the Second Amendment has become part of "normal" constitutional law, it is increasingly subject to the particular rules of legal argument. This is both the reward and the price of *Heller* – once rights are secured as legal entitlements, law tends to dominate other forms of discourse.[2]

THE SECOND AMENDMENT AS LEGAL DISCOURSE

Alexis de Tocqueville observed that "[s]carcely any political question arises in the United States that is not resolved, sooner or later, into a judicial question."[3] For most of the twentieth century, the Second Amendment generated a heated, often

[1] As noted above, scholarship has played a larger role in Second Amendment cases than in most other areas of constitutional law. *See* Chapter 2.

[2] *See* Robert M. Cover, *Nomos and Narrative*, 97 HARV. L. REV. 4, 40 (1983).

[3] ALEXIS DE TOCQUEVILLE, DEMOCRACY IN AMERICA 110 (Wordsworth Classics, ed., 1998).

acrimonious, political and moral conflict. But the law of the Second Amendment was fairly stable, even boring. The overwhelming judicial consensus was that the Second Amendment did not apply to the vast majority of gun regulations, because the Amendment reached only militia-related people, arms, and activities. *Heller* changed that. By adopting the private purposes reading, the Court made the political gun debate subject to law, transforming the right to keep and bear arms "into a judicial question."

Turning political issues into legal rules has consequences. Law empowers certain people, arguments, and evidence. It takes "certain policy choices off the table,"[4] as the *Heller* majority put it. Criminal defendants like Sean Masciandaro demand exoneration on Second Amendment grounds. Citizens like Otis McDonald seek to annul city and state regulations in federal court. Judges like Paul Niemeyer write opinions that become the law of the Second Amendment. Those cases, and the law they create, transcend the specific circumstances of the particular litigants, and generate legal propositions that bind future decision-makers.

But legal rules themselves conform to rules. Substantively, legal conclusions tend to be falsifiable in a way different from political or moral arguments. Assertions like "Immigrants have Second Amendment rights"; "Municipalities may regulate concealed carry"; "Stun guns are protected arms"; and "National parks are sensitive places" can be evaluated according to a body of ever-developing constitutional doctrine.

The same is true, perhaps even more so, of the method of legal argument. And it is these rules concerning legal method – not concrete legal conclusions – that are the subject of this chapter. Legal arguments are only valid if they respect the conventions of legal discourse. Legal claims, including constitutional ones, must be supported by a chain of legal reasoning, fashioned with legal tools that conform to American legal conventions.[5] Some kinds of arguments and evidence, while prevalent or persuasive in other arenas, are incomplete or inapplicable as a matter of constitutional law.

A legal brief that relied entirely on scripture or survey data, or a judicial opinion that rested solely upon such sources, would fail the basic requirements of legal justification in our system of law.[6] Even such venerable documents as the Declaration of Independence are not typically thought to provide enforceable legal entitlements separate from the Constitution. As Justice Kagan implied when asked about a "natural right" to a firearm during her confirmation hearings, judges are empowered to enforce the Constitution and laws of the United States, not

[4] District of Columbia v. Heller, 554 U.S. 570, 636 (2008).

[5] In pursuing this framework, we follow PHILIP BOBBITT, CONSTITUTIONAL FATE: THEORY OF THE CONSTITUTION (1982) [hereinafter BOBBITT, CONSTITUTIONAL FATE].

[6] *Id.* at 6; *see also* Lon L. Fuller, *The Forms and Limits of Adjudication*, 92 HARV. L. REV. 353, 368 (1978).

their own beliefs about the requirements of natural law, political ideology, or the most recent Gallup poll.[7]

Because only some forms of argument and evidence are legally valid in our constitutional system, a great deal of scholarly debate concerns the appropriateness of those forms and their relative priority. Originalism, for example, focuses on history, particularly that of the Founding era, as a guide to constitutional interpretation. Popular constitutionalism looks to the role of non-legal actors like advocacy organizations in shaping constitutional meaning. Common law constitutionalism emphasizes judicial precedent and its change over time.[8]

Our object is not to critique these interpretive methodologies, but rather to canvas the rudiments of constitutional grammar – what Philip Bobbitt calls the "modalities" of constitutional law[9] – that they utilize. In particular, we are interested in exploring how this grammar is used to create Second Amendment doctrine. Bobbitt identifies six modes that he says represent the sum total of constitutional argument: structural, textual, ethical, prudential, historical, and doctrinal.[10] Other scholars identify slightly different forms of argument, or combine them.[11]

In the Second Amendment context, we identify seven categories of permissible argument – *text*, *precedent*, *history*, *social practice*, *structure*, *analogy*, and *prudence*[12] – and explore each of them below. The Second Amendment presents unique challenges for these types of argument, and reflecting on these elements of grammar in turn can help illustrate what is unique about the Second Amendment. Our hope is that doing so helps show how the Second Amendment and the central questions of constitutional interpretation can shed light on one another.

Although legal professionals are schooled in this discourse, none of these forms of argument are confined to lawyers and judges. Indeed, as Tocqueville recognized, precisely because political questions tend to become legal ones in America, lawyers and non-lawyers alike eventually come to trade in "the ideas, and even the language" of the law.[13] Those who wish to participate in the conversation about Second

[7] *The Nomination of Elena Kagan to be an Associate Justice of the Supreme Court of the United States: Hearing Before the S. Comm. on the Judiciary*, 111th Cong. 284 (2010) (statement of Elena Kagan).

[8] *See generally* David A. Strauss, *Common Law Constitutional Interpretation*, 63 U. Chi. L. Rev. 877 (1996).

[9] *See generally* Philip Bobbitt, Constitutional Interpretation (1991) [hereinafter Bobbitt, Constitutional Interpretation]; Bobbitt, Constitutional Fate, *supra* note 5, at 6.

[10] Bobbitt, Constitutional Interpretation, *supra* note 9, at 12–13.

[11] *See* Richard H. Fallon, Jr., *A Constructivist Coherence Theory of Constitutional Interpretation*, 100 Harv. L. Rev. 1189 (1987).

[12] None of these are particularly unique to us. Most have been identified or defined by others, sometimes with slightly different emphasis or content. *See, e.g.*, Bobbitt, Constitutional Fate, *supra* note 5, at 7; Fallon, *supra* note 11; Lawrence B. Solum, *The Interpretation-Construction Distinction*, 27 Const. Comment. 95 (2010).

[13] De Tocqueville, *supra* note 3.

Amendment doctrine, then, should become familiar with the basic grammar of constitutional law.[14]

CONSTITUTIONAL GRAMMAR

Second Amendment cases used to be easily resolved by courts, because the militia reading of the Second Amendment provided clear answers. If the people, arms, and activities involved in a case did not closely connect to the functioning of a well-regulated militia, the challenges simply did not register as Second Amendment issues.

After *Heller* endorsed the private purposes reading, fundamental issues of coverage and protection became far more nuanced. An immigrant is a person, but is he one of "the people"? One can carry a pistol concealed, but is concealed carry "bear[ing]" arms? A person may wish to arm herself with a stun gun, but is a stun gun an "Arm"? Even if one answers yes to those coverage questions, there's the second question of how much the Second Amendment protects immigrants, concealed carry, or stun guns. The mechanics of those arguments, how one assembles reasons and evidence, and what makes them distinctly legal arguments, are the subjects of this chapter.

Text

Almost all constitutional questions start with the Constitution's text,[15] but few interesting ones end there. For easy cases, the text is all you need. A common example is Article I, section 3 of the Constitution, which specifies that "[t]he Senate of the United States shall be composed of two Senators from each State."[16] Each state has two senators, everyone knows what the number two means, and the legal effect of this provision is that no state may sit three senators at a time in Congress.

But not all portions of the Constitution are as clear as Article I, section 3. Some words are ambiguous because they can have more than one definition.[17] The word "State" in the Second Amendment could mean the specific geo-political units that comprise the United States, as it does in other provisions of the Constitution.[18] Or "State" could refer more generally to a "polity," as the majority says in *Heller*.[19]

14 BOBBITT, CONSTITUTIONAL FATE, *supra* note 5, at 6 (referring to the modalities as "legal grammar").

15 *See* Richard H. Fallon, Jr., *Precedent-Based Constitutional Adjudication, Acceptance, and the Rule of Recognition*, in THE RULE OF RECOGNITION AND THE U.S. CONSTITUTION 47 (Matthew D. Adler & Kenneth Einar Himma, eds., 2009); Curtis A. Bradley & Neil S. Siegel, *Constructed Constraint and the Constitutional Text*, 64 DUKE L.J. 1213 (2015).

16 U.S. CONST. art I, § 3.

17 Laurence B. Solum, *Originalism and Constitutional Construction*, 82 FORDHAM L. REV. 453, 469–70 (2013); Frederick Schauer, *A Critical Guide to Vehicles in the Park*, 83 N.Y.U. L. REV. 1109, 1116–17 (2008).

18 *Heller*, 554 U.S. at 597.

19 *Id.*

Some words are vague because people disagree about the relevant metric for their meaning.[20] The word "infringe," for example, could mean something binary, as "to violate," or it could mean something on a spectrum, as "to contract" or "to diminish."[21] For some, any regulation that results in a reduction or diminution of the ability to keep and bear arms, no matter how trivial, is an infringement of the Second Amendment; for others, it may require substantially more.[22]

Some words are both vague and ambiguous. "The people" in the Second Amendment could refer to all human beings, all adults, all adults with a connection to the United States, all citizens, all adult citizens, all law-abiding adult citizens, or some other category.[23] As noted in Chapter 3, *Heller* used "the people" in all these different ways.

Even when language is precise and unambiguous, it still may not answer the relevant legal question. In American constitutional practice, what the words say is not always what the law is.[24] Although constitutional doctrine rarely contradicts the text, it frequently departs from it in ways that may cause one to doubt the text's ability to constrain judicial discretion. Consider the first word of the First Amendment: "Congress shall make no law respecting an establishment of religion, or prohibiting the free exercise thereof; or abridging the freedom of speech." *Congress*. Not the President; not the Supreme Court of Florida; not the city of Akron. And yet judges have enforced the First Amendment against these non-congressional actors for more than a century.[25]

After *Heller*, some gun rights advocates insisted "the Second Amendment means what it says."[26] The statement may have political resonance, but it's not technically true of the Second Amendment any more than it is of the First. A citizen carrying

[20] *See* Laurence B. Solum, *Originalism and Constitutional Construction*, 82 FORDHAM L. REV. 453, 469–70 (2013); Schauer, *supra* note 17, at 1115–17.

[21] Joseph Blocher & Darrell A. H. Miller, *What is Gun Control? Direct Burdens, Incidental Burdens, and the Boundaries of the Second Amendment*, 83 U. CHI. L. REV. 295, 334 (2016).

[22] *See* Bob Owens, *This Lawsuit Could Shatter ALL Federal Gun Control Laws*, BEARING ARMS (Nov. 22, 2016, 12:43 PM), https://bearingarms.com/bob-o/2016/11/22/this-lawsuit-could-shatter-all-federal-gun-laws/ (arguing that "the Second Amendment meant the federal government in Washington had no power to constrain or regulate arms"); Patrick J. Charles, *The Second Amendment in the Twenty-First Century: What Hath* Heller *Wrought?*, 23 WM. & MARY BILL RTS. J. 1143 (2015) (documenting examples of Second Amendment absolutism); Joseph Blocher, *Gun Rights Talk*, 94 B.U. L. REV. 813 (2014).

[23] *Heller*, 554 U.S. at 579–81; *see also* Pratheepan Gulasekaram, *"The People" of the Second Amendment: Citizenship and the Right to Bear Arms*, 85 N.Y.U. L. REV. 1521 (2010).

[24] *See* Mitchell N. Berman, *The Tragedy of Justice Scalia*, 115 MICH. L. REV. 783, 787 (2017).

[25] David A. Strauss, *Foreword: Does the Constitution Mean What it Says?*, 129 HARV. L. REV. 1, 3–4 (2015); Mark P. Denbeaux, *The First Word of the First Amendment*, 80 NW. U. L. REV. 1156, 1156–57 (1986); Bradley & Siegel, supra, note 15, at 1244.

[26] *See* Michael Barone, *The Supreme Court Rules that the Second Amendment Means What It Says*, U.S. NEWS & WORLD REP. 9 June 27, 2008, 1:38 PM) www.usnews.com/opinion/blogs/barone/2008/06/27/the-supreme-court-rules-that-the-second-amendment-means-what-it-says; Randy E. Barnett, *News Flash: The Constitution Means What It Says*, WALL ST. J., June 27, 2008, at A13.

a dirty bomb in a satchel outside the White House meets the literal definition of each operative term in the Second Amendment. Citizens are "the people," meaning "persons who are part of a national community."[27] A dirty bomb is an "Arm," defined as a "weapon."[28] Keep means to "have"; "bear" means "to carry."[29] But a person carrying a dirty bomb could still be convicted for doing so,[30] notwithstanding the Second Amendment, because the *right* to keep and bear arms is not defined solely by the operative text of the Second Amendment. It does not protect all people, all weapons, all bearing, or all keeping, as *Heller* itself acknowledges.[31]

The words of the Amendment, standing alone, cannot answer all the questions surrounding *Heller*. This disjuncture is not necessarily a defect of the doctrine, any more than it is with respect to other constitutional rights. That the words cannot answer all questions doesn't mean they answer none. Nor does it mean they are incapable of curbing discretion or that they are unworthy of particular respect in our constitutional culture.[32] Courts still tend to structure their opinions around the Amendment's terminology – asking whether certain high-powered rifles are "Arms," for example, or whether concealed carrying falls within the scope of "keep and bear." Our constitutional practice is very heavily textually oriented. But sometimes the text is important not because it provides definite answers, but because it supplies "focal points"[33] for agreement and helps pare away idiosyncratic or implausible constructions.[34]

Precedent

Precedent is a specific type of history. History, tradition, and custom are precedential in the loose sense of offering guidance for today's decision makers based on what someone did in the past.[35] Legal precedent carries a stronger degree of obligation, requiring decision-makers to adhere to previous decisions even if they disagree with those decisions; therefore, legal precedent requires today's decision-makers to anticipate that they might well bind tomorrow's.[36]

Precedent is typically understood as coming in two forms: vertical and horizontal. Vertical precedent requires judges to follow the decisions of a higher court in the

[27] *Heller*, 554 U.S. at 580 (quoting United States v. Verdugo-Urquidez, 494 U.S. 259, 265 (1990)) (internal quotation marks omitted).

[28] *See id.* at 582 ("[T]he most natural reading of 'keep Arms' in the Second Amendment is to 'have weapons.'").

[29] *See id.* at 582–84.

[30] 18 U.S.C. § 2332h.

[31] *Heller*, 554 U.S. at 626–27.

[32] *See generally* Akhil Amar, *Foreword: The Document and The Doctrine*, 114 HARV. L. REV. 26 (2000).

[33] David A. Strauss, *Common Law Constitutional Interpretation*, 63 U. CHI. L. REV. 877, 910–11 (1996).

[34] *See* Justin Driver, *Constitutional Outliers*, 81 U. CHI. L. REV. 929 (2014).

[35] *See* Frederick Schauer, *Precedent*, 39 STAN. L. REV. 571, 572 (1987) [hereinafter Schauer, *Precedent*].

[36] *Id.* at 572–73.

judicial hierarchy, even in circumstances where the lower court thinks the higher court profoundly wrong. In the federal system, the Supreme Court sits atop the hierarchy, with the Courts of Appeals in the middle, and the District Courts below them. State courts are generally organized in a similar fashion. Federal and state judges are all bound by the federal constitution and the Supreme Court's interpretations thereof, so no judge – federal or state – can legitimately ignore *Heller*. A judge who refused to follow *Heller* because of a personal moral or political objection would be violating his or her oath to uphold the Constitution of the United States.[37]

But any decision's binding effect is directly related to the clarity of its guidance – a lower court cannot enforce a higher court's decision that it cannot understand – and in many respects *Heller* is not very clear.[38] Legal scholar Nelson Lund, who supports the central holding, has called the opinion "Delphic."[39] It is filled with internal contradiction; some conclusions lack reasons, or postpone those justifications for another day. Critics have noted, for instance, that the exclusions *Heller* carves out – the continued legality of felon-in-possession laws being a prominent example – are hard to justify on the basis of the majority's purported historical analysis.[40] On other issues, including major questions of coverage and protection, *Heller* is simply silent. This, Justice Scalia implied, is purposeful – *Heller* was not intended to "clarify the entire field."[41]

Whatever the reason, *Heller*'s opacity means that lower courts face significant challenges in hewing to the requirements of vertical precedent. And when precedent is unclear, the relative jurisprudential inclinations of lower court judges – caution or entrepreneurialism, skepticism or faith – tend to become more relevant. This is why Judge Wilkinson in *Masciandaro* questioned if there was a Second Amendment right outside the home at all. He didn't reject *Heller*, but concluded that a narrow decision – "saying a little less, rather than a little more" – was the wisest course given the stakes.[42] Of course, for every Wilkinson, there's another judge who doesn't see a

[37] See, for example, Alabama Chief Justice Roy Moore's suspension for his refusal to honor the Supreme Court's decision in *Obergefell*. Kent Faulk, *Moore Removal Upheld by State Supreme Court*, BIRMINGHAM NEWS, Apr. 21, 2017, at A6. Whether a judge can *ever* legitimately refuse to apply a legal rule he or she finds objectionable – the law of slavery being a prominent example – is a hard question, one we do not need to address here. *See generally* ROBERT COVER, JUSTICE ACCUSED: ANTISLAVERY AND THE JUDICIAL PROCESS (1975).

[38] See Nelson Lund, *No Conservative Consensus Yet: Douglas Ginsburg, Brett Kavanaugh, and Diane Sykes on the Second Amendment*, 13 ENGAGE: J. FEDERALIST SOC'Y PRAC. GROUPS 22, 24 (2012).

[39] *Id.*

[40] Joseph Blocher, *Categoricalism and Balancing in First and Second Amendment Analysis*, 84 N.Y.U. L. REV. 375, 423–29 (2009) (criticizing *Heller*'s categorical approach for failing to reflect any coherent Second Amendment value); Allen Rostron, *Justice Breyer's Triumph in the Third Battle over the Second Amendment*, 80 GEO. WASH. L. REV. 703, 729–32 (2012) (discussing increased scrutiny of felon-in-possession laws by judges and historians).

[41] *Heller*, 554 U.S. at 635.

[42] United States v. Masciandaro, 638 F.3d 458, 475 (4th Cir. 2011) (Wilkinson, J.).

"muddle[]"[43] in *Heller* as much as clear direction to vigorously and broadly protect the right to keep and bear arms. In this view, judicial modesty in the face of uncertainty is an abdication that relegates the Second Amendment to a "second-class right."[44] The debate between these views is inevitable to some extent, and turns on how broadly or narrowly one interprets *Heller*'s holding and its reasoning. Chapter 7 revisits it.

However one interprets *Heller*, as a matter of absolute numbers the supply of vertical precedent from the US Supreme Court is thin. More than 200 years after the Second Amendment's ratification, the Supreme Court has discussed it in detail only four times: *Miller*, *Heller*, *McDonald*, and 2016's decision in *Caetano v. Massachusetts*.[45] Federal courts of appeal have largely generated their own implementing doctrines for those cases, and those doctrines now provide vertical precedent for the district courts in each circuit.

Horizontal precedent – decisions made in the past by an equal or identical court within the system – is generally not as strongly binding as vertical precedent.[46] The US Supreme Court is not forever bound to follow even foundational cases like *Brown v. Board of Education*. *Brown* itself overturned a prior Supreme Court decision, *Plessy v. Ferguson*.[47] What makes *Brown*, *Heller*, or any prior Supreme Court decision different from history, custom, or other forms of experience is that American legal practice usually requires a decision maker to supply detailed and plausible reasons for overturning a prior generation's ruling on the issue.[48] For example, *Heller* declined to overturn *United States v. Miller*, despite *Miller's* apparent support for the militia-based reading, and instead went to great lengths to distinguish it.[49]

Horizontal precedent is covered by the principle of *stare decisis* (roughly "let the decision stand"). *Stare decisis* means that judges (or Justices) typically will not

[43] Lund, *supra* note 38, at 24.

[44] Duncan v. Becerra, 265 F. Supp. 3d 1106, 1115 (S.D. Cal. 2017).

[45] David Kopel has identified remarks in several other Supreme Court decisions, but they are not detailed decisions based on the Second Amendment. *See* David B. Kopel, *The Supreme Court's Thirty-Five Other Gun Cases: What the Supreme Court Has Said About the Second Amendment*, 18 St. Louis U. Pub. L. Rev. 99 (1999).

[46] A similar kind of *stare decisis* operates in the circuit court of appeals, albeit with a wrinkle. One panel of a circuit court *does* bind another panel. So, the *Masciandaro* court's decision in the Fourth Circuit about firearms in national parks horizontally binds other three-judge panels the Fourth Circuit. The difference is that within the circuit courts, a panel of three judges can have its decision voided by some larger group of judges – called an *en banc* panel – and then that *en banc* panel's opinion becomes the precedent within the circuit. *See, e.g.*, Binderup v. Attorney General United States of Am., 836 F.3d 336 (3rd Cir. 2016) (en banc).

[47] Brown v. Bd. of Ed. of Topeka, 347 U.S. 483, 494–95 (1954).

[48] *See* Schauer, *Precedent*, *supra* note 35; Jeremy Waldron, *Stare Decisis and Rule of Law: A Layered Approach*, 111 Mich. L. Rev. 1 (2012); *see also* Joseph Blocher & Margaret H. Lemos, *Practice and Precedent in Historical Gloss Games*, 106 Geo. L.J. Online 1 (2016).

[49] *Heller*, 554 U.S. at 621–25.

overturn a decision even if they think it is wrong, unless various other considerations are also satisfied.[50] Chapter 7 applies those factors to *Heller* itself.

Finally, judges may look to other courts for guidance – not because they are bound by their decisions, but because they find them persuasive along some other dimension. Such borrowing occurs among federal circuits, among state courts, and even across the federal-state divide. In the context of the Second Amendment, this kind of "persuasive precedent" has proven particularly important, precisely because *Heller*'s guidance (vertical precedent) is so scant or obscure, and lower courts initially had few of their own decisions (horizontal precedent) on which to draw. Eager for models, they often cited one another's opinions. The two-part test described in Chapter 4, for example, quickly spread across the federal courts of appeal not because it was binding, but because it was persuasive.

State constitutional law provides a potentially rich source of persuasive precedent, because the same kinds of questions now confronting federal constitutional law have been a part of state constitutional law for more than two centuries. Every state in the United States has its own constitution. Some states have constitutional provisions that track those of the federal constitution nearly word-for-word,[51] but as a legal matter they need not be interpreted in lockstep with their federal counterparts.[52] State courts can interpret state constitutions in ways that influence how the federal courts interpret federal constitutional provisions and vice versa. For example, the experience of several states in changing their constitutional guarantees in the area of criminal procedure eventually influenced the Supreme Court's reading of similar provisions in the federal constitution.[53]

With regard to the right to keep and bear arms, however, federal invocation of persuasive precedent from state courts has been peculiar. As Adam Winkler has demonstrated, state courts have historically given states latitude in regulating firearms, overwhelmingly applying what Winkler calls a "reasonable regulation" standard.[54] Under this standard, "[j]udicial review ... is limited to guarding against extreme, unfair, or nonsensical government action relating to guns and does not create any significant hurdles to gun control."[55]

Such state-level precedent has had little explicit influence on Second Amendment doctrine. The *Heller* majority did cite parallel state constitutional provisions as supporting its conclusion that the right to keep and bear arms was held by individuals,

[50] See Larry Alexander, *Constrained by Precedent*, 63 S. CAL. L. REV. 1, 59 (1989); Michael J. Gerhardt, *The Role of Precedent in Constitutional Decisionmaking and Theory*, 60 GEO. WASH. L. REV. 68, 73 (1991).

[51] Joseph Blocher, *Reverse Incorporation of State Constitutional Law*, 84 S. CAL. L. REV. 323, 327 (2011).

[52] JEFFREY SUTTON, 51 IMPERFECT SOLUTIONS: STATES AND THE MAKING OF AMERICAN CONSTITUTIONAL LAW (2018).

[53] Blocher, *supra* note 51, at 372.

[54] Adam Winkler, *The Reasonable Right to Bear Arms*, 17 STAN. L. & POL'Y REV. 597, 598 (2006).

[55] *Id.*

and not just the organized militia. But the majority gave short shrift to the long history of state standards of review concerning those parallel state provisions, seemingly assuming they had little bearing on the meaning of the Second Amendment when it was enacted. That said, the Court did not expressly reject these cases as persuasive precedent either – it simply declined to state an applicable level of review at all.[56] Given *Heller*'s narrow and conflicting application of state court precedent, some lower courts have used state decisions selectively – favoring state precedent from the antebellum South over cases from the North or more recent precedent.[57]

The role of precedent in Second Amendment doctrine will remain challenging, especially as it relates to other modes of legal reasoning. For most lawyers and judges, precedent is the most obvious and familiar form of constitutional reasoning. Lawyers are, after all, trained from the very first day of law school to parse cases. And as precedent develops, it has a tendency to displace other forms of argument, such as those based on history, structure, or even text, especially in lower courts subject to review by higher courts. This already seems to be happening in Second Amendment cases. Lower courts are scrutinizing phrases from *Heller* such as "public and private,"[58] "dangerous and unusual,"[59] and "M-16s and the like"[60] to get clues as to the meaning and breadth of the constitutional right. It is a process of what legal scholar Kim Roosevelt calls "constitutional calcification" – the tendency for the Court's opinions to become the predominant source of constitutional law.[61] In this way, *Heller*'s development into the law of the Second Amendment matches the development of constitutional law in other areas. But the right to keep or bear arms also presents unique challenges, from the relative lack of guidance from the Supreme Court in *Heller* itself to the largely untapped wealth of precedent in the state courts.

History

Many judges and scholars have concluded that history enjoys a privileged role in Second Amendment argument. Of course, *Heller* did not resolve all historical matters concerning the Second Amendment, but it has been understood to prescribe a special place for historical analysis in Second Amendment cases going forward. As is true of the broader debate about originalism, however, judges and scholars continue to disagree about the nature of that role and the answers it provides.

[56] *See Heller*, 554 U.S. at 628–29.

[57] Eric M. Ruben & Saul Cornell, *Firearm Regionalism and Public Carry: Placing Southern Antebellum Case Law in Context*, 125 YALE L.J. FORUM 121, 121–24 (2015).

[58] *See* Peruta v. Cty. of San Diego, 824 F.3d 919, 947(9th Cir. 2016), *cert. denied sub nom.* Peruta v. California, 137 S. Ct. 1995 (2017).

[59] Hightower v. City of Boston, 693 F.3d 61, 82 (1st Cir. 2012).

[60] Kolbe v. Hogan, 849 F.3d 114 (4th Cir. 2017).

[61] Kermit Roosevelt III, *Constitutional Calcification: How the Law Becomes What the Court Does*, 91 VA. L. REV. 1649 (2005).

Some want to use history to unearth the intentions or expectations of those who wrote or ratified the Constitution.[62] For example, James Madison's notes of the Constitutional Convention of 1787 – hastily written, schematic, and heavily revised by Madison himself years later – provide some information as to what the Framers intended or expected the Constitution to mean.[63] Second Amendment litigants have mined the writings of St. George Tucker, an early American lawyer and academic, to illuminate the intentions and expectations of the Founding generation with respect to the Amendment, often with predictably divergent conclusions. Private purposes scholars read Tucker to support an individual right in the Second Amendment; civic republicans read Tucker to advocate a right associated with militia service.[64]

The effort to use history to assess what the Framers wanted or expected to happen with their document largely has been abandoned in legal circles (in theory if not always in practice). The reasons are myriad, some of which have to do with proof: making definitive pronouncements about the intentions of a single person are difficult enough, and multiplying them to a body of men (like the delegates to the Constitutional Convention) or a body of voters (like the ratifiers) makes questions of intent virtually unanswerable.[65] Some have to do with democratic legitimacy: the Constitution was not ratified by anything like all the people in the eighteenth century, and even if it was, its status as law relies on today's acceptance, not yesterday's intentions. Perhaps most fundamentally, this mode of interpretation – giving conclusive weight to original intent or expectations – was not the mode practiced by the framing generation.[66]

Modern originalists tend to focus not on the Framer's intentions, but on the "original public meaning" of the Constitution.[67] Advocacy documents like *The Federalist Papers* provide evidence on that score, as do dictionaries, pamphlets, cases, popular usages in newspapers, and the like. This kind of exercise has its own challenges, not least of which is that some terms in the Constitution may

[62] *See* Thomas B. Colby, *The Sacrifice of the New Originalism*, 99 Geo. L.J. 713 (2011) (explaining how original intentions or expected applications gave way to other more linguistic conceptions of originalism).

[63] Mary Sarah Bilder, Madison's Hand: Revising the Constitutional Convention (2015) (demonstrating that Madison's notes, though given enormous weight in constitutional interpretation, were heavily revised).

[64] Saul Cornell, *St. George Tucker's Lecture Noes, The Second Amendment, and Originalist Methodology: A Critical Comment*, 103 Nw. U.L. Rev. 1541 (2009).

[65] *See* Kenneth J. Arrow, *A Difficulty in the Concept of Social Welfare*, 58 J. of Pol. econ. 328 (1950); *see also* Kenneth A. Shepsle, *Congress Is a "They," Not an "It": Legislative Intent as Oxymoron*, 12 Int'l Rev. L. & Econ. 239 (1992).

[66] *See* H. Jefferson Powell, *The Original Understanding of Original Intent*, 98 Harv. L. Rev. 885 (1985).

[67] *Masciandaro*, 638 F.3d at 470; *see also* NRA of Am v. Bureau of Alcohol, 700 F.3d 185, 194 (5th Cir. 2012). David B. Kopel & Joseph G.S. Greenlee, *The Federal Circuits' Second Amendment Doctrines*, 61 St. Louis U. L.J. 193, 229 (2017).

be specialized or idiomatic.[68] Dictionaries and other contemporary sources may not be reliable tools to reconstruct common understanding,[69] and parsing the Constitution term by term might actually disguise rather than reveal common understanding.[70]

Notwithstanding these challenges, Justice Scalia describes the project in *Heller* as an effort to recover how the Constitution's terms were understood at the time by the ordinary people to whom it applied,[71] and explained in *McDonald* that long-standing historical regulations "show the scope of the right."[72] Concealed carrying was traditionally prohibited, for example, and therefore concealed carry presumably does not qualify as part of the right to keep and bear arms.[73] The exclusion applies even though the Second Amendment does not specifically exclude concealed carry from its coverage (unlike some state constitutions, which have expressly permitted regulation of concealed carry[74]), despite the literal meaning of the word "bear," and irrespective of any benefit concealed carry may offer to the individual or society at large.

As with precedent, history presents difficulties when it comes to the Second Amendment. Whose history do we consult when construing the Second Amendment? *Heller* says the right "pre-exist[s]" the Constitution.[75] That could mean that the focus should be on English and Colonial history only up until the ratification of the Constitution. But *Heller* itself cited material from the nineteenth century. And now that *McDonald* has applied the Second Amendment to non-federal regulation through the Fourteenth Amendment, the historical focus on the late 1800s has further support. As one court put it, "when state- or local-government action is challenged, the focus of the original-meaning inquiry is carried forward in

[68] *See* Darrell A. H. Miller, *Text, History, and Tradition: What the Seventh Amendment Can Teach Us About the Second*, 122 Yale L.J. 852, 897–98 (2013) [hereinafter Miller, *Text, History and Tradition*] (discussing the necessity of an idiomatic reading of the Second Amendment); *see also* John O. McGinnis & Michael B. Rappaport, *The Constitution and the Language of Law*, San Diego Legal Studies Paper No. 17-262 (2017) (suggesting the Constitution may have included specialized legal terms of art).

[69] Darrell A. H. Miller, *Institutions and the Second Amendment*, 66 Duke L.J. 69, 112 (2016) ("'Excessive,' 'cruel and unusual,' and 'unreasonable' are vague and ambiguous terms whether one consults an eighteenth century dictionary or a modern one.").

[70] *See* Chris Thornton, *A Natural Cure for the Pet Fish Problem: Feature Emergence as a Classificatory Composition*, 35 Proceedings of the Annual Meeting of the Cognitive Science Society 1456 (2013) (describing the "Pet Fish" or "Guppy" problem where combinations of concepts create features that are not implicit in their components – we think of a pet fish as living in a bowl although we think of neither pets nor fish as normally living in bowls).

[71] *Heller*, 554 U.S. at 576–77.

[72] McDonald v. City of Chicago, 561 U.S. 742, 802 (2010) (Scalia, J., concurring); *see also Heller*, 554 U.S. at 626–27.

[73] *Heller*, 554 U.S. at 626.

[74] *See* Eugene Volokh, *State Constitutional Rights to Keep and Bear Arms*, 11 Tex. Rev. L. & Pol. 191 (2006).

[75] *Heller*, 554 U.S. at 592.

time; the Second Amendment's scope ... depends on how the right was understood when the Fourteenth Amendment was ratified [in 1868]."[76]

What about all the regulations that no one challenged, because no one thought there was any constitutional impediment to them?[77] If one object of history is to measure common understanding of the law at some point in the past, the unchallenged regulations may be as relevant as those struck down. What about the historical attitudes of African Americans, or women, or immigrants, toward the right to keep and bear arms? How should the court resolve conflicts between and within histories? For example, in 1870, Georgia prohibited firearms at church; in 1770, it required them.[78]

Despite its protestations to the contrary, *Heller* undoubtedly changed the doctrinal meaning of the Second Amendment. It was, after all, the first federal case in American history to strike down a law as violating the private purposes reading of the Second Amendment. What, then, should be made of the centuries of history that preceded it – a history that often was centered on issues other than private purposes? Relatedly, how much of that history should be considered Second Amendment law? English corporate charters allowed their members to arm themselves. Do corporations therefore have Second Amendment rights?[79] In the eighteenth century there was a limited privilege to resist an illegal arrest with force. Does that place a constitutional constraint on laws that prohibit resisting arrest?[80] Before the rise of the professional police force in the nineteenth century, private citizens enforced the law in specially assembled groups. Does the history of the posse comitatus, the hue and cry, or slave patrols figure into the scope or protection of the right to keep and bear arms?

Assuming lawyers and judges can amass the relevant historical materials and can understand what they are reading, there's always an antecedent question of the level of generality at which to evaluate these materials. As Judge Jeff Sutton has observed, "Level of generality is destiny in interpretive disputes."[81] A historical restriction on carrying arms in fairs, markets, and in the presence of the King's ministers could support regulations of wildly different scope: wherever people congregate, wherever the state is in control, wherever people buy things, or wherever government agents are stationed.[82]

[76] Ezell v. City of Chicago, 651 F.3d 684, 702 (7th Cir. 2011).

[77] *See* Strauss, *supra* note 33; *see also* Ruben & Cornell, *supra* note 57, at 122.

[78] *Compare* An Act to Preserve the Peace and Harmony of the People of this State, and for Other Purposes, no. 285, § 1, 1870 Ga. Laws 421 *with* An Act for the Better Security of the Inhabitants by Obliging the Male White Persons to Carry Fire Arms to Places of Public Worship, § 1 (1770), *in* 19 COLONIAL RECORDS OF THE STATE OF GEORGIA (1911).

[79] Darrell A. H. Miller, *Guns, Inc.:* Citizens United, McDonald, *and the Future of Corporate Constitutional Rights*, 86 N.Y.U. L. REV. 887 (2011).

[80] Darrell A. H. Miller, *Retail Rebellion and the Second Amendment*, 86 IND. L.J. 939 (2011).

[81] Thomas More Law Ctr. v. Obama, 651 F.3d 529, 560 (6th Cir. 2011) (Sutton, J., concurring in part and in the judgment), *abrogated by* Nat'l Fed'n of Indep. Bus. v. Sebelius, 567 U.S. 519 (2012).

[82] *See* Statute of Northampton, 2 Edw. 3, c. 3, § 3 (1328) (Eng.) (prohibiting persons from going or riding "armed by Night [or] by Day, in Fairs, Markets, [or] in the Presence of the Justices or other Ministers").

How much to privilege history over other forms of argument is a continuing question in Second Amendment cases. As noted in the prior chapter, some judges have taken the view that history, text, and tradition are the *only* legitimate forms of constitutional argument.[83] Privileging historical argument is not unheard of in constitutional law. The scope and coverage of the Seventh Amendment right to a civil jury, for example, is expressly determined by a "historical test."[84] But even with the Seventh Amendment, historical sources have never been applied with the kind of rigidity that some seek for the Second Amendment. Despite its numerous arguments from history, *Heller* does not counsel otherwise. Some of its justifications and exceptions can only be understood as stemming from contemporary considerations than some strict reading of the historical record.

Finally, that the right to keep and bear arms for private purposes did not prominently figure in federal constitutional law until 2008 means that the "constitutional" history of the private purposes reading is complicated. Consider age restrictions on bearing arms. While there are many historical regulations having to do with militia readiness – including age requirements of militia members, and requirements of arms-bearing – these regulations are of unknown significance in a post-*Heller* world. Courts are being asked, two centuries after the Second Amendment's ratification, to develop a doctrine focused on the private purposes of the right, even though most prior courts focused on the militia.

Social Practice

Constitutional law is not entirely divorced from a community's legal and political habits and norms – what we call its social practices.[85] In *Heller* and the cases that seek to implement it, community norms and practices already play an important, if sometimes uncredited, role in delineating the boundaries of the right to keep and bear arms.

James Madison predicted that social practice could be influential in building constitutional doctrine, writing that "it might require a regular course of practice to liquidate and settle the meaning" of some portions of the Constitution.[86] Whether we call the phenomenon social practice, custom, usage, convention,

[83] Heller v. District of Columbia (*Heller II*), 670 F.3d 1244, 1276 (D.C. Cir. 2011) (Kavanaugh, J., dissenting) ("The back and forth between the *Heller* majority opinion and Justice Breyer's dissent underscores that the proper Second Amendment test focuses on text, history, and tradition.").

[84] Miller, *Text, History, and Tradition*, *supra* note 68, at 856.

[85] Bobbitt's "ethical" modality does much the same work. *See* Bobbitt, Constitutional Fate, *supra* note 5.

[86] 3 The Records of the Federal Convention of 1787 435 (Max Farrand, ed., 1911) (quoting letter of Madison to Judge Roane Sept. 2, 1819); *see also* Paul G. Ream, *Liquidation of Constitutional Meaning Through Use*, 66 Duke L.J. 1645 (2017).

gloss, or tradition (and holding aside potential differences among those concepts),[87] the point is the same: some behaviors or understandings, occurring with some minimum level of frequency, by or among some group of persons, over some uncertain period of time, eventually take on features that judges recognize and incorporate into legal doctrine.

This kind of social practice has influenced doctrine for other constitutional rights. The Supreme Court has held, for example, that sectarian prayers to solemnize political events do not violate the First Amendment in part because they have long been part of American political culture.[88] Obscenity is unprotected when "'the average person, applying contemporary community standards' would find that the work, taken as a whole, appeals to the prurient interest."[89] Punishment violates the Eighth Amendment if it is both cruel and, in some sense, unusual by social standards.[90]

Social practice is likely to remain important in defining the Second Amendment's coverage and protection as well. In *Heller* and *McDonald*, the Court used social practice as a way to identify the values, objects, and behaviors the Second Amendment covers, as well as the regulations it prohibits. Sometimes this notion of social practice blends with arguments about history. For example, the Court suggested that the Second Amendment covers "*traditionally* lawful purposes, such as self-defense within the home."[91] But what other "traditional lawful purposes" it includes is not specified. Hunting has been a traditional practice in some areas of the country; it might even be protected, at least peripherally, by the Second Amendment.[92] A similar kind of reasoning may apply to the presumptive constitutionality of "longstanding" regulations, where "longstanding" could mean not only a regulation's longevity, but also its pervasiveness and enforcement.[93]

Modern forms of social practice could also be relevant. The Court in *Heller* suggested that gun regulation is presumptively constitutional in what it called "sensitive places." Contemporary customs may be useful in identifying those places. There was no national park system in 1791, for example, but the district court in *Masciandaro* specifically identified National Parks as "public properties where large numbers of people, often strangers (and including children), congregate for

[87] *See, e.g.*, Bradley & Siegel, *supra* note 15 (discussing "customary practice"); Adrian Vermeule, *The Third Bound*, 164 U. PA. L. REV. 1949 (2016) (discussing "conventions").

[88] Town of Greece v. Galloway, 134 S. Ct. 1811, 1818 (2014).

[89] Miller v. California, 413 U.S. 15, 24 (1973) (citation omitted).

[90] Miller v. Alabama, 567 U.S. 460, 469–70 (2012) (noting that the Eighth Amendment's central guarantee of proportionality is viewed "less through a historical prism than according to the evolving standards of decency that mark the progress of a maturing society") (quotation marks and citation omitted).

[91] *Heller*, 554 U.S. at 577 (characterizing the Respondent's Brief).

[92] *See* Joseph Blocher, *Hunting and the Second Amendment*, 91 NOTRE DAME L. REV. 133 (2015).

[93] *See* Darrell A.H. Miller, *Second Amendment Traditionalism and Desuetude*, 14 GEO. J. L. & PUB. POL'Y 223, 224–25 (2016).

recreational, educational, and expressive activities" and the roads and parking lots of those parks as "extensively regulated thoroughfares."[94] There could be other kinds of areas – airports or hospitals, perhaps – where, though there has not been a long history of specific regulation, there is a current and widespread perception of these places as "sensitive" and therefore less protected from regulation.[95]

The types of arms the Amendment covers also seem to depend on some notion of social practice. *Heller* stated that arms in "common use" for lawful purposes are covered by the Second Amendment.[96] Common use could be determined by what citizens today use for private purposes like self-defense.[97] Of course, as is true of any effort to define legality according to social practice, this leads to potential circularities, since social practices are themselves shaped by law.[98] Applying such a rule to the scope of "Arms," for example, could lead to the conclusion that the weapons either covered or protected by the Amendment are those weapons that are not legally prohibited.[99]

Circularity is not the only hazard, however. Using social practice in this way risks a peculiar ratcheting effect when it comes to constitutionally protected arms. Because bad guys illegally carry semiautomatic pistols, law abiding citizens need semiautomatic pistols; because the bad guys illegally carry AR-15s (to counter the semiautomatic pistols), civilians need AR-15s; and so on. If the potential bad guys include – as some commentators insist[100] – agents of the state or national government, including the police and the armed forces, this ratcheting would be hard to stop. The notion that law abiding citizens have a right to keep up in an arms race

[94] United States v. Masciandaro, 648 F. Supp. 2d 779, 790 (E.D. Va. 2009), *aff'd* 638 F.3d 458 (4th Cir. 2011).

[95] Federal regulation of firearms in airplanes is only about fifty years old, for example, although we venture most consider an airplane a sensitive place. *See* Act of Sept. 5, 1961, Pub. L. No. 87-197, 75 Stat. 466.

[96] *Heller*, 554 U.S. at 627.

[97] *Id.* at 629 ("Whatever the reason, handguns are the most popular weapon chosen by Americans for self-defense in the home, and a complete prohibition of their use is invalid.").

[98] *See McDonald*, 561 U.S. at 875 (Stevens, J., dissenting) ("For if it were really the case that the Fourteenth Amendment's guarantee of liberty embraces only those rights 'so rooted in our history, tradition, and practice as to require special protection,' ... then the guarantee would serve little function, save to ratify those rights that state actors have *already* been according the most extensive protection.") (emphasis in original) (citations omitted).

[99] *See Heller*, 554 U.S. at 721(Breyer, J., dissenting) ("On the majority's reasoning, if tomorrow someone invents a particularly useful, highly dangerous self-defense weapon, Congress and the States had better ban it immediately, for once it becomes popular Congress will no longer possess the constitutional authority to do so."); *id.* ("There is no basis for believing that the Framers intended such circular reasoning.").

[100] Sahil Kapur, *Ted Cruz: 2nd Amendment is 'Ultimate Check Against Government Tyranny'*, TALKING POINTS MEMO (Apr. 16, 2015, 12:57 PM) http://talkingpointsmemo.com/dc/ted-cruz-second-amendment-government-tyranny (Cruz: "The 2nd Amendment ... is a Constitutional right to protect your children, your family, your home, our lives, and to serve as the ultimate check against governmental tyranny – for the protection of liberty.").

with bad guys, however defined, is commonly deployed in political argument,[101] but courts now must address the matter as a legal one.

Structure

The grammar of constitutional law also recognizes that doctrine generates and is imbedded in political, legal, and social structures. As Philip Bobbitt has written, structural argument presumes that legal documents and unwritten legal norms expressly and implicitly designate certain institutions as constitutionally relevant, and govern to various degrees the interactions between those institutions and participants.[102]

Structural arguments underlie principles like the "separation of powers," even though no such term exists in the Constitution.[103] Structural arguments also support the notion that state and local governments have regions of authority that cannot be encroached upon by the national government, even when the precise placement of those regions are contested.[104]

Structural arguments in Second Amendment law used to be litigated around the proper balance between the militia and the private purpose interpretation of the Amendment. That has now been settled by *Heller* in favor of the private purpose interpretation. But *Heller* did not settle all structural questions regarding the right to keep and bear arms. If anything, it multiplied them. For example, the Justices unanimously agreed that the Second Amendment was adopted to protect the militia, but the majority then abandoned the militia when discussing the scope or protection of the right. Do militia purposes have any relevance with respect to the Second Amendment now? After *Heller*, some have invoked the militia to support coverage or protection of particularly powerful military grade weapons, or to extend Second

[101] *Ten Reasons Why States Should Reject "Assault Weapons" and "Large" Magazine Bans*, National Rifle Association Institute for Legislative Action (June 17, 2014), https://perma.cc/YPG7-HTCC ("Criminals could easily get around a limit on newly-manufactured magazines."); David C. Williams, *Constitutional Tales of Violence: Populists, Outgroups, and the Multicultural Landscape of the Second Amendment*, 74 Tul. L. Rev. 387, 473 (1999) ("[A] national policy that encourages and implements weapons ownership as a recognized means of self-defense invites a domestic arms race." (quoting Robert J. Spitzer, The Politics of Gun Control 192 (1995))); *see also* Amber Phillips, *Gun Control? Americans Increasingly See More Guns as the Solution, not the Problem*, Wash. Post: The Fix (July 27, 2015), http://perma.cc/96G3-E2QF; Donald J. Trump, Twitter (Jan. 7, 2015 2:29 pm), https://twitter.com/realdonaldtrump/status/552955292875759616?lang=en ("Remember, when guns are outlawed, only outlaws will have guns!").

[102] *See* Bobbitt, Constitutional Fate, *supra* note 5, at 74.

[103] *Id.* at 80–81.

[104] *See, e.g.*, Printz v. United States, 521 U.S. 898 (1997) (holding that provisions of the Brady Handgun Violence Prevention Act requiring local law enforcement to conduct background checks imposed unconstitutional obligations on state officials); Garcia v. San Antonio Metro. Transit Auth., 469 U.S. 528 (1985) (holding that application of the overtime and minimum-wage requirements of the Fair Labor Standards Act to state and local governments did not exceed Congress's authority under the Commerce Clause); Bobbitt, Constitutional Fate, *supra* note 5, at 74–75.

Amendment protections to teenagers,[105] but have resisted the militia as a tool to understand what kind of regulations are permitted.

More broadly, Second Amendment rights must be understood in various institutional contexts, including those involving other constitutional rights.[106] Demonstrations and protests on public land are covered by the First Amendment, so long as they are peaceable. But firearms at these events implicate these First Amendment guarantees, for example by raising the risk that speech and assembly will not be peaceable. Universities, too, may have special functions and privileges under the First Amendment,[107] which can come into conflict with the Second Amendment.[108] The free exercise of religion contemplates the kinds of institutions – churches, temples, mosques, and so on – that facilitate that exercise, but which might not always cut in favor of guns.

These kinds of structural arguments are sensitive to the fact that there are a number of institutions, of all kinds, that facilitate and constrain the right to keep and bear arms.[109] Structural arguments recognize the Second Amendment as doing something with the right to keep and bear arms narrower than confirming a naked natural right to self-defense, and broader than preserving a set of historically delineated regulations. Instead, it contemplates that the Second Amendment works within a constitutional and social system that requires judges to administer the right to keep and bear arms, alongside other constitutional rights, while also conserving valuable social and political institutions within that system.

Analogy

Reasoning by analogy is among the first skills students learn in law school, and is among the most fundamental tools in the lawyers' toolkit. It operates as a kind of universal modality in constitutional litigation, because lawyers make arguments by analogy when dealing with text, precedent, social practice or structure. Cass

[105] *See* Nat'l Rifle Ass'n, Inc. v. Bureau of Alcohol, Tobacco, Firearms, & Explosives, 714 F.3d 334, 339 (5th Cir. 2013) (per curiam) (Jones, J., dissenting from denial of rehearing en banc) ("History and tradition yield proof that 18- to 20-year olds had full Second Amendment rights. Eighteen year olds were required by the 1792 Militia Act to be available for service, and militia members were required to furnish their own weapons; therefore, eighteen year olds must have been allowed to 'keep' firearms for personal use."); Brief Amicus Curiae of Gun Owners of America, Inc. et al. in Support of Appellants and Reversal at 24–26, Heller v. District of Columbia, 670 F.3d 1244 (D.C. Cir. 2011) (No. 10-7036) (arguing that "assault rifles" and "high-capacity magazines" are protected because they are "reasonably related" to weapons employed in the militia).

[106] *Cf.* Gregory P. Magarian, *Speaking Truth to Firepower: How the First Amendment Destabilizes the Second*, 91 TEX. L. REV. 49 (2012); *see also* Luke Morgan, *Leave Your Guns at Home: The Constitutionality of a Prohibition on Carrying Firearms at Political Demonstrations*, 68 DUKE L.J. (forthcoming; unpublished manuscript on file with authors).

[107] Joseph Blocher, *Institutions in the Marketplace of Ideas*, 57 DUKE L.J. 821, 877–83 (2008).

[108] Darrell A. H. Miller, *Institutions and the Second Amendment*, 66 DUKE L.J. 69, 101–02 (2016).

[109] *See generally id.*

Sunstein describes the basic features of analogical reasoning as follows: we treat X in a particular way; Y is similar to X in some relevant respect; therefore, we should treat Y the same way as X.[110] X and Y could be rules, texts, litigants, or simply facts in the world – the "key step" is determining similarity or difference.[111]

Analogues of all kinds abound in *Heller*, and in post-*Heller* Second Amendment doctrine. For example, at the highest level of generality, courts sometimes analogize the Second Amendment with the First. Scalia wrote for the *Heller* majority that, "[j]ust as the First Amendment protects modern forms of communications ... the Second Amendment extends" to guns not in existence at the time of its ratification.[112] Scalia also utilized analogies to the First, Fourth, and Ninth Amendments to define the term "the people" in the Second.[113] Many lower courts have followed suit in invoking analogies to sources outside the Second Amendment.[114]

Heller also suggested that analogy could be used at a more granular level. During oral argument, Chief Justice Roberts speculated that some kind of reasoning by analogy might help determine what counts as an arm for Second Amendment purposes. He proposed that there may be some weapons that are "lineal descendants" of those arms protected when the Second Amendment was ratified, which presumably would also be protected.[115] Judge Brett Kavanaugh of the U.S. Court of Appeals for the D.C. Circuit later extended that reasoning. In a prominent dissent involving D.C.'s post-*Heller* revised gun regulations, he argued that the right way to adjudicate Second Amendment claims "is to reason by analogy from history and tradition."[116] Kavanaugh suggested that just as there are lineal descendants of the arms in use in 1791, "presumably there are lineal descend[a]nts of the restrictions [on firearms] as well."[117]

Analogy is the engine of the common law. The invocation of precedent, whether binding or persuasive, depends on establishing similarities or differences between a prior case and the present one. For example, *Heller* said that *Miller* was distinguishable in some relevant sense.[118] That left room for the *Heller* majority to hold the Second Amendment protects private purposes, without expressly overruling *Miller*. By contrast, lower courts have used analogy to extend *Heller*'s exclusions beyond those specifically identified in the case. For instance, *Heller* says that felons

[110] *See* Cass R. Sunstein, *On Analogical Reasoning*, 106 HARV. L. REV. 744, 745 (1993).

[111] EDWARD H. LEVI, AN INTRODUCTION TO LEGAL REASONING 2 (1949) ("The finding of similarity or difference is the key step in the legal process.").

[112] *Heller*, 554 U.S. at 582.

[113] *Id.* at 579.

[114] *See Marzzarella*, 614 F.3d at 96 n.15 ("[T]he First Amendment is a useful tool in interpreting the Second Amendment.").

[115] Transcript of Oral Argument at 77, District of Columbia v. Heller, 554 U.S. 570 (2008) (No. 07-290) (question of Roberts, C. J.).

[116] *Heller II*, 670 F.3d at 1275 (Kavanaugh, J., dissenting).

[117] *Id.* (citation omitted).

[118] District of Columbia v. Heller, 554 U.S. 570, 621–25 (2008).

are excluded from Second Amendment coverage. Most courts have concluded that some violent misdemeanants are relevantly similar to felons, and likewise should be carved out of Second Amendment coverage.[119]

The critical issue for analogical reasoning is what counts as "relevant."[120] Things can be similar or different in numerous ways, at various levels of abstraction. Helicopters and hummingbirds are analogous with regard to their ability to hover, but dis-analogous with regard to their weight. Houseboats have some features that resemble a house, and others that resemble a boat.[121] Relevance depends on some other source, whether social, biographical, emotional, political, or economic. The criteria of relevance might not be the kind people can articulate, or of which they are aware.[122] It may just be a bedrock part of human cognition, as Fred Schauer has explained, that we "group red bicycles with bicycles of other colors rather than with red ties and red meat."[123]

Reasoning by analogy assumes some principle or rule that explains what makes a factor relevant. For legal reasoning, this "rule of relevance" must typically adhere to the conventions of the legal profession – a biographical or emotional reason will not suffice – and it must be explained in a reasoned decision.[124] This means that the relevant similarity cannot be idiosyncratic or trivial. Take the argument that licenses for weapons should be unconstitutional because there is no analogous license required for books.[125] The First and Second Amendments are both provisions of the Bill of Rights, but that fact is inadequate to justify treating them similarly with respect to licensing. There must be some relevant factor that makes licensing a gun legally similar to licensing a book, or else the comparison is simply rhetorical.[126] Reference to some common value, principle or purpose could supply such a rule. We take up that issue in Chapter 6.

[119] *See, e.g.*, United States v. Chester, 2008 WL 4534210, *2 (S.D.W. Va. 2008), *vacated and remanded*, 367 F. App'x 392 (4th Cir. 2010), *opinion vacated on reh'g* 628 F.3d 673 (4th Cir. 2010), and *vacated and remanded* 628 F.3d 673 (4th Cir. 2010) ("The thrust of the majority opinion in *Heller* leaves ample room for the government to control the possession of firearms by misdemeanants found guilty of domestic violence. Indeed, the need to bar possession of firearms by domestic violent misdemeanants ... is quite often far greater than that of the similar prohibition ... on those who commit nonviolent felonies.").

[120] Sunstein, *supra* note 110, at 745.

[121] Fred Schauer, *Analogy in the Supreme Court:* Lozman v. City of Riviera Beach, Florida, 2013 SUP. CT. REV. 405 (2014) [hereinafter Schauer, *Analogy*].

[122] *Id.* at 422 (noting that people "draw their analogies ... often without ever going to or even seeing the level of abstraction or generalization that ... undergirds their judgments").

[123] Schauer, *Precedent*, *supra* note 35, at 584.

[124] Schauer, *Analogy*, *supra* note 121, at 422–23; *see generally* LLOYD L. WEINREB, THE USE OF ANALOGY IN LEGAL ARGUMENT (2005).

[125] *See* Sen. Ted Cruz, *Remarks During Senate Judiciary Committee Executive Business Meeting*, C-SPAN (Mar. 14, 2013 at 33:53 min.), www.c-span.org/video/?311493-1/senate-judiciary-cmte-continues-debate-gun-legislation&start=2027.

[126] *See* Richard A. Posner, *Reasoning by Analogy*, 91 CORNELL L. REV. 761, 768 (2006) (reviewing LLOYD L. WEINREB, LEGAL REASON: THE USE OF ANALOGY IN LEGAL ARGUMENT (2005)).

Prudence

Prudential arguments concern the institutional capacities and reputations of the courts as well as the facts they can rely upon to adjudicate a dispute. Such arguments can manifest in at least two related ways: As a reason to avoid constitutional rulings altogether, and as a reason to defer to the political branches.

Courts are not equipped to decide all matters, and being thrust into potentially fraught situations can undermine their legitimacy and standing. As Bobbitt has written, "a court's first responsibility is to decide whether it should decide."[127] *Heller* limits that decision to some degree. Second Amendment questions can no longer be completely avoided in favor of sub-constitutional rules. For example, when confronted with a Second Amendment challenge to the ban on possession by felons, a pre-*Heller* court might have resorted to a non-constitutional rule – finding that the law permits possession in situations involving necessity or self-defense, for example.[128]

After *Heller*, such prudential rulings are harder, because the right allows the claimant to control the terms of the challenge. While prudential arguments may be available for some peripheral matters – for example, whether the right to keep and bear arms has any bearing on negligently storing a firearm – judges increasingly have no choice but to answer questions lying near the core of the Second Amendment.[129]

In answering those questions, a second form of prudence comes into play. This kind of prudence concerns how much the court should defer to the considered judgment of another government actor that may be better positioned to acquire relevant information. Second Amendment litigation is suffused with questions of burdens and costs. It is the animating feature of the second part of the two-step process, which focuses on whether the regulation is sufficiently tailored to accomplish the goal. In the absence of clear instruction from some other source of law, including the Constitution, courts should generally defer to other institutional actors. If government actors want to support pro-gun legislation with credible criminological data showing a decrease in crime, judges cannot simply ignore or second-guess that data. The difficult cases are those where conflicting but credible data come before a court. In those cases, prudence typically counsels restraint and deference to the political process.[130]

[127] Bobbitt, Constitutional Fate, *supra* note 5, at 63.

[128] *See* United States v. Gomez, 92 F.3d 770, 778 (9th Cir. 1996) (justification defense is available to a felon convicted for the possession of a gun when that felon faced an unlawful and imminent threat of death).

[129] On the effect of the Second Amendment on these general tort principles, see Blocher & Miller, *supra* note 21, at 334.

[130] *See* Bobbitt, Constitutional Fate, *supra* note 5, at 68–73.

BUILDING SECOND AMENDMENT DOCTRINE

The preceding categories of arguments form the basic grammar of a constitutional Second Amendment. After *Heller*, they are the accepted forms of argument with regard to the right to keep and bear arms. In answering the many questions left open after *Heller* – some of which are sketched in Chapter 4 – these are the tools available to lawyers, judges, scholars, and others wanting to influence the law of the Second Amendment.

It should go without saying that these tools do not determine outcomes, except to the limited extent that arguments that do not employ them are not valid legal arguments. To say that a particular Second Amendment question should be answered by reference to history, in other words, is not to say what the answer should actually be. After all, Justice Scalia and Justice Stevens both relied on history in their *Heller* opinions, though they came to very different conclusions. The forms of Second Amendment argument might even point in different directions – First Amendment analogy might suggest that 18-year olds be given access to guns on the same basis as adults, as is true for most speech, while history- and social practice-based arguments could point to longstanding gun regulations suggesting otherwise.

But the grammar does have bite, and it can help channel disagreement into tractable and perhaps more soluble debates. A "legalized," "professionalized" Second Amendment limits – and sometimes even ignores – certain forms of argument, including arguments that rely solely on philosophical first principles, political popularity, emotion, or statistics.

As *Heller* has been litigated in the lower courts, judges and lawyers have used these various tools of legal reasoning to resolve questions of both coverage and protection. In doing so, they have begun to build a doctrine that implements the Second Amendment right mostly, but not exclusively, within the two-step framework described in Chapter 4.

Three cases, each focusing on a different key phrase of the Amendment, illustrate the modalities at work.

"the people"

Mariano Meza-Rodriguez grew up in Milwaukee, attending public schools until his senior year of high school, when he dropped out so as to provide for his girlfriend and their daughter.[131] He had worked in the city, but had some problems keeping a

[131] *See* Bruce Vielmetti, *Unlawful Immigrants Can Have Gun Rights, Appeals Court Rules*, MILWAUKEE J. SENTINEL, Aug. 25, 2015, at A4; *see also* Ian Millhiser, *Gun Rights Win A Major Victory In Federal Court, And That's Actually A Good Thing*, THINK PROGRESS (Aug. 21, 2015, 1:59 PM) https://thinkprogress.org/gun-rights-win-a-major-victory-in-federal-court-and-thats-actually-a-good-thing-a256927146o3#.jsj8zx1rw; Defendant's Brief at 3, United States v. Meza-Rodriguez, 798 F.3d 664 (7th Cir. 2015) (No. 14-3271).

job, and had a few scrapes with the law,[132] one of which ultimately led to a significant Second Amendment case.

Just before midnight on August 24, 2013, Milwaukee police responded to a complaint about a man with a gun at bar in the Mitchell Street District.[133] The man was gone by the time the police arrived, but he had been recorded on security video pointing what looked like a firearm into the bar's doorway.[134] Less than an hour later, a citizen flagged down the same officers to complain of a fight at a different bar.[135] The police arrived and, while breaking up the fight, identified Meza-Rodriguez as the man they'd seen in the surveillance footage earlier.[136]

Meza-Rodriguez ran.[137] After a short foot chase, the police caught him and found a single .22 caliber cartridge in his pocket.[138] For most Milwaukeeans, this likely would not have been a problem – Wisconsin's gun regulations are generally permissive.[139] But Meza-Rodriguez was unlike most Milwaukeeans in one critical respect. Although he had lived in Milwaukee for most of his life, he was born in Mexico. His parents had brought him into the United States illegally at age four, and he had never become an American citizen or a permanent resident.[140] Federal law prohibits undocumented immigrants like Meza-Rodriguez from possessing arms or ammunition, and a federal grand jury indicted him for violating that law.[141] Meza-Rodriguez sought to dismiss the indictment, arguing that the federal law unconstitutionally infringed his Second Amendment right to keep and bear arms.[142]

What would have been a relatively easy case before 2008 became much more difficult after *Heller* adopted the private purposes reading of the Second Amendment. The question was whether undocumented aliens counted as "the people" for purposes of the right to keep and bear arms. Three other courts of appeal had already held that they did not[143] – a strong degree of persuasive, but not binding, precedent. In Meza-Rodriguez's case, however, the US Court of Appeals for the Seventh Circuit held that undocumented aliens like Meza-Rodriguez were *not* categorically

[132] United States v. Meza-Rodriguez, 798 F.3d 664, 671 (7th Cir. 2015).

[133] *See* Jared Morgan, *2A Win Could Have Greater Implications for Immigrants*, GUNS (Aug. 21, 2015) www.guns.com/2015/08/21/second-amendment-win-could-have-greater-implications-for-illegal-immigrants/; Plea Agreement at 2, United States v. Meza-Rodriguez, 798 F.3d 664 (7th Cir. 2015) (No. 13-CR-192) [hereinafter Plea Agreement].

[134] Plea Agreement, *supra* note 133 at 2.

[135] *Id.*

[136] *Meza-Rodriguez*, 798 F.3d at 666.

[137] *Id.*

[138] *See* Morgan, *supra* note 133.

[139] *See Wisconsin Gun Laws*, NATIONAL RIFLE ASSOCIATION INSTITUTE FOR LEGISLATIVE ACTION (Nov. 12, 2014) www.nraila.org/gun-laws/state-gun-laws/wisconsin/.

[140] *See* Vielmetti, *supra* note 131.

[141] 18 U.S.C. § 922(g)(5).

[142] *Meza-Rodriguez*, 798 F.3d at 667.

[143] United States v. Carpio-Leon, 701 F.3d 974 (4th Cir. 2012); United States v. Flores, 663 F.3d 1022 (8th Cir. 2011); United States v. Portillo-Munoz, 643 F.3d 437 (5th Cir. 2011).

excluded from the Second Amendment. Because neither the text of the Second Amendment nor *Heller* itself directly resolved the question, the court had to rely on other justifications.

Reasoning from analogy, the Seventh Circuit recognized that the phrase "the people" appears in several different Amendments in the Bill of Rights. If used to mean one thing in one provision, then it presumably has the same meaning in another – the same argument the *Heller* majority invoked in favor of the private purposes reading. The "first ten amendments were adopted as a package," the *Meza-Rodriguez* court observed, and "identical phrasing" should be treated the same.[144]

But how had this language been treated in other areas? The court, having no clear vertical precedent on the matter, used analogy with another constitutional Amendment – the Fourth – to borrow precedent to build doctrine for the Second. In *United States v. Verdugo-Urquidez*, the Supreme Court had held that the Fourth Amendment applies to non-citizens "who are part of a national community or who have otherwise developed sufficient connection with this country to be considered part of that community."[145] The Seventh Circuit followed suit in holding that aliens are covered by the Second Amendment when they are part of, or have connection with, our national community. The court then looked to see whether Meza-Rodriguez met that standard. In finding that he did, the court implicitly used arguments based on social custom and practice. He'd lived in the United States for twenty years, attended public schools, worked, and built family connections.[146]

Having concluded that Meza-Rodriguez was covered by the Second Amendment the court went on to determine whether the law barring him from possessing a gun was nonetheless constitutional. The court did not clearly adopt the intermediate scrutiny test embraced by so many other courts, saying instead that the government needed to make – and had made – a "strong showing." In effect, the court concluded that Meza-Rodriguez may be covered by the Second Amendment, but was not protected. Undocumented immigrants were likely to evade the kinds of routine identification procedures common among citizens and lawful immigrants. Keeping guns out of the hands of those likely to misuse them was a sufficiently "strong" interest, as was "preventing people who already have disrespected the law" from possessing them.[147] This latter class included not only unauthorized immigrants, but also felons, fugitives, and domestic battery misdemeanants.[148]

[144] *Meza-Rodriguez*, 798 F.3d at 670.

[145] *Id.* at 670 (quoting United States v. Verdugo-Urquidez, 494 U.S. 259 (1990)). The Supreme Court had "obliquely" described this standard as involving the Second Amendment as well, but the *Meza-Rodriguez* court did not consider that one line as sufficient rationale to govern its decision. *Id.*

[146] *Id.* at 670–71.

[147] *Id.* at 673.

[148] *Id.* at 673.

In upholding this imperfect prohibition, despite its undoubted overbreadth, the Seventh Circuit deferred to the legislature's judgment about the risks associated with undocumented aliens in possession of firearms – a nod to prudential considerations.

"keep and bear"

Edward Peruta describes himself as "not a guy who backs down too easy ... if I know I'm right."[149] Peruta, a former Marine, firearms instructor, and police officer, had skirmished with all levels of municipal government in two different states, including school boards, zoning boards, parking authorities, and police departments.[150] Although he owned homes in Connecticut and Florida,[151] for most of the year he lived in a mobile home close to Fiesta Bay in San Diego.[152]

The motocross track operator/private detective/public access television show host applied for a concealed carry license to protect himself while in pursuit of hot news stories (another of his careers). San Diego officials denied his application because, among other reasons, he had not shown the "good cause" that California requires for the license.[153] Peruta sued, arguing that the "good cause" requirement violated the Second Amendment right to bear arms.[154]

Peruta won his first appeal. A panel of the Ninth Circuit ruled that California's "good cause" requirement for obtaining a concealed carry permit, considered in conjunction with California's ban on open carry, violated the Second Amendment. The opinion, written by Judge Diarmuid O'Scannlain, was a sixty-page tour-de-force of Second Amendment originalism.

Judge O'Scannlain framed the question before the court as whether the Second Amendment's word "bear" encompasses bearing arms for confrontation beyond the home, and found the answer primarily in history. What the court did with this historical material was revealing, and showed just how difficult it can be to harmonize the various forms of argument in a concrete case. The panel recognized that "every historical gloss on the phrase 'bear arms' furnishes a clue of that phrase's original or customary meaning."[155] But the court also recognized that some of this history did not neatly fit with what it understood as *Heller*'s precedential command. As the panel said, *Heller* held that "keeping and bearing of arms is, *and has always been*, an

[149] Peter Rowe, *Ed Peruta: 'I'm Not a Guy Who Backs Down Too Easy,'* SAN DIEGO UNION TRIBUNE, Nov. 16, 2014, at A1.
[150] *Id.*
[151] *Id.*
[152] Complaint at 3, Peruta v. Cty. of San Diego, 742 F.3d 1144 (9th Cir. 2014) (No. 09CV01235).
[153] *Id.* at 4.
[154] *See* Peruta v. Cty. of San Diego, 758 F. Supp. 2d 1106 (S.D. Cal. 2010), *rev'd and remanded*, 742 F.3d 1144 (9th Cir. 2014), *on reh'g en banc*, 824 F.3d 919 (9th Cir. 2016), *and aff'd*, 824 F.3d 919 (9th Cir. 2016).
[155] Peruta v. Cty. of San Diego, 742 F.3d 1144, 1155 (9th Cir. 2014).

individual right ... Any contrary interpretation of the right, whether propounded in 1791 or just last week, is error."[156]

Trimming was therefore in order. Citing George Orwell, the majority candidly judged that while all historical materials are "equally relevant" to determine meaning, "some cases are more equal than others."[157] And so the majority proceeded to chop historical authority into categories. In the first category were "authorities that understand bearing arms for self-defense to be an individual right." In the second category were "authorities that understand bearing arms for a purpose *other than* self-defense to be an individual right." In the third category were "authorities that understand bearing arms not to be an individual right at all."[158] Cases in the third category – those that employed a militia-based interpretation of the Second Amendment – were entitled to no weight, those in the second were given marginal weight, and those in first category were fully valued.

Having weighted the history and precedent in this fashion, the majority then concluded that "bear," when combined with the strict dictionary meaning (to "carry"), clearly meant a right to carry arms for confrontation out of doors. San Diego County's regulation, combined with California's restrictions, had all but destroyed this right, because no one could get a license without good cause, and no one was allowed to carry firearms outside of the home otherwise. The regulation could not stand.

In dissent from the panel, Judge Thomas, like Judge Wilkinson in *Masciandaro*, thought a narrow construction of the question was the more prudent route. Does the good cause requirement for concealed carry infringe the Second Amendment? He thought it did not. When the Ninth Circuit heard the case *en banc*, Judge William Fletcher, writing for the majority, agreed. After vacating O'Scannlain's opinion, the *en banc* court proceeded to answer the narrower question – not about public carry generally but about concealed carry specifically. "Based on the overwhelming consensus of historical sources, we conclude that the protection of the Second Amendment [whatever its scope] ... simply does not extend to carrying of concealed firearms in public by members of the general public."[159]

As the initial panel opinion had done, Judge Fletcher acknowledged the importance of history to Second Amendment adjudication. *Heller* and *McDonald* had treated "historical analysis as determinative."[160] But on the question of a Second Amendment right to concealed carry, the history was conclusively against Peruta: "The right of a member of the general public to carry a concealed firearm in public is not, and never has been, protected by the Second Amendment."[161]

[156] *Id.*
[157] *Id.* (citing George Orwell, Animal Farm 118 (2009) (1945)).
[158] *Id.* at 1156.
[159] *Peruta*, 824 F.3d at 927.
[160] *Id.* at 929.
[161] *Id.*

What followed was an exhaustive march through nearly six centuries of Anglo-American history, from Edward I's requirement that those going armed obtain a special license from the King,[162] to New Jersey's 1686 regulation forbidding the private wearing of any "pocket pistol,"[163] to Mississippi's 1890 Constitution, which expressly permitted the legislature to "regulate or forbid carrying concealed weapons."[164] Fletcher concluded that the overwhelming press of history showed there was no right to concealed carry. The only contrary conclusion, a court decision in Kentucky, was later negated.[165] In this regard, the *Peruta* court's conclusion fit squarely with the majority of other circuits.[166] There may be a right to open carry, the court concluded, but that was not a question before the court, and not a question to be answered by extending the Second Amendment to a right of concealed carry that history clearly did not support.[167]

A concurrence written by Judge Graber emphasized the virtues of prudence, pointing to the disputed statistical evidence concerning concealed firearms. Some studies show a decrease in crime, some show an increase. Some trace law-abiding behavior to concealed carry permits, but it could be this law-abiding behavior is created *because* of the regulations.[168] In such a hotly contested area, Judge Graber argued that the wisest route was deference to the political branches.[169]

"Arms"

Jaime Caetano lived in fear. Her ex-boyfriend persistently harassed her, even after she fled her home for a hotel, and despite multiple court orders to leave her alone.[170] He regularly showed up outside the club where she worked to intimidate, threaten, and embarrass her.[171] After Caetano described her situation to a fellow hotel lodger, the man handed her a stun gun. "You don't have to use it," he assured her, "but it'll scare him enough to leave you alone."[172]

The statement proved prophetic. Caetano's ex-boyfriend showed up at work again and started screaming until he was removed by a bouncer.[173] He waited for her

[162] *Id.* (citing 4 Calendar of the Close Rolls, Edward I, 1296–1302, at 318 (Sept. 15, 1299, Canterbury) (H. C. Maxwell-Lyte, ed., 1906)).
[163] *Id.* at 933 (9th Cir. 2016) (quoting An Act Against Wearing Swords, &c. N. J. Laws Chap. IX (1689)).
[164] *Id.* at 937 (quoting Miss. Const. art. III, § 12 (1890)).
[165] *Id.* at 939.
[166] *Id.*
[167] *Id.* at 942.
[168] *Id.* at 943–44 (Graber, J., concurring).
[169] *Id.* at 944 (Graber, J., concurring).
[170] Caetano v. Massachusetts, 136 S. Ct. 1027, 1028 (2016) (Alito, J., concurring).
[171] Substitute Brief and Record Appendix for the Defendant On Appeal from the Framingham Division of the District Court Department at 4–6, Com. v. Caetano, 26 N.E.3d 688 (Mass. 2015) (SJC-11718) [hereinafter Substitute Brief].
[172] *Id.* at 4.
[173] *Id.*; *Caetano*, 136 S. Ct. at 1028 (Alito, J., concurring).

outside and resumed his tirade. A foot taller and a hundred pounds heavier, Caetano's harasser "towered over her,"[174] but she stood firm. "I'm not gonna take this anymore[,]" she said, showing him the stun gun.[175] "Somebody ... gave me this and I don't wanna have to do it to you, but if you don't leave me alone, I'm gonna have to."[176] He backed off and left.[177]

Sometime later, Caetano was sitting in the passenger seat of a car outside a supermarket in Ashland, Massachusetts, when the police approached her on suspicion of shoplifting.[178] They asked to search her purse and found the stun gun inside.[179] At the time, electrical weapons were illegal in Massachusetts, and she was charged with unlawful possession of the weapon.[180] She sought to dismiss the charge on grounds that the stun gun was an arm protected by the Second Amendment.[181]

Caetano lost her initial appeal in the Massachusetts Supreme Judicial Court. Stun guns, according to the Massachusetts justices, were not "the type of weapon contemplated by Congress in 1789 as being protected by the Second Amendment."[182] The Massachusetts court cited *Heller*'s categorical prohibition on "dangerous and unusual weapons,"[183] finding that stun guns fit within that category because, first, they were not "in common use at the time" the Second Amendment was ratified. The reliance on *Heller*'s "common use" test – a matter of vertical precedent – was clear. The Supreme Judicial Court took this as a near verbatim quote from *Heller*. Stun guns had only become generally available in the early 1990s, and the first patent for such a weapon wasn't until 1972.[184] They were a "thoroughly modern invention."[185]

The Massachusetts justices also noted that, as a matter of social practice, sales of lethal firearms – a weapon clearly in common use and protected by the Second Amendment – far eclipsed sales of electronic weapons.[186] Because of their relative commercial novelty, and because they were not traditionally weapons in the military, such arms were unusual. Therefore, they were unprotected under the Second Amendment.

In an unsigned per curiam opinion, the Supreme Court reversed.[187] The Justices reiterated that the test for coverage was not whether the weapon was in common use at the time the Second Amendment was ratified, because – as *Heller* explained – the

[174] *Caetano*, 136 S. Ct. at 1028 (Alito, J. concurring).
[175] *Id.*
[176] Substitute Brief, *supra* note 171, at 6.
[177] *Id.*
[178] *Id.* at 3.
[179] *Id.* at 4.
[180] Mass. Gen. Laws Ann. ch. 140 § 131J (West 2004).
[181] Com. v. Caetano, 26 N.E.3d 688, 690 (Mass. 2015).
[182] *Id.* at 691.
[183] *Id.* at 692.
[184] *Id.* at 693.
[185] *Id.* at 693–94.
[186] *Id.* at 693.
[187] *Caetano*, 136 S. Ct. 1027.

Amendment extends "prima facie[] to all instruments that constitute bearable arms, even those that were not in existence at the time of the founding."[188] In other words, the Supreme Court focused on that part of its decision that pointed outward, to the text and to *contemporary* social practice, rather than backward, to those kinds of weapons and their "lineal descendants" that could be gleaned from history.

Justice Alito, joined by Justice Thomas, wrote a concurrence pillorying the state court decision. Justice Scalia had, after all, said that limiting the Second Amendment's protections to weapons in existence at the time of its ratification was an argument "bordering on the frivolous."[189] Justice Alito found that "each step" of the Massachusetts court's analysis "defied *Heller*'s reasoning"[190] and argued that the "reasoning of the Massachusetts court poses a grave threat to the fundamental right of self-defense."[191]

The concurrence also argued from structure and analogy. Stun guns were constitutionally covered – not because they were popular, but because they were used by the US military, as well as "law enforcement and correctional officers ... for such purposes as nonlethal crowd control."[192] This kind of crowd control, pursued by military and law enforcement officials with nonlethal weapons, is the same kind of activity that the traditional militia would have engaged in. Hence, they presumably should be protected when possessed by private persons.[193]

Caetano demonstrates how the recognized forms of legal argument often compete with one another and with themselves. Depending on where one dives into *Heller*, it points in different directions with respect to how to identify arms covered by the Second Amendment. Justice Alito's concurrence in *Caetano* tries to harmonize them, but would create its own set of problems. If covered weapons include those weapons commonly used by government officials to accomplish crime control and military objectives, then why does coverage end at stun-guns? Why doesn't it extend to "M-16s and the like," which Heller presumes are *not* covered? It is possible that some analysis of protection, using some other set of legal tools, would say that such powerful weapons are covered, but not protected, but then the doctrine would definitely drift beyond the kind of categorical approach *Heller* tended to favor.

TO WHAT END?

In *Meza-Rodriguez*, *Peruta*, and *Caetano*, judges used legal tools to resolve concrete legal disputes. In doing so, they generated Second Amendment doctrine – the kind of precedent that gives shape to the law, and is either persuasive or binding for courts

[188] *Heller*, 554 U.S. at 582.
[189] *Caetano*, 136 S. Ct. at 1030 (Alito, J., concurring).
[190] *Id.* at 1030 (Alito, J., concurring).
[191] *Id.* at 1033 (Alito, J., concurring).
[192] *Id.* at 1032 (Alito, J., concurring).
[193] *Id.* at 1032–33 (Alito, J., concurring).

in future cases. In a post-*Heller* world where the private purpose interpretation of the Second Amendment is not just a political argument, but an enforceable legal provision, those kinds of legal arguments are necessary.

Necessary, but not sufficient. Law, including constitutional law, is a practice with a purpose.[194] Individuals use the kinds of grammar laid out in this chapter to make legal arguments to pursue some kind of goal. The goals of a constitutional provision then become justifications for legal doctrine. As cases are litigated and the doctrine develops one case at a time, the doctrine is justified by new purposes that the constitutional provision is supposed to advance. For example, may of the first cases to successfully challenge speech regulations were cases having to do with political participation. Other litigants used decisions involving political participation to challenge restrictions on academic freedom or expressive association, which in turn gave rise to new justifications for freedom of speech and, correspondingly, new doctrine.

Which comes first – the purpose or the grammar – may be an impossible question to answer. The grammar of legal argument both presupposes and helps create understandings of the Constitution's goals. As noted above, for a litigant or judge to apply a historical modality assumes the specific history advanced is relevant. And a judgment about the relevance of a historical argument turns in part on what the Second Amendment is for. If it is about a right to personal safety, then the history that matters is the interaction between rights and personal safety regulations. If it is a right to defy tyrannical government, then the relevant history will be different, as will the arguments that flow from that history. The same can be said for all of the categories of argument identified here.

What is remarkable about the Second Amendment in a post-*Heller* world is that the doctrine is not mature enough to determine the purposes of the right, and the purposes of the right are not sufficiently theorized to determine the doctrine. Identifying those theories of the Second Amendment, and thinking how they reflect or reject the emerging doctrine, is the topic of the next chapter.

[194] Lon L. Fuller, The Morality of the Law (1964).

6

What Is the Second Amendment For?

On April 28, 2017, President Donald Trump walked on stage to address the National Rifle Association Leadership Forum in Atlanta, Georgia.[1] Not since Ronald Reagan had the President of the United States come to speak to the NRA's annual meeting, and not since Reagan had the gun rights group so visibly embraced a presidential candidate. The NRA spent more than $30 million in support of Trump's 2016 presidential bid, twice the amount it had spent on Mitt Romney's 2012 race, and more than any other interest group spent on a single candidate that year.[2]

Though the NRA spent more money in the 2016 cycle, its message was much the same as in previous elections. In 2012, President Obama was the head of a "conspiracy" to "destroy the Second Amendment." In 2016, Hillary Clinton was set to "launch an all-out war on the Second Amendment."[3] In 2012, President Obama was an "elitist hypocrite" for having security protect his daughters at school.[4] In 2016, Clinton was "an out-of-touch hypocrite," protected by "armed guards" while she plotted to disarm everyone else.[5]

[1] Meghan Keneally, *President Trump 'Proud' to be 1st President to Address the NRA in 34 Years*, ABC News (Apr. 28, 2017), http://abcnews.go.com/Politics/president-trump-proud-1st-president-address-nra-34/story?id=47080710.

[2] Mike Spies & Ashley Balcerzak, *The NRA Placed Big Bets on the 2016 Election, and Won Almost All of Them*, OpenSecrets: OpenSecrets Blog (Nov. 9, 2016), www.opensecrets.org/news/2016/11/the-nra-placed-big-bets-on-the-2016-election-and-won-almost-all-of-them/.

[3] Sean Lengell, *NRA Official: Obama Wants to Outlaw Guns in 2nd Term*, Wash. Times: Inside Politics (Feb. 10, 2012), www.washingtontimes.com/blog/inside-politics/2012/feb/10/nra-official-obama-wants-outlaw-guns-2nd-term/; Paul Bedard, *NRA: Clinton Wants 'Post Freedom America'*, Wash. Examiner (Oct. 28, 2016), www.washingtonexaminer.com/nra-clinton-wants-post-freedom-america.

[4] J. K. Trotter, *Why the NRA Said Obama's Daughters Have Armed School Guards (They Don't)*, Atlantic (Jan. 18, 2013), www.theatlantic.com/politics/archive/2013/01/nra-obama-daughters-armed-guards-school/319322/.

[5] Glenn Kessler, *The NRA's False Claim That Hillary Clinton Doesn't Believe Americans Can Keep Guns at Home*, Wash. Post: Fact Checker (Aug. 15, 2016), www.washingtonpost.com/news/fact-checker/wp/2016/08/15/the-nras-false-claim-that-hillary-clinton-doesnt-believe-americans-can-keep-guns-at-home/?utm_term=.eb20d8455ef4.

On the stump, Trump amplified these attacks. Clinton "wants to destroy [the] Second Amendment"; she "doesn't want guns"; he suggested her security detail should disarm and see "what happens to her"[6] and hinted that "Second Amendment people" could do something about a Clinton presidency.[7] He lambasted "gun free zones" as a "catastrophe"[8] and promised to "get rid of gun free zones at schools"[9] if he became president. Now he came to Atlanta in triumph, to speak before an adoring and appreciative crowd, with all the power of the presidency behind his pledge to "cherish" the Second Amendment.[10]

But off stage, the messages were more complicated. Outside the venue where the President would speak, a sign announced: "Hall A3 is under the jurisdiction of the U.S. Secret Service during the Leadership Forum ... [T]he following items are prohibited inside of Hall A3." Among those items: "Ammunition," "Firearms," "Knives," "Mace/pepper spray," "Weapons of any kind," and "Any other item determined to be potential safety hazards."[11] While NRA attendees could remain armed in the convention center,[12] and even as gun-rights supporters bet violent crime would drop during the Forum,[13] those entering the hall would be disarmed.

Trump's gun-free zone at a gun rights convention – and the almost total lack of organized protest by gun rights supporters – was fodder for online sniping and charges of hypocrisy.[14] But snark doesn't address the merits of the policy, its

[6] Jessica Taylor, *Trump's Second Amendment Rhetoric Again Veers Into Threatening Territory*, NPR (Sept. 16, 2016), www.npr.org/2016/09/16/494328717/trumps-second-amendment-rhetoric-again-veers-into-threatening-territory.

[7] Sarah McCammon, *Trump Campaign Says 'Dishonest Media' Misinterpreted His Second Amendment Comment*, NPR (Aug. 9, 2016), www.npr.org/2016/08/09/489364948/trump-appears-to-suggest-second-amendment-could-stop-clinton.

[8] Charlotte Alter, *Donald Trump Says Gun-Free Zones Are 'Target Practice for Sickos'*, TIME (Oct. 29, 2015), http://time.com/4091988/republican-debate-donald-trump-guns/.

[9] Jenna Johnson, *Donald Trump: 'I Will Get Rid of Gun-Free Zones on Schools'*, WASH. POST (Jan. 8, 2016), www.washingtonpost.com/news/post-politics/wp/2016/01/08/donald-trump-i-will-get-rid-of-gun-free-zones-on-schools/?utm_term=.3e91ca9252bf.

[10] Jeremy Diamond, *Donald Trump Goes After Hillary Clinton on Guns*, CNN (May 20, 2016), www.cnn.com/2016/05/20/politics/donald-trump-national-rifle-association/index.html.

[11] Dean Weingarten, *Knife Check at the NRA Meeting in Atlanta, Georgia*, AMMOLAND (May 1, 2017), www.ammoland.com/2017/05/knife-check-at-the-nra-meeting-in-atlanta/#axzz4i1NH33Km.

[12] NRA ANNUAL MEETING FIREARMS POLICY, www.nraam.org/attendee-info/firearms-policy/ [https://perma.cc/2JKA-ZLKS] (last visited Oct. 4, 2017).

[13] Steve Sheldon, *81,846 NRA Members Showed Up ... and Nothing Happened*, TOWNHALL (May 4, 2017), https://townhall.com/notebook/stevesheldon/2017/05/04/this-is-what-happens-when-over-80-000-nra-members-are-in-one-place-n2320698 ("The safest wager anywhere is that, just like every other year, rates of violent crime went down in the vicinity of the convention center during this year's NRA Annual Meeting in Atlanta."); A. J. Willingham, *Inside 'freedom's safest place'*, CNN, www.cnn.com/interactive/2017/04/politics/nra-convention-cnnphotos/.

[14] *See, e.g.*, Matt Novak, *Guns Banned at President Trump's NRA Speech*, Gizmodo (Apr. 28, 2017), https://gizmodo.com/guns-banned-at-president-trumps-nra-speech-1794734765. Months earlier, during Trump's appearance at the Republican National Convention in Cleveland, Ohio, similar rules were put into effect. Even then, the outcry amounted to little more than some online complaints and a liberal troll by a group called Americans for Responsible Open Carry. *Nearly 20,000 Support Petition*

justification, or the Second Amendment issues that Trump himself raised. What if someone had brought a Second Amendment challenge to the Secret Service's regulations, or had violated them and raised a constitutional defense?[15]

It is hardly unprecedented for a person to challenge a government-designated "sensitive place"; *Masciandaro* is one of many examples.[16] And we know from the previous chapter the legal arguments that would have been deployed. The word "bear" would have been examined in all its linguistic nuance. The Statute of Northampton, the medieval law that prohibited the carrying of arms "in the presence of" the King's ministers, would have been cited as analogous to the modern regulation.[17] The practice of banning weapons in the vicinity of the President would have been evaluated to see how "longstanding" it was. The government's interest in protecting the head of state would have been considered in light of the individual's interest in carrying a gun.

We know the legal grammar. But this grammar must be used with some end in mind – some sense of the *point* of the Second Amendment. A judge cannot accommodate public and private interests without knowing how each one fits with the Amendment's objective. An interest in protecting the audience and an interest in protesting the President weigh differently if the purpose of the right is checking government rather than self-protection. Historical arguments require some lens through which to read the historical materials. Evidence that colonists possessed the latest military-grade technology might be unimportant if the right is more about deterring burglars than about deterring despotic governments. Some theory of the right is needed to understand which "policy choices [are] off the table,"[18] whether those choices are made by school boards or by the Secret Service.

Yet, even ten years after *Heller*, the Second Amendment has a surprisingly thin theoretical foundation. Other areas of constitutional doctrine rest on theories that have built up over generations. The First Amendment's free speech guarantee and the Fourteenth Amendment's guarantee of equal protection have been subject to a century's worth of debate involving courts, scholars, and the public. Those debates about constitutional purpose in turn feed back into the doctrine itself. By comparison, an account of the Second Amendment's purpose remains schematic. *Heller*

to Allow Guns at Republican National Convention, FOX NEWS (Mar. 26, 2016), www.foxnews.com/us/2016/03/26/nearly-20000-support-petition-to-allow-guns-at-republican-national-convention.html; Arden Farhi, *Surprising Source of GOP Convention Guns Petition*, CBS NEWS (Mar. 29, 2016), www.cbsnews.com/news/surprising-source-of-gop-convention-guns-petition/.

[15] 18 U.S.C. § 1752 & 3056 and implementing regulations, 31 C.F.R. § 408.3, are generally understood as the source of this authority.

[16] *See, e.g.*, Bonidy v. U.S. Postal Service, 790 F.3d 1121 (10th Cir. 2015); U.S. v. Masciandaro, 638 F.3d 458 (4th Cir. 2011); DiGiacinto v. Rector & Visitors of George Mason Uni., 281 Va. 127 (2011).

[17] Statute of Northampton, 1328, 2 Edw. 3, c. 3 (Eng.).

[18] McDonald v. City of Chicago, 561 U.S. 742, 790 (2010) (quoting District of Columbia v. Heller, 554 U.S. 570, 636 (2008)).

and *McDonald* provide some broad strokes, identifying "self-defense," especially in the home, as the "core" and "central component" of the right.[19] But, as explained below, self-defense is too vague, ambiguous, and contested a concept to fill the void. Scholars have so far done little to help – pre-*Heller* Second Amendment theory mainly focused on the militia versus private purposes debate described in Chapter 2. A few pre-*Heller* pieces attempted to transcend this dispute,[20] but few theorists have engaged with the Second Amendment on its own terms after *Heller* codified the private purposes reading of the right.[21]

The theoretical vacuum is not just a jurisprudential problem; it's also a political one. Many liberals have failed to grapple with the positive values animating the Second Amendment. Many conservatives have not moved beyond broad generalizations, typically couched in the rhetoric of self-defense. Constructive debate about gun policy continues to falter in part because of basic disagreement over what the right to keep and bear arms is for. Consider "smart guns" – weapons that work only when activated by an authorized user.[22] Reaction to even the *availability* of such weapons, much less their requirement, has been swift and caustic.[23] But the discussion often takes place in a fog of unarticulated or imprecise notions of Second Amendment values.

Some people oppose smart guns because they think such weapons are unsafe or unsuitable. Smart gun technology isn't all that smart, they say, and may fail at a crucial moment, rendering the weapon inadequate for self-protection. Some oppose them because they threaten personal freedom. Even if the technology is reliable, smart guns may prevent a person from choosing the kind of weapon he thinks best. Some simply do not trust the government. Even if the technology works, even if the ability to choose a weapon has no intrinsic value, smart gun technology inches the nation closer to universal registration or confiscation of personal firearms.

These objections – one premised on personal safety, one on autonomy, and one on anti-tyranny – represent three different views of the Second Amendment's central value. Understanding them can help clarify disagreements about particular gun laws, and may

[19] *See McDonald*, 561 U.S. at 744–45; *Heller*, 554 U.S. at 599, 630.

[20] *See, e.g.*, Sanford Levinson, *The Embarrassing Second Amendment*, 99 YALE L.J. 637 (1989); Carl T. Bogus, *The Hidden History of the Second Amendment*, 31 U.C. DAVIS L. REV. 309 (1998).

[21] One of the few in the legal literature is Michael S. Green, *Why Protect Private Arms Possession – Nine Theories of the Second Amendment*, 84 NOTRE DAME L. REV. 131 (2008).

[22] *See, e.g.*, N.J. Stat. § 2C:39-1(dd); N.J. Stat. § 2C:58-2. The New Jersey legislature has recently attempted to amend these statutes because these statutes have caused "smart gun" research to halt. Samantha Marcus, *N.J. Lawmakers Act to Put a 'Smart Gun' in Every Gun Shop*, NJ.COM (Dec. 7, 2015), www.nj.com/politics/index.ssf/2015/12/senate_passes_bill_requiring_retailers_stock_smart .html.

[23] Michael Rosenwald, *Threats Against Maryland Gun Dealer Raise Doubts about Future of Smart Guns*, WASH. POST (May 2, 2014), www.washingtonpost.com/local/threats-against-maryland-gun-dealer-raise-doubts-about-future-of-smart-guns/2014/05/02/8a4f7482-d227-11e3-9e25-188ebe1fa93b_story.html?utm_term=.c119405b64c4.

help resolve them. These arguments are also deeply intertwined with the forms of constitutional argument described in Chapter 5. If a putative theory of the Second Amendment cannot be expressed in the grammar of constitutional law, so much the worse for the theory. And to the degree that a theory has purchase, it may in turn constrain the use of modalities that don't support it. Through this process, a kind of reflective equilibrium,[24] we can develop more insight about the purpose of the right than can be gleaned from examining the legal tools alone, and a more precise account of the right can emerge than is currently offered by an undifferentiated assertion of "self-defense."

"SELF-DEFENSE" IS NOT ENOUGH

"Self-defense" is the starting place for any Second Amendment theory. *Heller* and *McDonald* identify self-defense as the "core" and "central component" of the Second Amendment.[25] And, at a high level of generality, this is undoubtedly true. "[T]he natural right of resistance and self-preservation" welds together the prefatory militia clause and the operative right to keep and bear arms.[26] As this broad level, self-defense unifies the history of gun rights and regulation, from the Framers' fear of a despotic government to the Freedmen's fear of hostile militias and the Klan, to Otis McDonald's fear of drug dealers and thieves.[27]

But the more that self-defense is stretched to accommodate all the different histories, institutions, and motivations along this continuum, the less satisfying it is as a workable theory of the Second Amendment. First, self-defense is too abstract. Defense against whom? Or, in the terms of *Heller*, a right to arm against what kind of confrontation? Saying the Second Amendment's purpose is self-defense is like saying that the Fourteenth Amendment's purpose is equality or the First Amendment's purpose is free expression – the concept is so capacious as to be unhelpful. "[S]elf-defense," as Justice Breyer said in *Heller*, "is the beginning, rather than the end, of any constitutional inquiry."[28]

Second, self-defense is both broader and narrower than the right to keep and bear arms. It's broader in that self-defense covers far more persons and circumstances than the Second Amendment. A prison inmate, for example, has a legal and moral right to defend himself if another inmate attacks him. The government should not make the prisoner choose between "death through violent attack now or statutorily

[24] *See* JOHN RAWLS, A THEORY OF JUSTICE (1971).

[25] *Heller*, 554 U.S. at 630; *McDonald*, 561 U.S. at 745.

[26] *Heller*, 554 U.S. at 599, 629; *see also* David Williams, *Death to Tyrants:* District of Columbia v. Heller *and the Uses of Guns*, 69 OHIO ST. L. J. 647 (2008).

[27] *Cf.* David B. Kopel, *The Second Amendment in the Nineteenth Century*, 1998 B.Y.U. L. REV. 1359, 1454 n.358 ("The Framers ... saw community defense against a criminal government as simply one end of a continuum that began with personal defense against a lone criminal.").

[28] *Heller*, 554 U.S. at 687 (Breyer, J., dissenting).

mandated death ... [for] murder later."[29] But no one would conclude that the inmate therefore has a right to keep or carry a weapon.[30] Similarly, felons and the mentally ill can claim moral and legal rights to self-defense, and yet *Heller* specifically carves them out from Second Amendment coverage.[31] Federal law does the same for other groups with self-defense rights, including minors.[32]

Self-defense is also narrower than the right to keep and bear arms. Self-defense is legally justified only when it is both necessary and proportionate to respond to an imminent and unavoidable threat.[33] Generally, you cannot preemptively attack another person on a suspicion that he may harm you in the future. Neither are you permitted to respond with deadly force to a minor threat.[34] But the right to keep and bear arms – as opposed to the right to shoot them at someone – is not limited by necessity or proportionality.[35] *Heller* protects a right to keep a handgun in the home, even with no imminent and unavoidable threat, and irrespective of whether deadly force is a proportionate response.

Finally, self-defense is an unstable and contested historical, philosophical, and legal concept. Self-defense did not justify homicide until relatively recently in Anglo-American law.[36] "At early common law," the Supreme Court has written, "only those homicides committed in the enforcement of justice were considered justifiable; all others were deemed unlawful and were punished by death."[37] Although this severe approach relaxed over time, Framing-era sources still categorized pure self-defense as a blameworthy (but excusable) homicide, rather than a faultless (hence, justified) homicide – presumably, in Blackstone's words, "to caution men how they venture to kill another upon their own private judgment."[38] Philosophers and political theorists

[29] Griffin v. Martin, 785 F.2d 1172, 1186 n.37 (4th Cir. 1986), *opinion withdrawn by* 795 F.2d 22 (4th Cir. 1986). *But see* Rowe v. DeBruyn, 17 F.3d 1047, 1052 (7th Cir. 1994) ("[W]e find no precedent establishing a constitutional right of self-defense in the criminal law context."), *vacated by* 1994 U.S. App. LEXIS 10069 (7th Cir. 1994).

[30] Darrell A. H. Miller, *Institutions and the Second Amendment*, 66 DUKE L.J. 69, 80 (2016).

[31] *Heller*, 554 U.S. at 626–27 (felons and the mentally ill).

[32] Nat'l Rifle Ass'n of Am., Inc. v. Bureau of Alcohol, Tobacco, Firearms, & Explosives, 700 F.3d 185, 203 (5th Cir. 2012).

[33] MODEL PENAL CODE § 3.04(1) (AM. LAW INST., 1962) ("[T]he use of force upon or toward another person is justifiable when the actor believes that such force is immediately necessary for the purpose of protecting himself against the use of unlawful force by such other person on the present occasion."). An exception to this may be the doctrine permitting some battered spouses to attack or kill their batterers without the threat being strictly imminent. *See, e.g.*, Ohio Rev. Code Ann. § 2901.06 (West 2017).

[34] MODEL PENAL CODE § 3.04(2)(b) (AM. LAW INST., 1962). *See* State of Florida v. Curtis Reeves, No. 140216CFAES, http://curtisreevestrial.com/ (describing case involving second degree murder charges for shooting a person who threw popcorn at the defendant in a movie theater).

[35] Public carry licenses, by contrast, can and often do impose a requirement that a person show "good cause" for carrying a gun outside the home. *See* Joseph Blocher, *Good Cause Requirements for Carrying Guns in Public*, 127 HARV. L. REV. F. 218 (2014).

[36] *See* Joseph H. Beale, Jr., *Retreat from a Murderous Assault*, 16 HARV. L. REV. 567, 567 (1903).

[37] Mullaney v. Wilbur, 421 U.S. 684, 692 (1975).

[38] 4 WILLIAM BLACKSTONE, COMMENTARIES ON THE LAWS OF ENGLAND *187.

continue to debate the ethical and political roots of self-defense,[39] and the legal predicates for permissible self-defense are changing even today.[40]

That said, self-defense is undoubtedly "deeply rooted" in American law,[41] and rests at the "core" of the right to keep and bear arms. Any theory of the Second Amendment that ignores self-defense would be wrong. But so, too, would a theory that fails to address the complications, contradictions, and uncertainties in such an approach. A post-*Heller* theoretical debate about the purposes of the right to keep and bear arms must go beyond a naked moral claim to individual self-defense. That debate by necessity will move past the extensive pre-*Heller* scholarship. That scholarship, understandably, largely addressed the single question of whether the right protected the militia or private purposes. Little of it is suitable for the post-*Heller* era when litigation is no longer about the existence of private rights, but about the scope, nature and reasons for those rights. In that sense, Second Amendment self-defense today is where First Amendment free expression was in the 1930s – a proposition awaiting further theoretical elaboration.

We focus on three reasons the Second Amendment may protect a right to keep and bear arms: safety, autonomy, and anti-tyranny. These three theories are all consistent with the "private purposes" reading of the Second Amendment, but can lead to different conclusions with regard to its *coverage* and *protection* – the two doctrinal dimensions explored in Chapter 4. The theories do not line up neatly with any particular form of argument explored in Chapter 5, although there are some natural affinities. Our aim, in any event, is not to say any particular theory must necessarily correspond any specific form of constitutional grammar, but rather to explore the ways in which the theories harmonize or clash with recognized conventions of legal argument and with *Heller* itself.

We recognize that these three theories could be broken into sub-categories and may include other categories, such as preventing foreign invasion, or hunting.[42] But, given the timbre of Second Amendment thought after *Heller*, we think these three are the most salient. We also recognize that many details or objections to these theories will be left unaddressed. But as our goal is to encourage the theoretical debate, not to end it, we consider that to be a virtue rather than a vice.

SAFETY

Otis McDonald wanted a pistol to defend himself, even though he had other firearms in the home.[43] Jaime Caetano wanted a stun gun to scare off her abusive

[39] *See* Tyler Doggett, *Recent Work on the Ethics of Self Defense*, 6(4) PHIL. COMPASS 220, 220–33 (2011).

[40] Adam Weinstein, *How the NRA and Its Allies Helped Spread a Radical Gun Law Nationwide*, MOTHER JONES (June 7, 2012), www.motherjones.com/politics/2012/06/nra-alec-stand-your-ground/ (detailing nationwide spread of "stand your ground" laws).

[41] *McDonald*, 561 U.S. at 768.

[42] *See* Green, *supra* note 21.

[43] Debra Cassens Weiss, *Why Otis McDonald Is Lead Plaintiff in High Court Gun Rights Case*, ABA J. (Feb. 1, 2010), www.abajournal.com/news/article/why_otis_mcdonald_is_lead_plaintiff_in_supreme_court_gun_rights_case/.

ex-boyfriend.[44] Sean Masciandaro wanted to carry his pistol into a park, because he sometimes slept in his car. For each of these individuals, gun ownership was largely about *personal safety*. That is, they chose to be armed because of a personal judgment that possessing a gun would make them safer from threat. Personal safety is undoubtedly what most people associate with the concept of "self-defense."

But personal protection is not the only kind of safety the Second Amendment might contemplate. Under a slightly different reading of the safety rationale, one focusing on *public safety*, the effect of each private decision to possess a firearm leads to greater security for society as a whole. As the saying goes, "an armed society is a polite society."[45]

These two versions of the safety rationale rest on notions of arms, force, and deterrence operating within what might be thought of as a *marketplace of violence*. The marketplace of violence metaphor echoes the "marketplace of ideas" metaphor that drives so much thinking about the First Amendment. The animating principle of the latter is that "the best test of truth is the power of the thought to get itself accepted in the competition of the market."[46] Speech must be free to enable this competition, and the competition will more likely lead in the end to truth, a public good.[47] As Justice Louis Brandeis put it: "[F]reedom to think as you will and to speak as you think are means indispensable to the discovery and spread of political truth."[48] The desired end – truth – emerges from the market-like competition between ideas, some of them good and some of them bad.

The marketplace of violence operates similarly. On this theory, the state does not possess a monopoly on violence.[49] The Second Amendment empowers individuals to own and carry the tools of violence and to threaten violence by owning and carrying those tools.[50] Personal choices about violence contribute to personal safety in roughly the same way that personal choices about speech contribute to truth. Some

44 Defendant's Substitute Brief at *5–7, Commonwealth v. Caetano, 470 Mass. 774 (2015) (No. SJC-11718), 2014 WL 5911422.

45 Robert Heinlein, Beyond This Horizon (1948); *see also* Firmin DeBrabander, *The Freedom of an Armed Society*, N.Y. Times: The Stone (Dec. 16, 2012), https://opinionator.blogs.nytimes.com/2012/12/16/the-freedom-of-an-armed-society/?_r=0 (noting that the Heinlein quote is a "favorite gun rights saying").

46 Abrams v. U.S., 250 U.S. 616, 630 (1919) (Holmes, J., dissenting).

47 *Cf.* Stanley Ingber, *The Marketplace of Ideas: A Legitimizing Myth*, 1984 Duke L. J. 1 (1984).

48 Whitney v. California, 274 U.S. 357, 375 (1927) (Brandeis, J., concurring).

49 *See* Max Weber, Politics as Vocation (1919), available at http://anthropos-lab.net/wp/wp-content/uploads/2011/12/Weber-Politics-as-a-Vocation.pdf; *see also* Donald W. Dowd, *The Relevance of the Second Amendment to Gun Control Legislation*, 58 Mont. L. Rev. 79, 99 (1997); George P. Fletcher, *Domination in the Theory of Justification and Excuse*, 57 U. Pitt. L. Rev. 553, 570 (1996); David C. Williams, *Constitutional Tales of Violence: Populists, Outgroups, and the Multicultural Landscape of the Second Amendment*, 74 Tulane L. Rev. 387, 459 (1999).

50 *See* Daniel M. T. Fessler, Colin Holbrook, & Jeffrey K. Snyder, *Weapons Make the Man (Larger): Formidability Is Represented As Size and Strength In Humans*, 7(4) PLoS ONE (2012) (showing that "knowing that an individual possesses a gun ... leads observers to conceptualize him as taller, and generally larger and more muscular").

violence – like some speech – will be undesirable, but undesirable violence will be mitigated by desirable violence, such as threatened or actual self-defense. Over time, desirable exercises of the right (self-defense or truth) will win out over undesirable exercises (crime or falsehoods),[51] leading to a better equilibrium than could be achieved by government regulation. In the free speech context, Brandeis summed up faith in this market when he said the proper remedy for lies is not legal intervention, but "more speech."[52] The NRA's Wayne LaPierre, sounding like a Second Amendment Brandeis, echoed that theme after Sandy Hook: "The only thing that stops a bad guy with a gun is a good guy with a gun."[53]

Of course, at the heart of this safety rationale lay both an empirical question – does gun ownership make the individual or society safer? – and a normative question – to what degree does it matter? Neither has a certain answer. As to the former, the experimental data is hotly contested. Economist John Lott has argued that more guns equal less crime, and some polls suggest that a majority of Americans agree.[54] But scholars like Ian Ayres and John Donohue dispute Lott's findings.[55] Some say that the available data is inconclusive,[56] or that relaxing certain gun regulations leads to more fatalities.[57] As to the latter, one view is that the Second Amendment renders the empirical question moot. As the *Heller* majority put it, the Second Amendment "is the very *product* of an interest-balancing by the people" that occurred at the Founding.[58] On this view, United States decided in 1791 that the benefits of private ownership of the tools of violence would always outweigh the costs, and this weighing cannot be done again without amending the Constitution.[59]

[51] Joseph Blocher & Darrell A. H. Miller, *What is Gun Control? Direct Burdens, Incidental Burdens, and the Boundaries of the Second Amendment*, 83 U. CHI. L. REV. 295, 302, 352–54 (2016).

[52] Whitney v. California, 274 U.S. 357, 377 (Brandeis, J., concurring).

[53] Peter Overby, *NRA: 'Only Thing That Stops A Bad Guy With A Gun Is A Good Guy With A Gun,'* NPR (Dec. 21, 2012), www.npr.org/2012/12/21/167824766/nra-only-thing-that-stops-a-bad-guy-with-a-gun-is-a-good-guy-with-a-gun; *see also* Green, *supra* note 21, at 146 (identifying one theory of the Second Amendment as "constitutionaliz[ing] the empirical judgment that private arms possession promotes public safety").

[54] *See* JOHN R. LOTT JR., MORE GUNS, LESS CRIME: UNDERSTANDING CRIME AND GUN-CONTROL LAWS (1998); *see also Guns: Suppose more Americans were allowed to carry concealed weapons if they passed a criminal background check and training course. If more Americans carried concealed weapons, would the United States be safer or less safe?*, GALLUP (Oct. 7–11, 2015), www.gallup.com/poll/1645/guns.aspx (finding that 56 percent of Americans would feel safer if more citizens carried guns lawfully in public).

[55] Ian Ayres & John J. Donohue III, *Shooting Down the "More Guns, Less Crime" Hypothesis*, 55 STAN. L. REV. 1193 (2003); *see also* Abhay Aneja, John J. Donohue III, & Alexandria Zhang, *The Impact of Right to Carry Laws and the NRC Report: The Latest Lessons for the Empirical Evaluation of Law and Policy*, NBER Working Paper 18294 (Issued 2012, Revised 2014).

[56] FIREARMS AND VIOLENCE: A CRITICAL REVIEW, NATIONAL RESEARCH COUNCIL (2005).

[57] John J. Donohue, Abhay Aneja, & Kyle D. Weber, *Right-to-Carry Laws and Violent Crime: A Comprehensive Assessment Using Panel Data and a State-Level Synthetic Controls Analysis*, NBER Working Paper No. 23510 (Issued June 2017, Revised January 2018).

[58] *Heller*, 554 U.S. at 635.

[59] *Id.* at 635–36.

But that is not the only view, nor is it enough to answer the questions the Second Amendment raises. The Founders may have decided that some gun ownership contributes to personal or public safety, but that does not mean that they necessarily decided how that balance applies to specific questions about which weapons may be owned, who can own them, and where and how they may be carried. From that perspective, it would be odd for a right that promotes public safety through private gun ownership to disregard public safety when considering these unanswered questions. The public safety rationale for the right is predicated on the idea that gun ownership generates externalities, after all. Some are positive, like the legitimate defensive use of weapons or the reduction of crime. But some are negative, like accidents, unjustified shootings, or avoidance behaviors caused by fear.[60] As Justice Stevens pointed out in his dissent in *McDonald v. City of Chicago*, "*[y]our* interest in keeping and bearing a certain firearm may diminish *my* interest in being and feeling safe from armed violence."[61]

The concept of government regulation in this marketplace of violence is not inconsistent with a constitutional right that encodes the right to keep and bear arms for safety reasons. Even the most skeptical view of government regulation recognizes that state intervention is sometimes necessary to prevent or remedy "market failures."[62] In this view, the fact that firearms unquestionably are used for legitimate defensive purposes is an input to the Second Amendment inquiry, but not the only relevant input. The Amendment clearly takes certain choices off the table, like banning all arms, but the goal is still safety, and that may permit limits on individual choice. The right is not being reweighed, but actually contemplates this weighing.

Heller seems to recognize that some safety assessments are permissible. For example, *Heller* recognizes limits on firearms in "sensitive places." The safety rationale provides content to "sensitive places" by allowing greater regulation of firearms in those places where negative externalities are higher, as, for example, in a theater, restaurant or on a crowded street. The safety purpose also is consistent with the historical record, which has revealed widespread and thorough regulation of firearms and ammunition in densely populated areas since at least the middle ages.[63]

A Second Amendment whose primary purpose is safety may also guide questions about which arms are covered by the Second Amendment and which are the kinds of "dangerous and unusual" weapons that may be banned. For example, if a certain kind of weapon generates great risks but only marginal benefits – a

[60] *See* CTRS. FOR DISEASE CTRL. AND PREVENTION, NATIONAL VITAL STATISTICS REPORTS 84 (vol. 64.2, Feb. 16, 2016) (finding 33,636 deaths by firearms in 2013; Eric Ruben, *Justifying Perceptions in First and Second Amendment Doctrine*, 80 LAW & CONTEMP. PROBS. 149 (2017).

[61] *McDonald*, 561 U.S. at 891 (Stevens, J., dissenting).

[62] Joseph Blocher, *Institutions in the Marketplace of Ideas*, 57 DUKE L.J. 821 (2008). *Cf.* Jens Ludwig, *Gun Self-Defense and Deterrence*, 27 CRIME AND JUSTICE 363 (2000).

[63] Joseph Blocher, *Firearm Localism*, 123 YALE L.J. 82 (2013).

high-powered rifle in a subway station, say – then the government might have more leeway to regulate precisely because it has left us with sufficient alternative means of self-protection.[64] A First Amendment analogy might be warranted here, since the Supreme Court's free speech cases suggest that the "adequate alternatives" inquiry may be more deferential to the state when the right is claimed in a public rather than a private setting.[65]

The safety rationale also provides a way to implement *Heller*'s rule that the Second Amendment covers weapons in "common use." As noted previously, that rule raises hard questions: Common use by whom, and for what? From the perspective of a safety theory, one might simply consider whether a weapon is in common use *for personal safety*. Although there may be many long guns in common use for reasons unrelated to safety – target shooting, hunting, or collecting, for example[66] – only those that are designed and owned primarily for personal safety purposes would receive the maximum constitutional protection. For example, the D.C. law at issue in *Heller* effectively banned handguns, but permitted private individuals to own an arsenal of long guns. Opponents of the law maintained that rifles are not reliable for self-defense.[67] If it is true, as these arguments suggest, that certain long guns are not commonly or properly used for personal safety, then their Second Amendment protection should be correspondingly weaker.

Of course, one's faith in the marketplace may also correlate with skepticism of safety-focused government interventions. Although this skepticism could arise out of a sense that the Amendment is about safety, objections in practice might quickly

[64] Blocher & Miller, *supra* note 51, at 292.

[65] City of Ladue v. Gilleo, 512 U.S. 43, 56, 58 (1994) ("[W]hereas the government's need to mediate among various competing uses, including expressive ones, for public streets and facilities is constant and unavoidable, its need to regulate temperate speech from the home is surely much less pressing.").

[66] Heller v. District of Columbia (*Heller II*), 670 F.3d 1244, 1261 (D.C. Cir. 2011) ("We think it clear enough in the record that semi-automatic rifles and magazines holding more than ten rounds are indeed in 'common use' .... Nevertheless, based upon the record as it stands, we cannot be certain whether these weapons are commonly used or are useful specifically for self-defense or hunting."); *see also* David B. Kopel & Richard E. Gardner, *The* Sullivan Principles: *Protecting the Second Amendment from Civil Abuse*, 19 SETON HALL LEGIS. J. 737, 755 (1995); Michael O'Shea, *The Right to Defensive Arms After* District of Columbia v. Heller, 111 W. VA. L. REV. 349, 388 n.182 (2009); Ray Long & Rafael Guerrero, *Lawmakers Clash Over Assault Weapons Ban*, CHI. TRIB., Mar. 1, 2013, at 1.7.

[67] *See, e.g.*, Brief for Amici Curiae Disabled Veterans for Self-Defense and Kestra Childers at 29–30, District of Columbia v. Heller, 554 U.S. 570 (2008) (No. 07-290) (noting that rifles are more dangerous to keep in the home because of their relative muzzle velocity); Brief Amicus Curiae of the Heartland Institute at 16–17, District of Columbia v. Heller, 554 U.S. 570 (2008) (No. 07-290) (noting that "[t]he vast majority of American gun owners prefer handguns to other firearms for self-defense" and that "the FBI found that handguns accounted for over 83 percent of all firearms used in legally justified defensive homicides by private citizens, while shotguns and rifles together accounted for less than 7.5 percent of such"); Brief of Amici Curiae Se. Legal Found., Inc. et al. at 17–21 District of Columbia v. Heller, 554 U.S. 570 (2008) (listing reasons why "[h]igh powered rifles are not recommended for self-defense," including (1) the fact that dialing 911 while aiming one is difficult, (2) they are awkward to get into action quickly, and (3) they are less useful in close quarters (internal quotations omitted)).

shade into concerns that are rooted in autonomy or anti-tyranny as well. First, one might be dubious of regulation on the basis of *competence*: the government is simply incapable of ensuring an optimal amount of safety for everyone, and the invisible hand of the market will provide better (that is, safer) results.[68] For those with competence objections, gun regulations designed to promote safety are likely to be ineffectual precisely because the government is unable to achieve optimal safety, even when it regulates in good faith and with the public welfare in mind.[69]

Second, one might resist regulation on the basis of *equality*. Such objections emphasize the tension between recognition of the inherent worth of every individual and the tendency for safety regulations to favor the safety of some people over others. Even if a government had the ability to design a regime that would increase total safety, one may say that it is inequitable to elevate the safety interests of, for instance, armored car drivers over school bus drivers. Presidents should have no more rights to personal safety than other politicians, and politicians should have no more rights than the citizenry at large. The core concern of these arguments is safety, but infused with something like autonomy or dignity. Such objections suggest that, if distinctions between persons can be made at all, they require extraordinary justification.

Third, one may be skeptical of government regulation due to fear of *corruption*. To these skeptics, the government should not be able to regulate firearms, even to achieve safety, because its policies will inevitably skew toward the protection of insiders – including police, political supporters, and the military.[70]

The point is not that the safety rationales lead to easy answers about the scope and protection of the Second Amendment, let alone the resolution of particular legal disputes. But they do focus the inquiry, drawing attention to particular aspects of history, precedent, policy, and social practice that speak to a safety purpose rather than to other purposes like autonomy.

AUTONOMY

Most people probably believe that the Second Amendment is a right primarily for reasons of personal safety. But that's a rather new development. Indeed, until very recently, only a minority of gun owners said that personal protection was their primary reason for owning a firearm.[71] If the Amendment protects a right for reasons other than the utility of the firearm itself, then the right is really about a power to choose, and that's a matter of autonomy.

[68] *See, e.g.*, Lott, *supra* note 54.

[69] *See* Martin H. Redish, The Adversary First Amendment (2013).

[70] David C. Williams, The Mythic Meanings of the Second Amendment: Taming Political Violence in a Constitutional Republic (2003).

[71] *Why Own a Gun? Protection Is Now Top Reason*, Pew Research Ctr. (Mar. 12, 2013), www.people-press.org/2013/03/12/why-own-a-gun-protection-is-now-top-reason/.

"Autonomy" is derived from a Greek word that roughly translates as "self-rule." References to autonomy suffuse Second Amendment rhetoric.[72] Frequently that rhetoric is joined with appeals to the early classical liberalism of John Locke, and his notion that every person is inalienably his own master.[73]

Many rights besides the right to keep and bear arms are said to promote dignity and autonomy,[74] among them the First Amendment right to free speech,[75] the right to privacy,[76] and the Fourth Amendment right to be free from unreasonable searches and seizures.[77]

But autonomy is a difficult foundation on which to rest a constitutional right. For one thing, it is an incredibly contested concept – perhaps more so even than self-defense. At least there's an ascertainable legal doctrine for self-defense. There is no corresponding "doctrine of autonomy," and judges cannot be expected to agree on the contours of the concept with any more precision than philosophers.

Even to the degree that judges' and philosophers' notions of autonomy overlap, however, that agreement may not provide much insight. On the one hand, autonomy provides too little guidance – most constitutional rights protect "self-rule" of one kind or another, and that recognition does little to resolve concrete cases. On the other hand, it proves too much. If every constitutional right is whatever the right-holder says it is, then it's hard to discern a principle of the constitutional right that is not trivial (you have a right so long as it doesn't interfere with another's right) or anarchic (no one can gainsay your claim to a right). For the most part, then, autonomy tends to bolster *other* normative theories, rather than resting on its own bottom.

The strongest version of Second Amendment autonomy renders irrelevant the reasons for an individual's exercise of the right to keep and bear arms. Persons want

[72] Green, *supra* note 21, at 158–59 n.96; Clark M. Neily III, *The Right To Keep and Bear Arms in the States: Ambiguity, False Modesty, and (Maybe) Another Win for Originalism*, 33 HARV. J.L. & PUB. POL'Y 185, 193 (2010) (calling the Second Amendment a pledge about "spiritual" and "physical autonomy"); Robert Weisberg, *The Utilitarian and Deontological Entanglement of Debating Guns, Crime, and Punishment in America*, 71 U. CHI. L. REV. 333, 337 (2004) (noting the "association of the gun with a form of individual autonomy" (reviewing GUNS, CRIME, AND PUNISHMENT IN AMERICA (Bernard E. Harcourt, ed., 2003))).

[73] Green, *supra* note 21, at 154; Steven J. Heyman, *Natural Rights and the Second Amendment*, 76 CHI.-KENT L. REV. 237; *see also* Todd C. Hughes & Lester H. Hunt, *Liberal Basis of the Right to Keep and Bear Arms*, 14 PUB. AFFAIRS QUART. 1, 3 (2000).

[74] *See* Lawrence v. Texas, 539 U.S. 558, 567, 574–75 (2003); Stanley v. Georgia, 394 U.S. 557, 566 (1969); *cf.* Burwell v. Hobby Lobby, 134 S. Ct. 2751 (2014). *See generally* Neomi Rao, *Three Concepts of Dignity in Constitutional Law*, 86 NOTRE DAME L. REV. 183 (2011); Reva B. Siegel, *Dignity and the Politics of Protection: Abortion Restrictions under* Casey/Carhart, 117 YALE L.J. 1694 (2008).

[75] *See generally* ED BAKER, HUMAN LIBERTY AND FREEDOM OF SPEECH (1989); Martin H. Redish, *The Content Distinction in First Amendment Analysis*, 34 STAN. L. REV. 113 (1981).

[76] *See, e.g.*, Ann L. Schiavone, *Unleashing the Fourteenth Amendment*, 2016 WIS. L. REV. FORWARD 27 (2016); William M. Beaney, *The Right to Privacy and American Law*, 31 LAW & CONTEMP. PROBS. 253 (1966).

[77] *See, e.g.*, Robert James McWhirter, *Border Searches, Aliens, and the Fourth Amendment*, 17 CRIM. JUST. 25 (2003); Osmond K. Fraenkel, *Concerning Searches and Seizures*, 34 HARV. L. REV. 361.

to keep and bear arms for all kinds of reasons: they might consider guns beautiful, they might want them for reasons of nostalgia or kinship, they might want to hunt or target shoot, or they might want to express contempt for government. They might have no purpose in owning a gun other than to exercise a right to own a gun. Indeed, in one recent poll, 2 percent of Americans said they owned firearms because of the Second Amendment – about as non-instrumental a reason as can be imagined.[78]

The strong autonomy view of the right to keep and bear arms says that the choice itself deserves respect. Any instrumental reason to own a weapon – for hunting or even for protection, for example – is unnecessary. Any impact on safety, either personal or public, good or ill, is irrelevant. All that matters is the fact that person wants the gun.

Autonomy reasoning often echoes Second Amendment arguments rooted in equality.[79] The equality mantra is summed up in the chestnut about Samuel Colt, who made the revolver broadly available: "God created man – Colonel Colt made them equal."[80] Each person has inherent dignity to make choices, to be self-directed, and not to be thwarted in those choices by other people. A person has a right to keep and bear arms because they are tools best designed to make that person equal to others. The right to keep and bear arms for self-defense prevents the government from keeping the most physically vulnerable from living as autonomous a life as the strongest.[81] Even beyond this reason, the ability to keep and bear firearms may serve as a token of equality for each individual. Denying weapons to minorities, women, immigrants, or the disabled is wrong not only because of its impact on their actual or perceived safety, but because it communicates their inferiority as persons.[82]

Embracing autonomy as the purpose of the Second Amendment has concrete implications for doctrine. If the Second Amendment elevates autonomy over all other considerations, then the adequacy of alternative weapons is all but irrelevant. It would be no answer to tell a person that he could carry pepper spray or some nonlethal alternative to a firearm, because his choice as to what is "adequate" trumps all other considerations.[83]

Or consider the ongoing battles about the constitutionality of laws that require a "good cause" in order to obtain a permit for public carrying. The laws' defenders argue that they are a legitimate means of ensuring that only people with sufficient reason are allowed to take their guns out in public.[84] Critics answer that the Second Amendment is its own permit,[85] which explains the movement for what is sometimes

[78] *Why Own a Gun? Protection Is Now Top Reason*, *supra* note 71.

[79] Green, *supra* note 21, at 152.

[80] GARY KLECK, POINT BLANK: GUNS AND VIOLENCE IN AMERICA 156 (Aldine Translation 2009) (1991).

[81] Hughes & Hunt, *supra* note 73, at 15.

[82] *See* Pratheepan Gulasekaram, *Aliens with Guns: Equal Protection, Federal Power, and the Second Amendment*, 92 IOWA L. REV. 891 (2007); WILLIAMS, *supra* note 70, at 174-76..

[83] Blocher & Miller, *supra* note 51, at 291–92.

[84] *See* Blocher, *supra* note 35.

[85] *Id.* at 218–19.

called "constitutional carry"[86] – the notion that the only license one needs to own or carry a firearm "was signed in 1791." The underlying theory here can be traced to an autonomy rationale: the Second Amendment covers a right to keep and bear arms for any reason, or for no reason at all.

Defenders of good cause restrictions might respond by emphasizing that such laws tend to apply only to the *public* use of weapons, preserving a zone of autonomy at home. That division, and the greater protection for autonomy in the home, is deeply ingrained in constitutional law, from the Fourth Amendment warrant requirement,[87] to the First Amendment protection of obscenity in the home,[88] to the Due Process protection for the "sanctity" of the bedroom.[89] Sometimes the freedom to make choices in private settings is referred to as the right of "privacy," but the import is the same. The notion is that there's a place – the home – within which, for the majority of cases, no reason-giving is required and no consequences are relevant.[90]

If the Second Amendment rests on the sanctity of individual choices regarding firearms, then it should support that choice in either direction. It should, in other words, support a right *not* to keep or bear arms.[91] A person could choose not to have a gun because of a belief the gun makes the person less safe – if so, it falls within the personal safety rationale discussed above. But that doesn't need to be the reason. Perhaps a person doesn't want a gun because it interferes with his sense of self. For example, an organization of pacifists, even pacifists who own a restaurant or furniture company, may not want to have a gun on their property for reasons that have nothing to do with safety and everything to do with their identity as pacifists.[92] Even if having or allowing the gun made the person or society safer, the autonomy rationale would say that the individual choice should be respected. Just as a person has a right not to be forced by government to speak, or to associate with speech with which the person disagrees, the person has a right not to arm themselves or to associate with those who want to be armed.[93]

Perhaps surprisingly, such a notion has practical significance, because some laws either require people to arm, require them to constructively possess guns carried by others, or else make it hard for them to disassociate from firearms. In 1982,

[86] *See* Adam Weinstein, *Understanding 'Constitutional Carry,' the Gun-Rights Movement Sweeping the Country*, THE TRACE (Feb. 28, 2017), www.thetrace.org/2017/02/constitutional-carry-gun-rights-movement-explained/.

[87] U.S. Const. amend. IV ("The right of the people to be secure in their persons, *houses*.") (emphasis added).

[88] Stanley v. Georgia, 394 U.S. 557 (1969).

[89] Griswold v. Connecticut, 381 U.S. 479, 485–86 (1965).

[90] Darrell A. H. Miller, *Guns as Smut: Defending the Home-Bound Second Amendment*, 109 COLUM. L. REV. 1278 (2009).

[91] *See* Joseph Blocher, *The Right Not to Keep or Bear Arms*, 64 STAN. L. REV. 1 (2012).

[92] *Cf.* Burwell v. Hobby Lobby, 134 S. Ct. 2751 (2014).

[93] Boy Scouts v. Dale, 530 U.S. 640 (2000) (association); Wooley v. Maynard, 430 U.S. 705 (1977) (speech). *See generally* Joseph Blocher, *Rights To and Not To*, 100 CAL. L. REV. 761 (2012).

in response to gun regulations in Morton Grove, Illinois, the city of Kennesaw, Georgia – a small community about thirty minutes from Atlanta – passed a law that required nearly every household to possess a firearm and ammunition.[94] It was not the only one; a few authorities in other states have proposed or enacted similar regulations.[95]

Much of this legislation was political theater. The Kennesaw ordinance was not intended to be enforced, and no one was ever prosecuted for violating it.[96] That said, the Brady Center to Prevent Gun Violence was successful in getting another Georgia town to amend its mandatory gun possession law so as to state that "the Constitution protects the rights of Americans to choose not to possess a firearm or bring one into the home."[97]

Nevertheless, directly requiring private persons to possess a gun is only the most extreme example of regulation that may be placed along a continuum of burdens on the right not to keep or bear arms. Some states, for example, have "take your gun to work," "parking lot," or "forced entry" laws that require private employers to permit private firearms onto their property. The goal, ostensibly, is to allow employees to carry guns with them to work and leave them in their cars, but the laws are not always written so precisely.[98] Some regulations make it illegal for the employer to ask about whether their employees possess such weapons on the premises.[99] At least one state threatened criminal penalties for violation of its "guns to work" law.[100] Some legislators have sponsored legislation that would make private businesses that

[94] Anna Fifield, *Kennesaw, Where Everyone is Armed by Law*, FIN. TIMES (Sept. 25, 2010), www.ft.com/cms/s/2/5c1b6a72-c5eb-11df-b53e-00144feab49a.html #axzz16d4dQ5T3.

[95] *See* Associated Press, *Kansas Community Requires Households to Have Guns*, USA TODAY (Nov. 23, 2003), http://usatoday30.usatoday.com/news/nation/2003-11-23-kansas-guns_x.htm; Glenn Reynolds, *A Rifle in Every Pot*, N.Y. TIMES A21 (Jan. 16, 2007), www.nytimes.com/2007/01/16/opinion/16reynolds.html; *Town in Utah Requires Owning Guns*, ABC NEWS (Nov. 5, 2000), http://abcnews.go.com/US/story?id=95092&page=1; *see also* Joanna Mareth, *Vermont's Right Not to Bear Arms*, AM. PROSPECT (Dec. 19, 2001), www.prospect.org/cs/articles?article=vermonts_right_not_to_bear_arms (describing similar bill proposed in Vermont).

[96] Larry Copeland, *Georgia Town Not Alone In Using Gun Law as 'Deterrent,'* USA TODAY, Apr. 2, 2013, at A.3; Fifield, *supra* note 94.

[97] Nick Wing, *Georgia City Loses Battle Over Mandatory Gun Ownership Law, Affirms Right Not To Bear Arms*, HUFF. POST. (Aug. 23, 2013), www.huffingtonpost.com/2013/08/23/nelson-georgia-guns_n_3805292.html; *see also* Settlement Agreement and Release, available at www.bradycampaign.org/sites/default/files/Georgia-Settlement.pdf.

[98] *See* Alaska Stat. § 18.65.800 (2011); Ariz. Rev. Stat. Ann. § 12-781 (2011); Fla. Stat. Ann. § 790.251 (West 2011), invalidated in part by Fla. Retail Fed'n, Inc. v. Attorney Gen., 576 F. Supp. 2d 1301, 1303 (N.D. Fla. 2008); Ga. Code Ann. § 16-11-135 (2011); Ind. Code Ann. § 34-28-7-2 (West 2011); Kan. Stat. Ann. § 75-7c11 (2009) (repealed 2010); Ky. Rev. Stat. Ann. § 237.106 (West 2011); La. Rev. Stat. Ann. § 32:292.1 (2011); Minn. Stat. Ann. § 624.714 (West 2011); Miss. Code Ann. § 45-9-55 (2011); Okla. Stat. tit. 21, § 1289.7a (2011).

[99] Fla. Stat. § 790.251(4)(b) (2012).

[100] Ramsey Winch Inc. v. Henry, 555 F.3d 1199, 1202 (10th Cir. 2009) (rejecting challenges on takings, preemption, due process, and vagueness grounds).

bar guns from their property strictly liable for any gun violence that occurs there, essentially using tort liability to effect a forced entry law.[101]

These laws illustrate government interference with people's autonomous choices about gun possession and ownership. They also show how theories of the Amendment can frame not only gun regulation but also gun *protection*. As Chapter 7 explores in more detail, such pro-gun regulation (or "anti-gun control") is an increasingly prominent feature of the legal landscape, and may implicate the Second Amendment in novel and unexpected ways, as with the right not to keep or bear arms.

The autonomy-protecting purpose of the Second Amendment, like the safety purpose, is subject to a number of complications, especially when one thinks of it as a method of shaping future doctrine. The first and most obvious complication – a difficulty it shares with autonomy-based theories of free speech – is its overbreadth. It is plain the Second Amendment does not cover all claims rooted in individual autonomy. Numerous courts have upheld good cause restrictions, for example, meaning that people *can* be required to give reasons for their ownership and use of guns.[102] Likewise, it is unimaginable that a court would recognize a Second Amendment claim to some highly destructive weapon simply because a person really and truly wanted it – an explosive vest, for example.[103]

It is therefore likely that Second Amendment autonomy values may only be pursued within some set of constraints – individual choice within a limited set of arms, in a limited number of places.[104] The strength of those constraints may be keyed to other factors that do not sound in autonomy, such as the risk to others or interaction with other institutions or constitutional values. Subscribing to an autonomy view of the Second Amendment does not necessarily mean all forms of gun regulation are unconstitutional, any more than an autonomy view of the First Amendment means that speakers can determine for themselves what constitutes free speech. The real challenge going forward will be how to delineate the scope of those constraints, their sources, and the reasons that may be offered for them.

ANTI-TYRANNY

One rather jarring slogan encapsulates a third possible value of the Second Amendment: the right to keep and bear arms "isn't about hunting ducks; it's about hunting politicians."[105] The notion is that government, not burglars or thieves, is the

[101] Lauren McGauhy, *Texas Businesses that Ban Guns Should be Liable if Unarmed Patrons Are Hurt, Dallas Senator Says*, DALL. MORNING NEWS (Aug. 8, 2016), www.dallasnews.com/news/texas-politics/2016/08/08/texas-businesses-ban-guns-liable-unarmed-patrons-hurt-senator-says.

[102] *See* Blocher, *Good Cause Requirements*, *supra* note 35.

[103] Consider "The Professor" in JOSEPH CONRAD, THE SECRET AGENT (1907).

[104] *See* Frederick Schauer, *Too Hard: Unconstitutional Conditions and the Chimera of Constitutional Consistency*, 72 DENV. U. L. REV. 989, 999 (1995) (discussing constitutional "side-constraints").

[105] David C. Williams, *The Militia Movement and Second Amendment Revolution: Conjuring with the People*, 81 CORNELL L. REV. 879, 894 (1996) (quoting Linda Thompson, *Six O'Clock Newscast*,

primary antagonist one must prepare to confront with arms. As Judge Alex Kozinski once remarked in a dissenting opinion: "The Second Amendment is a doomsday provision, one designed for those exceptionally rare circumstances where all other rights have failed .... However improbable these contingencies may seem today, facing them unprepared is a mistake a free people get to make only once."[106] The implication is that the Second Amendment protects not personal or public safety, nor even individual autonomy, but democracy itself.

This view has intense popular currency in some circles,[107] and has some historical foundation. Most of the Founding era debates about the right to keep and bear arms didn't talk of burglars, but of the evils of a standing army and the need to ensure that the militia could reliably check a potentially despotic government.[108] *Heller*'s more heady passages rhapsodize about the idea of an armed citizenry standing as a bulwark against government: "[W]hen the able-bodied men of a nation are trained in arms and organized, they are better able to resist tyranny."[109] Even when confronted with the uncomfortable implications of this view – that people should have access to military-grade weapons ("M-16s and the like") – the majority rejected the practical conclusion, but not the theory.[110]

Reconstruction expanded the potential targets of the anti-tyranny purpose to include state and local governments. During the debates over the Civil Rights Act of 1866 and the Fourteenth Amendment, the agents of repression were not the federal government or the US military, but the unreconstructed Southern state militias or their paramilitary allies.[111] In three episodes in 1866 alone, local police forces joined with former Confederates and white supremacists to disarm and butcher African American freedmen and pro-Union political sympathizers.[112] Stephen Halbrook, who has written extensively on Reconstruction-era attitudes, argues that Republican sentiment and the Fourteenth Amendment "championed the right of freedmen to keep arms in opposition to searches and seizures of arms by state militias."[113]

INDIANAPOLIS EYEWITNESS NEWS (May 1, 1995)); *see also* Sen. Rand Paul (@RandPaul), Twitter (June 23, 2016, 9:48 AM), https://twitter.com/RandPaul/status/746022114042478592 (".@Judgenap: Why do we have a Second Amendment? It's not to shoot deer. It's to shoot at the government when it becomes tyrannical!").

[106] Silveira v. Lockyer, 328 F.3d 567, 570 (9th Cir. 2003) (Kozinski, J., dissenting from denial of hearing en banc).

[107] *See* Joseph Blocher, *Gun Rights Talk*, 94 B.U. L. REV. 813, 826–27 (2014).

[108] *See* Chapter 1.

[109] *Heller*, 554 U.S. at 598.

[110] *Id.* at 627–28.

[111] *See* Akhil Reed Amar, *The Bill of Rights and the Fourteenth Amendment*, 101 YALE L.J. 1193, 1217 (1992).

[112] Darrell A. H. Miller, *Retail Rebellion and the Second Amendment*, 86 IND. L.J. 939, 959 (2011).

[113] STEPHEN P. HALBROOK, FREEDMEN, THE FOURTEENTH AMENDMENT, AND THE RIGHT TO BEAR ARMS, 1866–1876, 69 (1998).

That the Second Amendment's purpose was primarily to resist despotic government took on an undeniable racial cast in the mid-to late twentieth century. Historian Akinyele Omowale Umoja recounts how African Americans living in Mississippi turned to armed self-defense to counter racial violence and oppression during the Civil Rights Movement. "[A]rmed resistance," he writes, "was critical to the efficacy of the southern freedom struggle and the dismantling of segregation and Black disenfranchisement."[114] Individual acts of defense against racial oppression in the 1950s and early 1960s became organized in groups like the Deacons for Defense in the mid-1960s.[115] Even as late as the 1970s, groups like the United League used arms to fight the racial violence of the Ku Klux Klan.[116]

Malcolm X famously called on African Americans to defend themselves "by any means necessary." In doing so, he claimed authority from the Constitution itself: "Article number two of the constitutional amendments provides you and me the right to own a rifle or a shotgun."[117] The Black Panthers, distrustful of all levels of American government – from the local police to the FBI – expressly called for members to assert Second Amendment rights and arm themselves. "We believe we can end police brutality in our black community by organizing black self-defense groups," they wrote in their 1966 Party Platform: "[A]ll black people should arm themselves for self-defense."[118]

Today, there is no shortage of organizations that advocate and organize around bearing arms to counter what they understand to be tyrannical government. The New Black Panther Party (NBPP), a group identified as racist and anti-Semitic by the Southern Poverty Law Center,[119] believes in arming communities against institutions like the police.[120] An anti-federal government militia group associated with Cliven Bundy and his family took over the Malheur National Wildlife Refuge in Harney County, Oregon with force of arms in 2016.[121]

Sometimes this kind of anti-tyranny ideology takes a dark and deadly turn. Timothy McVeigh murdered more than a hundred people in his attack on the Oklahoma City Murrah Federal Building in April 1995. (The NRA's unwillingness to distance itself from McVeigh, and its criticism of federal officials as "jack-booted

[114] Akinyele Omowale Umoja, We Will Shoot Back: Armed Resistance in the Mississippi Freedom Movement 2 (2013).

[115] *Id.* at 130–47 (describing the Deacons of Defense); *id.* at 186–91 (describing the Provisional Government of the Republic of New Africa).

[116] *Id.* at 211–53.

[117] Adam Winkler, Gunfight: The Battle over the Right to Bear Arms in America 233 (2013) (internal quotations omitted).

[118] *What We Want, What We Believe*, October 1966 Black Panther Party Platform and Program, reprinted in The Black Panthers Speak (Philip S. Foner, ed., 1995); *see also* Winkler, *supra* note 117, at 234.

[119] *New Black Panther Party*, Southern Poverty Law Center, available at www.splcenter.org/fighting-hate/extremist-files/group/new-black-panther-party.

[120] *Id.*; *see also New Black Panther Party*, available at www.cbpm.org/nbpp.html.

[121] *Oregon Standoff Timeline: 41 Days of the Malheur Refuge Occupation and the Aftermath*, The Oregonian (Feb. 15, 2017), www.oregonlive.com/portland/index.ssf/2017/02/oregon_standoff_timeline_41_da.html.

thugs," spurred President George H. W. Bush to renounce his NRA life membership.[122]) On July 7, 2016, Micah Johnson, a gunman claiming to sympathize with the Black Lives Matter movement, ambushed and killed police offers after a march in Dallas, Texas.[123] A year later, James Hodgkinson, angry at the policies of Republicans and President Trump, opened fire at a GOP baseball practice, severely injuring the majority whip of the House.[124] The list goes on.

The rhetoric surrounding the right to keep and bear arms is persistently sprinkled with the "paranoid style" of American politics.[125] But distrust of government is not uniform in intensity, consequence, or justification. Short of actual attacks on the agents of government – which are widely condemned when they occur – the anti-tyranny value of the Second Amendment has a number of gradations, from the strongest to the most limited. At one end of the spectrum there are those like United States Senate candidate Sharron Angle, who notoriously warned that "people are really looking toward those Second Amendment remedies" if Congress didn't change course.[126] Fox News Commentator Andrew Napolitano offered something similar, suggesting that the American colonists won the Revolutionary War because "they possessed weapons equivalent in power and precision to those of the British government."[127] Consequently, he argued, the Second Amendment "protects the right to shoot tyrants, and it protects the right to shoot at them effectively, with the same instruments they would use upon us."[128]

This is an internally consistent position, albeit a startling one. If it was translated into Second Amendment doctrine it would mean that any kind of weapon that is available to the US military must be available to each individual citizen of the United States. Certainly "M-16s and the like," which *Heller* says are presumptively *not* covered by the Amendment, would be included.[129] But "weapons equivalent in power and precision" would not necessarily be limited to fully automatic rifles. Despotic regimes worldwide employ weapons like guided missiles, landmines, and nerve gas against civilian populations.[130] The implication is that individuals must have access to these weapons as well.

[122] *Letter of Resignation Sent by Bush to Rifle Association*, N.Y. TIMES, May 11, 1995, B10.

[123] Joshua Holland, *Dallas Shooter Micah Johnson Showed What the NRA's 'Insurgency Theory' of Gun Rights Really Looks Like*, THE NATION (July 11, 2016), www.thenation.com/article/dallas-shooter-micah-johnson-showed-what-the-nras-insurgency-theory-of-gun-rights-really-looks-like/.

[124] Jessica Lussenhop, *James T Hodgkinson: What We Know About Virginia Suspect*, BBC NEWS (June 15, 2017), www.bbc.com/news/world-us-canada-40280034.

[125] Richard Hofstadter, *The Paranoid Style in American Politics*, HARPERS MAG., Nov. 1964, at 77.

[126] Tierney Sneed, *Trump Just the Latest on Hard Right To Call For '2nd Amendment Remedies'*, TALKING POINTS MEMO (Aug. 11, 2016), http://talkingpointsmemo.com/dc/trump-second-amendment-people-context (providing similar examples).

[127] Andrew Napolitano, *The Right to Shoot Tyrants, Not Deer*, WASH. TIMES, Jan. 10, 2013, at B1.

[128] *Id.*

[129] *Heller*, 554 U.S. at 627.

[130] *Dozens of Civilians Killed in Alleged "Poison Gas" Attack*, CBS NEWS (Apr. 4, 2017), www.cbsnews.com/news/syria-alleged-poison-gas-chemical-attack-khan-sheikhoun-idlib-civilians/;

While many commentators agree that the Second Amendment exists in part to prevent despotism, most are unwilling to concede that individuals have a right to possess such weapons of mass destruction.[131] A somewhat more modest democracy-protective argument for the Second Amendment value benchmarks the right to some less powerful government institution, such as the police. Under this view, the right to keep and bear arms is limited to those kinds of arms that ordinary law enforcement officials possess.[132] The emphasis is on *ordinary* law enforcement, recognizing that elite units of law enforcement such as SWAT teams may have weapons that are functionally identical to those possessed by the military.[133]

Further along the spectrum is the position that the prevention of tyranny is the central value of the Second Amendment, but that it has no real implications for the types of weapons the Amendment covers, which remain properly limited to those "in common use" and not "dangerous and unusual." This view of the anti-tyranny value of the Second Amendment might seem, to the most impassioned, a shadow of the Founding era conception of the right. But the idea could be that private arms need only offer some minimal deterrent to a potentially tyrannical government, even if they are unlikely to be effective to defeat the standing army. As Justice Scalia put it in *Heller*, "It may be true that no amount of small arms could be useful against modern-day bombers and tanks. But the fact that modern developments have limited the degree of fit between the [militia] and the [right to keep and bear arms] cannot change our interpretation of the right."[134]

While the anti-tyranny, democracy-protecting value of the Second Amendment resonates in history, scholarship, portions of *Heller* itself, and certainly with certain segments of the population, translating it into workable legal doctrine is challenging. Indeed, it is almost impossible to fully square the anti-tyranny view with *Heller*, with most of criminal law, and with fundamental political theories of the state.

For example, *Heller* indicates that guns can be prohibited in "sensitive places," including "government buildings."[135] But these "sensitive places" include the very locations where a show of force would be most useful to check a potentially tyrannical government. Similarly, in many states it is a crime to resist an arrest, even an

Christopher Woody, *A Dangerous Weapon from Wars that are Long Over is Still Wreaking Havoc Around the World*, BUS. INSIDER (Aug. 18, 2016), www.businessinsider.com/land-mines-still-dangerous-around-the-world-and-used-by-isis-2016-8.

[131] *See, e.g.*, Nelson Lund, *The Second Amendment and the Inalienable Right to Self-Defense*, THE HERITAGE FOUNDATION (Apr. 17, 2014); Glenn Reynolds, *Second Amendment Limitations*, 14 GEO. J.L. & PUB. POL'Y 233, 243 (2016); *see generally* Michael P. O'Shea, *Modeling the Second Amendment Right to Carry Arms (I): Judicial Tradition and the Scope of "Bearing Arms" for Self-Defense*, 61 AM. U. L. REV. 585 (2012).

[132] *See generally* O'Shea, *supra* note 131.

[133] Dan Bauman, *Campus Police Acquire Military Weapons*, N.Y. TIMES (Sept. 21, 2014), www.nytimes.com/2014/09/22/world/americas/campus-police-acquire-military-weapons.html.

[134] *Heller*, 554 U.S. at 627–28.

[135] *Id.* at 626.

unlawful one, by displaying a weapon, even though such a display would doubtlessly deter lawless government agents.[136] Many states punish assaults against officers of the law more severely than other crimes.[137] In reaction to police shootings, there has even been a movement to treat crimes against these government agents as hate crimes – reflecting a widespread feeling that armed opposition to government is to be vilified, not celebrated.[138] It is unlikely all these principles of social stability and governmental authority have been swept away by the Second Amendment – after all, the same people who wrote the Second Amendment also specified treason as a capital offense.[139] Perhaps recognizing these difficulties, even *Heller* seems to minimize the anti-tyranny and democracy-preserving rationales in favor of individual self-defense against ordinary criminals.[140]

The keeping and bearing of lethal arms to deter government officials may be connected to the Second Amendment, but it is likely that the value is primarily moral or political, rather than a judicially administrable constitutional entitlement. It could be that the democracy preserving aspect of the Second Amendment is not a right to "wage war,"[141] or a right to weapons effective to wage war, but simply to have some kind of weapon to prove that the holder will not submit without a fight – no matter how futile that fight may be. The right is an incidental benefit of creating some limited caution in government agents, even if the total scope of the anti-tyranny value of the right cannot be directly administered as constitutional law.

CHOOSING A THEORY

How is one supposed to choose among these theories of the Second Amendment? The theories themselves cannot provide an answer. Selecting a theory of the Second Amendment (or the First, Fourteenth, or any other Amendment) depends on interpretive commitments that are in some sense prior to those that we address here. Originalists who believe that the purpose of constitutional provisions is fixed at the

[136] Miller, *supra* note 112, at 944.

[137] *See, e.g.*, N.C. Gen. Stat. Ann § 15A-1340.16(d)(6) (2016) (listing as an aggravating factor "the offense was committed against or proximately caused serious injury to a present or former law enforcement officer").

[138] Rebecca Beitsch, *Is Killing a Police Officer a Hate Crime?*, PBS NEWSHOUR: THE RUNDOWN (Aug. 3, 2016), www.pbs.org/newshour/rundown/killing-police-officer-hate-crime/.

[139] U.S. CONST. art. III, § 3; *see also* JOSEPH STORY, CHARGE OF MR. JUSTICE STORY ON THE LAW OF TREASON, DELIVERED TO THE GRAND JURY OF THE CIRCUIT COURT OF THE UNITED STATES 7 (1842) (describing treason as bearing arms "for the express purpose of overawing or intimidating the public," even where "no actual blow has been struck, or engagement has taken place"); *see also* Crimes Act of 1790, 1 Stat. 112 (defining treason as a capital offense).

[140] *See* David C. Williams, *Death to Tyrants:* District of Columbia v. Heller *and the Uses of Guns*, 69 OHIO ST. L.J. 641 (2009); *cf. Heller*, 554 U.S. at 627 (suggesting the weapons most effective against a national government, "M-16 rifles and the like," can be banned, as opposed to weapons most effective against a common criminal).

[141] *Heller*, 554 U.S. at 586.

time they are ratified may choose the theory that best reflects those original understandings. Those who believe that our constitutional commitments can be found in contemporary practices or doctrine will look elsewhere. And all of these theories operate within a much broader philosophical framework far outside the scope of this book.

Perhaps there is no one best theory of the Second Amendment. In First Amendment circles, there seems to be increasing agreement that there is simply no way to understand free speech doctrine as reflecting a single animating value.[142] As Fred Schauer put it in *The Second-Best First Amendment*, "the very idea of free speech is a crude implement, to the core, protecting acts that its background justifications would not protect, and failing to protect acts that its background justifications would protect."[143] Those background justifications are themselves diverse, as Robert Post notes: "There is in fact no general free speech principle."[144]

It seems possible, if not inevitable, that the modern Second Amendment will always be animated by a similar plurality of values. The three theories we have elaborated here – safety, autonomy, and anti-tyranny – are likely to be the leading contenders. To the degree that a priority can be established, safety likely has pride of place, because it seems to best capture the popular understanding of the Amendment as a provision dedicated to personal self-defense against private violence and it best unifies the various strands of the *Heller* opinions. But just as a century of debate has not settled the central purpose of free speech, we should not expect a single theory of the Second Amendment to be established any time soon.

What is clear that *Heller* itself does not provide a definitive answer. Because our goal in this book is to provide an account of Second Amendment law and theory that makes the most of the existing materials, we have tried to stay within *Heller*'s framework. But the Court's decision is hard to reconcile with any particular theory of the Second Amendment. If it is about personal safety (as opposed to safety overall), why should felons and the mentally ill be carved out? If it is about the preservation of democracy, why should "sensitive places like government buildings" be carved out? *Heller* and *McDonald* put self-defense at the "core" of the right, but have left the elaboration of that concept to others. We've started that conversation here, but we have no illusions that ours will be the last word.

Choosing a theory of the Second Amendment will not answer all the doctrinal questions raised in Chapters 4 and 5. In particular, certainty about a theory does not necessarily lead to particular conclusions about the constitutionality of regulations. For example, one can believe strongly that the Second Amendment is rooted in a theory of safety, and yet believe that the government has leeway to determine what

[142] This discussion is adapted from Joseph Blocher, *Second Things First: What Free Speech Can and Can't Say About Guns*, 91 TEX. L. REV. 37 (2012).

[143] Frederick Schauer, *The Second-Best First Amendment*, 31 WM. & MARY L. REV. 1, 13 (1989).

[144] Robert Post, *Recuperating First Amendment Doctrine*, 47 STAN. L. REV. 1249, 1271 (1995).

balance of rights and regulation best accomplish that goal. Alternatively, one may strongly believe that the Second Amendment is about autonomy, but deny any right not to keep and bear arms.

To illustrate, let us return to the hypothetical at the beginning of this chapter: The bold gun rights advocate raising a Second Amendment challenge to the Secret Service regulations preventing guns at President Trump's speech to the NRA. How do the modalities look when viewed through the lens of the three theories outlined here?

From the perspective of the *safety* rationale, our constitutional challenger would argue from the *text* that he is engaged in precisely the activity that *Heller* defined as "bearing" – carrying a weapon "in case of confrontation." Doing so is protected by clear Supreme Court *precedent*, since it effectuates the interest of personal self-defense that the Court located at the "core" of the right to keep and bear arms. And, as a matter of *social practice*, the exercise of that creates positive benefits, as demonstrated by the belief that crime rates fall in the vicinity of the NRA convention.[145]

Seeking to defend the regulation through the lens of safety, the government would point to a long *history* of public safety regulations in crowded public places, beginning perhaps with the "fairs and markets" covered by the Statute of Northampton. That history, the government would say, is reflected in *precedent* by *Heller*'s conclusion that weapons can be banned in "sensitive places" like "government buildings," which in this context should mean any building where the President is speaking. Disputing the challengers' account of *social practice*, the government would argue that carrying weapons into crowded rallies is not widespread, nor should it be. The government might add that as a matter of *structure* the constitutionally sanctioned mechanism for political expression is "peaceable" assembly under the First Amendment, not armed assembly under the Second.[146]

The *autonomy rationale* would, if anything, make the dispute even more stark. Our challenger might *analogize* to free speech cases, arguing that the possession of a gun at the rally is simply a way of actualizing and expressing his identity. After all, millions of Americans think about gun ownership as an important part of who they are, a longstanding *social practice* and *tradition* that supports each individual's right to choose for him or herself what weapon to carry and where.

The government might respond to the *analogy* by arguing that even free speech cases do not fully embrace an autonomy rationale – one cannot say whatever one desires, as a supposed means of self-actualization – and that, in those areas where it arguably does, the externalities of conduct are much lower than they are with gun

[145] *See 2016 NRA Annual Meeting: The Crime Report*, GUN FREE ZONE (May 26, 2012), http://gunfreezone.net/index.php/2016/05/26/2016-nra-annual-meeting-the-crime-report/.

[146] Gregory Magarian, *Speaking Truth to Firepower: How the First Amendment Destabilizes the Second*, 91 TEX. L. REV. 49 (2012).

ownership. And the *precedent* of *Heller* clearly does not include a broad autonomy-based right to keep and bear arms.

Arguments based on the *anti-tyranny* rationale would approach the question from an entirely different angle. On this theory, our challenger would assert that his actions fall squarely within the purpose of the Second Amendment, given his effort to engage with and influence a political actor. Arguing from *history* and *precedent,* he would say that modern day Americans, like the Englishmen of old, are "jealous of their arms" because of government attempts to take them, which is precisely why the NRA annual meeting must be held. He should be able to attend all parts of that meeting armed, and especially those parts of the meeting where agents of the government are present.

The government would respond with a strong argument from *precedent,* pointing again to *Heller*'s approval of gun bans in "sensitive places" like "government buildings" – an exception that makes no sense on the challenger's reading of the democracy rationale for the right to keep and bear arms. *Analogizing* to free speech, the government might argue that just as democracy permits the establishment of "free speech zones" at political conventions, so, too, can weapons be limited to particular places and times.

The matter can be resolved in a number of different ways, and our goal is not to advocate one or another. Primarily, our task is to explore how each of these Second Amendment values employs and direct the kinds of legal arguments identified in Chapter 5, and how the values differ from each other. The present and future of the Second Amendment law will continue to be shaped by the slow, case-by-case interaction between accepted forms of legal argument and the constitutional theories they respond to and reveal.

7

Second Amendment Law and the Gun Debate

On Saturday, June 11, 2016, more than 300 people were packed into Pulse, a gay nightclub in Orlando, for "Latin Night." At 2:00 the next morning, as the bartenders were announcing last call, Omar Mateen entered the club and began shooting.[1] Terrified patrons sought refuge anywhere they could: some hid in bathroom stalls; others sheltered under bodies on the dance floor.[2] The security officer on site – a uniformed off-duty police officer – was outgunned and called for help. Police responded swiftly, but reported their shields were useless against the gunfire.[3] In a call from his cell phone, Mateen claimed affiliation with the Islamic State, then searched online for news reports of the mayhem he was causing.[4] After a three-hour stand-off, police stormed the building and shot Mateen – the final casualty of what was, at that point, the deadliest mass shooting in modern US history.[5] Forty-nine people were killed and fifty-three injured by one person in one night.[6] (Just over a year later, in Las Vegas, another single gunman in another mass shooting would kill and injure even more.[7])

[1] Michael Scherer, *Why Did They Die?*, TIME MAG. (June 27, 2016), at 32; *see also* Thomas Gibbons-Neff, *Rifle Used in Shooting Looks Like an AR-15 on the Outside But Differs Internally*, WASH. POST, June 16, 2016, at A12. Ariel Zambelich, *3 Hours in Orlando: Piecing Together An Attack And Its Aftermath*, NPR (June 26, 2016, 5:09 PM), www.npr.org/2016/06/16/482322488/orlando-shooting-what-happened-update; Gal Tziperman Lotan, Charles Minshew, Mike Lafferty and Andrew Gibson, *Orlando Nightclub Shooting Timeline: 4 Hours of Terror Unfold*, ORLANDOSENTINEL.COM (May 31, 2017), www.orlandosentinel.com/news/pulse-orlando-nightclub-shooting/os-orlando-pulse-nightclub-shooting-timeline-htmlstory.html.

[2] Zambelich, *supra* note 1; Sam Greenfield, *Clubbers Ran for Lives or Played Dead*, DAILY MAIL (UK), June 14, 2016, at 8.

[3] Tziperman Lotan, *supra* note 1.

[4] *Id.*

[5] *Id.*

[6] *Id.*

[7] Holly Yan, Madison Park and Darran Simon, *Las Vegas Shooting: Bodycam Footage Shows First Response*, CNN (Oct. 7, 2017), www.cnn.com/2017/10/03/us/las-vegas-shooting-investigation/index .html

Nine days after the Orlando shooting, a bipartisan group of senators called for banning the sale of guns to suspected terrorists on the "no-fly list."[8] Senator Lindsey Graham of South Carolina explained his support for the proposal in straightforward terms: "[I]f you're on a no-fly list – if the government has determined it's too dangerous for you to get on an airplane, I believe you shouldn't be able to buy a gun but have a process to challenge that determination in court."[9] Like the effort to expand background checks after Sandy Hook, the "no fly, no buy" proposal initially enjoyed overwhelming support from the American public. Early polls indicated that 86 percent of registered voters agreed with the proposal, including 83 percent of "voters in households where there is a gun."[10]

But, as with background checks, many opinion leaders sympathized with the goals while believing that the means would violate the Second Amendment.[11] Chris Cox, executive director of the NRA Institute for Legislative Action, argued that the regulation would provide "a dangerous sense of false security" and "destroy the right of law-abiding Americans to defend [themselves]."[12] Senator Chuck Grassley of Iowa declared, "The Second Amendment right to bear arms is a fundamental right, and any legislative action must start and finish with recognition of this fact."[13] Representative John Culberson, a Republican from Texas, described the measure as infringing "one of the most fundamental rights Americans have."[14]

Whatever might be said about the merits of the policy and its constitutional vulnerabilities – especially those involving due process[15] – the response to the no fly, no buy proposal demonstrates the power and influence of Second Amendment rhetoric

[8] David M. Herszenhorn, *Bipartisan Senate Group Suggests Gun Compromise*, N.Y. TIMES, June 22, 2016, at A12.

[9] David Sherfinski, *Lindsey Graham Praises Donald Trump on Proposed Gun Ban for No-fly List*, THE WASH. TIMES (June 16, 2016), www.washingtontimes.com/news/2016/jun/16/lindsey-graham-praises-trump-gun-ban-no-fly-list/.

[10] *See, e.g.*, Press Release, Quinnipiac Univ. Poll, *Overwhelming Support for No-Fly, No Buy Gun Law, Quinnipiac University National Poll Finds; Support for Background Checks Tops 90 Percent Again* (June 30, 2016), https://poll.qu.edu/national/release-detail?ReleaseID=2364.

[11] Senator John Cornyn of Texas, for example, said, "Every single senator wants to deny terrorists access to guns they use to harm innocent civilians, but there's a right way to do things and a wrong way." Lisa Mascaro & Jill Ornitz, *Senate Rejects New Gun Sales Restrictions*, L.A. TIMES (June 21, 2016), at A8. He offered his own amendment to the proposal which, he said, would keep guns out of the hands of terrorists, "and it upholds the Second Amendment to the Constitution of the United States." 162 CONG. REC. 98, S4.345 (daily ed., June 20, 2016).

[12] Chris W. Cox, *Gun Laws Don't Deter Terrorists: Opposing View*, USA TODAY, June 14, 2016, at A7.

[13] 162 CONG. REC. S4, 349 (daily ed., June 20, 2016).

[14] Matthew Nussbaum, *House Committee Rejects 'No Fly, No Buy' Gun Amendment*, POLITICO (June 22, 2016), www.politico.com/story/2016/06/gun-control-terror-suspects-house-spending-committee-224669.

[15] *See* Hina Shamsi & Christopher Anders, ACLU, *The Use of Error-Prone and Unfair Watchlists Is Not the Way to Regulate Guns in America* (June 20, 2016), www.aclu.org/blog/washington-markup/use-error-prone-and-unfair-watchlists-not-way-regulate-guns-america; *see also* Joseph Greenlee, *No Fly, No Buy (And No Due Process)*, THE FED. SOC. (Feb. 17, 2016), www.fed-soc.org/blog/detail/no-fly-no-buy-and-no-due-process.

in the gun debate. The Second Amendment-fueled opposition prevailed, and no fly, no buy joined Manchin-Toomey in the dustbin.[16]

The debates on Capitol Hill after the Pulse nightclub murders were just one scene in a larger legal and political drama concerning the future of the Second Amendment itself. In February 2016, Justice Scalia, the author of *District of Columbia v. Heller*, died in his sleep at a ranch in Texas. His death precipitated an unprecedented and ultimately successful year-long effort by the GOP to keep the Supreme Court seat empty, which in turn made the Court – and the Second Amendment – a key issue in the presidential campaign. In May 2016, then-candidate Donald Trump warned that the Second Amendment was in peril if Hillary Clinton were to pick the next justice.[17] Even before Scalia's death, Texas Senator Ted Cruz claimed that: "[If] Hillary Clinton gets one more Supreme Court justice ... the Supreme Court would say you and I and every individual American have no constitutional right under the Second Amendment at all and either the federal government or a state government could make it a crime to possess a firearm."[18]

Congressional paralysis and apocalyptic campaign rhetoric are but two manifestations of how the Second Amendment has distorted the gun debate. The Second Amendment is misunderstood, misrepresented, or wielded as a rhetorical weapon, when it can and should be used to set the boundaries of permissible policy. Too often the Second Amendment is used as a shibboleth, a method of distinguishing "us" versus "them." Too often it is invoked to end a policy discussion rather than to guide one.

The gun debate and the Second Amendment deserve better. Nothing in American history or constitutional law requires a choice between the Second Amendment and gun regulation, nor the other absolutes that the gun debate presents. One can conclude that a gun regulation is unwise, and still believe that *Heller* permits it. Conversely, one can believe that a regulation would save lives, but is unconstitutional. One can support the Second Amendment, and also think that *Heller* is a flawed opinion.

Most fundamentally, one's view of the Second Amendment, or of its interpretation in *Heller*, need not and should not simply be the result of personal and political preferences regarding guns. If anything, the gun debate would be improved if the causation ran more in the other direction – if, that is, politics took more cues from constitutional law. A clearer understanding of what Second Amendment law requires, and of what questions remain open, can help ameliorate some of the gun debate's worst pathologies, including its absolutism, distrust, and inability to recognize consensus and guide policy-making.

This does not mean there is no mechanism of exchange between Second Amendment law and the politics of gun rights and regulation. *Heller* itself is largely

[16] *See* Mascaro & Ornitz, *supra* note 11.

[17] *See* Nick Corasaniti & Maggie Haberman, *Trump Suggests Gun Owners Act Against Hillary Clinton*, N.Y. Times, Aug. 10, 2016, at A1.

[18] Ted Cruz, Transcript, CNN (Jan. 7, 2016), http://edition.cnn.com/TRANSCRIPTS/1601/07/cnr.03.html.

a product of Second Amendment politics,[19] and constitutional law will undoubtedly continue to draw on political and policy debates. When courts evaluate the constitutionality of good cause requirements for public carrying, they consider the breadth and depth of public carry restrictions, the contemporary empirical debates about their effectiveness, and other political factors. Likewise, the political choice to deregulate certain weapons, making them more broadly available, in turn can impact whether those guns are in common use and protected by the Second Amendment. Recognizing how Second Amendment doctrine channels these political debates into constitutional law will help clarify the stakes of the political debate and also help keep the doctrine from becoming inflexible and unresponsive.

It is certain that Second Amendment politics will continue to inform Second Amendment law and vice versa. Our constitutional culture is largely based on these kinds of interactions.[20] But politics and constitutional law each have their own rules and grammar, their own institutions and personnel, and those must be respected in order for each to retain its integrity.

This book has attempted to explain the history, doctrine, and values that inform Second Amendment law. Its goal has been to clarify what *Heller* requires, the questions it leaves open, and how those questions might be answered using the doctrinal and theoretical tools of constitutional adjudication and theory. In this final chapter, we return to the relationship between Second Amendment law and the broader gun debate. We argue that both sides of that debate have something to learn – and something to gain – from constitutional law. *Heller* is politically and legally secure, and advocates of gun regulation must recognize and accept that fact. Gun rights advocates must likewise accept that most contemporary gun regulation complies with *Heller*'s mandate, and that constitutional law is most legitimate and successful when it mediates political disputes instead of trying to supplant them. Our hope is that a clearer understanding of the substance and method of the law might make the gun debate less toxic and more productive, and Second Amendment doctrine clearer and more secure. With that hope in mind, we offer the following propositions.

THE RIGHT TO KEEP AND BEAR ARMS FOR PRIVATE PURPOSES IS FIRMLY ENTRENCHED IN AMERICAN CONSTITUTIONAL LAW

One way in which law can clear the air with respect to Second Amendment politics is by addressing fear that the right to keep and bear arms is just one judicial nomination away from destruction. Even after *Heller*, some believe that the right is

[19] *See* Reva Siegel, *Dead or Alive: Originalism as Popular Constitutionalism in* Heller, 122 HARV. L. REV. 191, 192–93 (2008) (describing how *Heller* "enforces understandings of the Second Amendment that were forged in the late twentieth century through popular constitutionalism").

[20] *See generally* Robert Post & Reva Siegel, *Democratic Constitutionalism, in* THE CONSTITUTION IN 2020 (Jack Balkin & Reva Siegel, eds., 2009).

hanging by a thread.[21] Although no amount of open and repeated support for the Second Amendment will satisfy those with political or financial incentives to claim otherwise, anxieties about the right's future are largely unfounded, and stand in the way of useful discussions about gun rights and regulation. Certainly, important questions of Second Amendment scope and protection remain, but the core holding of *Heller* is politically and legally secure, and everyone should accept that fact.

Heller *Enjoys Broad Political Support*

A central function of any enforceable constitutional right is to take some political choices off the table by placing constraints on government action. Constitutional rights are in that sense counter-majoritarian, which means that unpopular rights and rights-holders tend to be the focus of constitutional law, theory, and debate.

The Second Amendment is something of an outlier in this regard. Although a shrinking minority of Americans are gun owners,[22] the essential holding of *Heller* – that individuals have a right to keep and bear arms for private purposes – has the overwhelming support of the American public. One poll conducted just before the oral argument in *Heller* asked, "Do you believe the Second Amendment to the U.S. Constitution guarantees the rights of Americans to own guns, or do you believe it only guarantees members of state militias such as National Guard units the right to own guns?" Seventy-three percent chose the former, while just 20 percent said that the right is limited to members of the state militias.[23] A poll taken a year after *Heller* found similar results, with 77 percent supporting an individual right to gun ownership and only 21 percent supporting a limited militia-centered right.[24] Americans believe not only that the Second Amendment *does* protect private purposes like self-defense, but that it *should*. A 2008 poll conducted just after *Heller* found that 78 percent of respondents would oppose amending the US Constitution to ban individual gun ownership, compared to only 17 percent in favor.[25] Given the public support for the private purposes reading of the Second Amendment, it is unsurprising that political leaders have overwhelmingly embraced it as well. The Court decided *Heller* in the midst of the 2008 presidential

[21] *See* Dan Baum, Gun Guys: A Road Trip 256 (2013) ("The NRA's American Rifleman magazine warned, bizarrely, that after *Heller*, 'our firearm freedoms may be in greater danger.'").

[22] *See* Christopher Ingraham, *American Gun Ownership Drops to Lowest In Nearly 40 Years*, Wash. Post Wonkblog (June 29, 2016), www.washingtonpost.com/news/wonk/wp/2016/06/29/american-gun-ownership-is-now-at-a-30-year-low/.

[23] Jeffrey Jones, *Public Believes Americans Have Right to Own Guns*, Gallup (Mar. 27, 2008), www.gallup.com/poll/105721/public-believes-americans-right-own-guns.aspx.

[24] CNN/Opinion Research Corporation Poll, May 14–17, 2009, available at www.pollingreport.com/guns2.htm.

[25] Press Release, Quinnipiac University Polling Institute, *American Voters Oppose Same-Sex Marriage Quinnipiac University National Poll Finds, But They Don't Want Government to Ban It* (July 17, 2008), www.qu.edu/news-and-events/quinnipiac-university-poll/national/release-detail?ReleaseID=1194.

race, and both John McCain and Barack Obama registered their support for the decision.[26]

The stalled nomination of Judge Merrick Garland for Justice Scalia's former seat on the Supreme Court shows just how little political appetite there is for calling *Heller* into question, much less overturning it. During his time as a judge on the D.C. Circuit, Garland wrote no Second Amendment opinions, and participated in only two cases that implicated gun rights. In one, he voted for the full circuit to rehear *Parker v. District of Columbia* after a D.C. Circuit panel handed held that the Second Amendment includes an "individual" right to bear arms.[27] The full court decided not to rehear the case, however, and the Supreme Court upheld the panel's decision, which by then had been renamed *District of Columbia v. Heller*.[28] In the other, Garland joined the majority in *National Rifle Association v. Reno*. In that case, the court held that the Justice Department's practice of keeping background-check data for six months did not violate a 1968 federal law forbidding the creation of a national gun registry, nor did it "produce constitutional violations."[29]

The NRA and its allies characterized these opinions as demonstrating Garland's "strong hostility to gun owner rights" and providing positive proof that he would vote to overturn *Heller*.[30] The NRA declared that if Garland were to be confirmed to the Supreme Court, it would "mean the end of the fundamental, individual right of law-abiding Americans to own firearms for self-defense in their homes."[31] Garland's supporters countered that the NRA's position was "based on an extraordinary misrepresentation" of his record.[32] They argued that two cases were a flimsy basis for characterizing Garland's entire record on guns, particularly since the vote to rehear *Parker* wasn't even a vote on the merits.[33] Some conservative legal observers like Miguel Estrada (whom George W. Bush once nominated to the D.C. Circuit, the Court on which Garland sits[34]) agreed that Garland's record was being distorted.[35]

[26] *See* Dina-Temple Raston, *Supreme Court: Individuals Have Right to Bear Arms*, NPR (June 26, 2008), www.npr.org/templates/story/story.php?storyId=91911807.

[27] *See* Olivia Li, *Gun Advocates Already Slamming Merrick Garland Over Two Pivotal Cases*, THE TRACE (Mar. 16, 2016), www.thetrace.org/2016/03/merrick-garlands-record-on-guns-a-problem-for-conservatives/. Only one other federal appeals court had ever so held.

[28] *Id.*

[29] NRA of Am., Inc. v. Reno, 216 F.3d 122, 135 (2000).

[30] Carrie Severino, *The 'Moderates' Are Not So Moderate: Merrick Garland*, NAT'L REV. BENCH MEMOS (Mar. 11, 2016, 8:21 PM), www.nationalreview.com/blog/bench-memos/432716/moderates-are-not-so-moderate-merrick-garland.

[31] Chris W. Cox, *Gun Rights in the Balance*, WASH. POST (Mar. 19, 2016), at A19.

[32] Mike DeBonis, *Garland's Gun Record has been Distorted by NRA, Second Amendment Experts Say*, WASH. POST (Apr. 1, 2016), at A12; *see also* Nina Totenberg, *Why Merrick Garland's Judicial Record Slips Through Critics' Fingers*, NPR (Mar. 27, 2016), www.npr.org/2016/03/27/472051889/a-look-at-garlands-judicial-record-reveals-few-hot-buttons (quoting Mar. 31, 2016 Scholars Letter to the Senate Judiciary Committee).

[33] *Id.*

[34] Elsa Walsh, *Minority Retort*, THE NEW YORKER (Aug. 8, 2005), at 49.

[35] Totenberg, *supra* note 32

But partisan distortion of judicial records is nothing new. What is notable is what was *not* said. No one embraced the allegations regarding Garland and touted him as a likely vote to overturn *Heller*. Calls to overturn Supreme Court decisions were on the Democratic Party agenda, just as reversal of *Roe v. Wade* has been a GOP plank for decades. But *Heller* was notably not on the list. Contrast this with the open and prominent calls to overturn decisions like *Citizens United v. FEC*.[36] In a campaign speech in July 2016, Hillary Clinton pledged to "appoint Supreme Court justices who understand that this decision [*Citizens United*]was 'a disaster for our democracy.'"[37] At the Democratic National Convention, Bernie Sanders cheered Clinton's goal to "nominate justices to the Supreme Court who are prepared to overturn *Citizens United* and end the movement toward oligarchy in this country."[38]

Even the major gun violence prevention groups like the Brady Center, Everytown for Gun Safety, the Violence Policy Center, the Law Center Against Gun Violence, and Americans for Responsible Gun Ownership seem to have accepted *Heller*'s authority.[39] Although many of them argued against the private purposes reading at the time,[40] and criticize and fight particular interpretations of the Second Amendment today, to date none have launched an effort to overturn *Heller*. If there was truly a groundswell of support to overturn *Heller*, we would have seen in the last decade a multi-pronged campaign analogous to the one waged by gun rights groups that led to *Heller* in the first place. Instead, we have broad public acceptance (if not outright celebration) that *Heller* is the law of the land. Perhaps gun violence groups recognize that overturning the case could represent a political setback rather than a victory.[41] In any event, there are plenty of issues that divide mainstream gun

36 *See* Citizens United v. FEC, 558 U.S. 310 (2010).

37 *Clinton to Madison: Get Me Rewrite*, WASH. POST. (July 20, 2016), at A14.

38 Michael McGough, *Democrats United in (Over) Promising to Reverse Citizens United*, L.A. TIMES (July 26, 2016), www.latimes.com/opinion/opinion-la/la-ol-citizens-sanders-20160726-snap-story .html. Hillary Clinton's campaign website argued that *Shelby County* "gutted one of the most important parts of the Voting Rights Act of 1965." Hillary Clinton, Press Release, A Republican President Could Transform the Supreme Court – and Upend Our Most Fundamental Rights (March 17, 2016), archived at www.presidency.ucsb.edu/ws/index.php?pid=116783.

39 *See Gun Regulation and the Second Amendment*, Law Center to Prevent Gun Violence (Nov. 2008), available at http://smartgunlaws.org/gun-regulation-and-the-second-amendment/; Chris Good, *Interview: Brady Campaign President Paul Helmke on Why the Gun Ruling Isn't So Bad*, THE ATLANTIC (June 28, 2010), www.theatlantic.com/politics/archive/2010/06/interview-brady-campaign-president-paul-helmke-on-why-the-gun-ruling-isnt-so-bad/58849/.

40 *See* Brief for the Brady Center to Prevent Gun Violence as Amici Curiae, District of Columbia v. Heller, 2008 WL 157193 (U.S.), 4 (U.S., 2008) ("[T]he Framers did not envision the guarantee of a right to possess guns for private purposes as the means of arming the militia."); Brief for the Violence Policy Center as Amici Curiae, Parker, v. District of Columbia, Appellees., 2006 WL 5846067 (C.A.D.C.), 3 ("In short, the Second Amendment confers no individual fight [sic] to own or use firearms for purposes unrelated to militia service.").

41 Adam Winkler, *Why the Supreme Court Won't Impact Gun Rights*, THE ATLANTIC (June 7, 2016), www .theatlantic.com/politics/archive/2016/06/why-the-supreme-court-wont-restrict-gun-rights/485810/ ("Several [gun-control advocates] have told me they would not ask the Court to overturn *Heller*" because of the ensuing popular backlash.).

rights supporters and proponents of gun regulation. The future of *Heller*'s central holding is not among them.

There Is No Strong Legal Argument to Overturn Heller's *Central Holding*

In a 2011 interview, then-retired Justice John Paul Stevens said that of all his dissents, the one he would most like to turn into a majority was his dissent in *Heller*, where he concluded that the right to keep and bear arms is limited to militia service.[42] The following year, Justice Ginsburg reportedly told an audience that she hoped Stevens' dissent would be adopted by "a future, wiser Court."[43] And Justice Breyer observed in *McDonald* that "historians, scholars, and judges have continued to express the view that the Court's historical analysis was flawed" in *Heller*. He asked, "why would the Court not now reconsider *Heller* in light of these more recently published historical views?"[44]

Although there is broad political support for *Heller's* core holding that the Second Amendment covers privately owned weapons kept for private purposes, not everyone thinks the case was rightly decided. Most notably, some judges have joined with Justices Stevens, Ginsburg, and Breyer in criticizing *Heller*.[45] Hence, while *Heller*'s core holding may be politically secure – given its widespread acceptance and popularity among American citizens – one might still be concerned about the *legal* case for its continuing vitality.

We think there's no compelling legal justification to overturn *Heller* today. Even if it were possible to show with certainty that *Heller*'s private purposes holding was wrong – and we have doubts about the feasibility of such a showing – there is a significant difference between thinking that a case was poorly reasoned, or even wrongly decided, and thinking that it should be overturned.[46] Ensuring the stability and predictability of constitutional law is a responsibility the Justices take seriously, even when they disagree about what that duty requires. As Justice Brandeis once

[42] *See* Belinda Luscombe, *10 Questions for John Paul Stevens*, TIME, Oct. 31, 2011, at 92.

[43] Chris W. Cox, *Justice Ginsburg Reminds Us What Is at Stake in November*, NAT'L RIFLE ASS'N-INST. FOR LEGISLATIVE ACTION (Feb. 13, 2012), www.nraila.org/news-issues/articles/2012/justice-ginsburg-reminds-us-what-is-at-stake-in-november.aspx. Ginsburg called *Heller* a "very bad decision" and suggested the court could reconsider it. Adam Liptak, *Ginsburg Has a Few Words About Trump*, N.Y. TIMES, July 11, 2016, at A1.

[44] McDonald v. City of Chicago, 561 U.S. 742, 914, 916 (2010) (Breyer, J., dissenting).

[45] *See, e.g.*, Richard Posner, *In Defense of Looseness*, NEW REPUBLIC, Aug. 27, 2008, at 32; J. Harvie Wilkinson III, *Of Guns, Abortions, and the Unraveling Rule of Law*, 95 VA. L. REV. 253, 267–71 (2009).

[46] Larry Alexander, *Constrained by Precedent*, 63 S. CAL. L. REV. 1, 59 (1989) ("[I]f incorrectness were a sufficient condition for overruling, there would be no precedential constraint in statutory and constitutional cases."); Michael J. Gerhardt, *The Role of Precedent in Constitutional Decisionmaking and Theory*, 60 GEO. WASH. L. REV. 68, 73 (1991) (supporting the "traditional view that precedents should be overruled only when the prior decision was wrongly decided *and* there is some other important disadvantage in respecting that precedent").

said, "in most matters it is more important that the applicable rule of law be settled than that it be settled right."[47]

This is the principle of *stare decisis*, which is a notoriously slippery concept to define, let alone operationalize. But the law does provide some guidance. In *Casey v. Planned Parenthood*, the Supreme Court invoked the principle of *stare decisis* and refused to overturn *Roe v. Wade*. In doing so, the Court identified a list of relevant factors to consider: whether the central holding is unworkable, whether overturning the decision would frustrate public reliance interests, whether the law has developed away from the legal rule in a way that renders it antiquated or anachronistic, and whether the facts in the world are so different from when the case was decided that the decision is no longer suitable to decide contemporary legal disputes.[48]

If *Casey* is any guide, *Heller* is not likely to be overruled in the foreseeable future. First, nothing about *Heller's* central holding has proven "unworkable" in practice.[49] This is unsurprising, because most state constitutions have long recognized the right to keep and bear arms for private purposes. In that sense, *Heller* effectively federalized what was already the overwhelming rule in the states.[50] There are difficult challenges regarding implementation, to be sure, but those challenges are not so different in type or difficulty than those confronting the freedom of speech or other constitutional rights.

Whether overturning *Heller* would work a "special hardship" on individuals or the public is less clear, although we think this factor also tips in favor of upholding *Heller*.[51] In one sense, *Heller* is so new that no one has had time to build a reliance upon it. It is (for the time being) akin to decisions like *Furman v. Georgia* and *South Carolina v. Gathers*, both of which were overruled just a few years after being decided.[52] On the other hand, if Justice Scalia is correct that *Heller* simply codified a preexisting understanding of the right to keep and bear arms that many have relied upon, then it seems more plausible to say that a change would work a hardship.

Third, no principles of law have changed since *Heller* that would make it a "remnant of abandoned doctrine."[53] It is difficult to imagine what those changes could be, except perhaps for some radical, constitutional expansion in the federal law of self-defense that would render the Second Amendment superfluous.

47 Burnet v. Coronado Oil & Gas Co., 285 U.S. 393, 406 (1932) (Brandeis, J., dissenting).

48 Planned Parenthood of Southeastern Pennsylvania v. Casey, 505 U.S. 833, 854 (1992).

49 *Id.*

50 *Cf.* Eugene Volokh, *State Constitutional Rights to Keep and Bear Arms*, 11 TEX REV. L & POL. TEX. REV. L. & POL. 191 (2006).

51 *Casey*, 505 U.S. at 854.

52 *Furman*, 408 U.S. 238 (1972), which effectively struck down every death penalty scheme in the United States, was effectively overruled by Gregg v. Georgia, 428 U.S. 153 (1976). *Gathers*, 490 U.S. 805 (1989), which limited the use of victim impact statements during the sentencing phase of a trial, was overruled by Payne v. Tennessee, 501 U.S. 808 (1991).

53 Casey, 505 U.S. at 854.

Fourth and finally, *Casey* asks whether "facts have so changed, or come to be seen so differently, as to have robbed the old rule of significant application or justification."[54] This factor depends, in part, on what one understands the Amendment to be for. If, in some inconceivable future, the United States no longer permitted any government agent to possess arms, then *Heller* might no longer seem relevant as an anti-tyranny provision. If, as is more likely, the Amendment primarily concerns personal safety, then the necessary change in facts might include proof that gun ownership for private purposes makes people less safe always and everywhere. And while there is strong empirical evidence that gun ownership is correlated with increased risk both to gun owners and to others, that evidence does not preclude the possibility that some gun owners, in some situations, will be made safer by guns. Alternatively, if nonlethal weapons could provide safety equally well or better, then courts might be more willing to uphold restrictions on weapons specifically designed to be lethal.[55] But that would mean tweaking doctrine (giving superior protection to nonlethal weapons, for example), not overturning *Heller*'s core (which would still guarantee a right to arms for private purposes like self-defense).

In sum, none of the factors commonly used to evaluate *stare decisis* currently support overturning *Heller*, even if one assumes that it was wrongly decided on day one. Plus, one must remember that *Casey* upheld the "central holding" of *Roe* even in the face of sustained pressure by many political actors to see it overturned. There is no comparable political pressure to undo *Heller*.

This does not mean that there is nothing left to argue about. *Casey*, after all, refused to overturn *Roe*, but replaced its trimester framework with the "undue burden" test.[56] A subsequent Supreme Court could decide certain questions of coverage or protection differently than the Justices who made up the *Heller* majority. But so long as *Heller* is not expressly repudiated, that simply means the relevant questions are about what it means to faithfully implement *Heller*, not whether to overturn the Court's central holding that the Second Amendment includes the right to keep and bear arms for private purposes, including self-defense.

[54] Planned Parenthood v. Casey, 505 U.S. 833, 855 (1992); *see also* Stuart M. Benjamin, *Stepping into the Same River Twice: Rapidly Changing Facts and the Appellate Process*, 78 Tex. L. Rev. 269, 281 (1999) ("Judicial opinions are not proclamations of general principles from an ethereal body; they are situated in a particular factual context, and a transformation of that context necessarily affects the opinion that builds upon it.").

[55] *See* Joseph Blocher & Darrell A. H. Miller, *Lethality, Public Carry, and Adequate Alternatives*, 53 Harv. J. on Legis. 279, 301 (2016).

[56] *See, e.g.*, Richard M. Re, *Narrowing Precedent in the Supreme Court*, 114 Colum. L. Rev. 1861, 1895 (2016) ("Instead of reaffirming *Roe*'s actual trimester-based analysis, the controlling plurality in *Casey* adopted a new 'undue burden' inquiry that afforded governments somewhat greater ability to regulate abortions.").

THE SECOND AMENDMENT IS NOT A SECOND CLASS RIGHT, AND IS NOT BEING TREATED AS SUCH

Heller is not in peril of being overturned. Whether *Heller* is being faithfully followed is a harder question, because it rests on intertwined claims about how courts *are* treating Second Amendment claims and how they *should* treat them. Some Justices, judges, advocates, and scholars have argued that the Second Amendment is being treated like a "second class right," that some courts are undermining *Heller*, and that the judiciary – including the Supreme Court – must do more to defend the right to keep and bear arms.

A certiorari petition filed by dozens of members of Congress is representative: "[S]econd-class treatment of the Second Amendment pervades the lower courts .... The Court must act to ensure that citizens have a means of enforcing their individual right to keep and bear arms when legislative bodies infringe that right."[57] Other briefs and opinion pieces have echoed the "second class" language.[58] Some have used even more pointed terms, charging "massive resistance" to gun rights by lower courts – a phrase generally used to describe white segregationist resistance to school integration.[59]

A related criticism suggests that the lower courts are not openly defying *Heller*, but rather hollowing it out – an example of what legal scholar Barry Friedman calls "stealth overruling."[60] Heller's lawyer Alan Gura makes the argument with particular verve, calling *Heller* and *McDonald* "optional precedents" that "have in practice proven meaningless in the face of near-total resistance throughout the federal courts,

[57] Brief of Members of Congress as Amici Curiae in Support of the Petition for a Writ of Certiorari, Drake v. Jerejian, 2014 WL 636382 (U.S.) (No. 13-827), 4–5.

[58] Amicus Curiae Brief of National Rifle Association of America in Support of Petitioner, Walker v. United States of America, 2016 WL 1130019 (U.S.) (No. 15-1027), 22; Reply Brief for Petitioner, National Rifle Ass'n of America, Inc. v. McCraw, 2014 WL 411544 (U.S.) (No. 13-390), 3; Amicus Curiae Brief of the American Civil Rights Union in Support of Petitioners, Kachalsky v. Cacace, 2013 WL 522039 (U.S.) (No. 12-845), 4; *see also* Petitioners' Reply Brief, Bonidy v. United States Postal Service, 2016 WL 722179 (U.S.) (No. 15-746), 2; Petition for Writ of Certiori, Jackson v. City and County of San Francisco, 2014 WL 7169757 (U.S.) (No. 14-704), 12.

[59] This claim has been repeated in briefs, scholarship, and major editorials. Petition for Writ of Certiorari, Drake v. Jerejian, 2014 WL 117970 (U.S.) (No. 13-827), 3 (describing "lower courts' massive resistance to *Heller*"); Petition for Writ of Certiorari, Friedman v. City of Highland Park, 2015 WL 4550385 (U.S.) (No. 15-133), 24 (same); Alice Marie Beard, *Resistance by Inferior Courts to Supreme Court's Second Amendment Decisions*, 81 TENN. L. REV. 673, 673 (2014) ("In the wake of the Supreme Court's *District of Columbia v. Heller* ('Heller I') and *McDonald v. Chicago* decisions that clarify, expand, and protect Second Amendment rights, federal and state inferior courts have been engaging in massive resistance."); Editorial, *Massive Gun Resistance*, WALL ST. J., Apr. 13–14, 2013, at A14. Along the same lines, some have suggested an analogy between the position of contemporary gun owners and that of black schoolchildren in the 1950s. *See* Alan Gura, *The Second Amendment as a Normal Right*, 127 HARV. L. REV. F. 223 (2014) (comparing post-*Heller* developments in gun rights to the struggle for racial equality after Brown v. Board of Education); David B. Kopel, *Does the Second Amendment Protect Firearms Commerce?*, 127 HARV. L. REV. F. 230 (2014) (same).

[60] *See* Barry Friedman, *The Wages of Stealth Overruling*, 99 GEO. L.J. 1 (2010).

in combination with the transparent lack of interest" by the Supreme Court.[61] Legal scholar Richard Re calls the treatment of *Heller* a prime example of "narrowing Supreme Court precedent from below," and suggests that "the passage of time has seen *Heller*'s legacy shrink to the point that it may soon be regarded as mostly symbolic," although Re notes that, because "*Heller* left vast room for interpretation," the lower courts' treatment of it has been "defensible."[62]

The charges of "second class" treatment and "massive resistance" have found a sympathetic ear in Justice Clarence Thomas. Thomas has advanced the "second class" line in his opinions,[63] and his concern about gun rights prompted him to break a decade-long silence at oral argument.[64] Thomas' sense that the Second Amendment is being slighted has led him to repeatedly call for the Justices to grant certiorari in a Second Amendment case. As he said in a recent opinion: "Despite the clarity with which we described the Second Amendment's core protection for the right of self-defense, lower courts ... have failed to protect it. Because Second Amendment rights are no less protected by our Constitution than other rights enumerated in that document, I would have granted this petition."[65]

If lower courts were uniformly thumbing their noses at *Heller*, it would be a cause for concern as much as ignoring rights related to same sex marriage, and would surely increase the Court's willingness to grant cert on another Second Amendment case.[66] To be sure, there are cases that are hard to square with *Heller*'s methodology,[67] and occasional decisions that stray far from it – recall *Caetano*, described in

[61] Alan Gura, *The Court After Scalia: The Next 'Conservative' Justice May Not Save the Second Amendment*, SCOTUSBLOG (Sept. 6, 2016, 12:50 PM), www.scotusblog.com/2016/09/the-court-after-scalia-the-next-conservative-justice-may-not-save-the-second-amendment/.

[62] Richard M. Re, *Narrowing Supreme Court Precedent from Below*, 104 Geo. L.J. 921, 962 (2016).

[63] Voisine v. United States, 136 S. Ct. 2272, 2292 (Thomas, J., concurring) ("In construing the statute before us expansively so that causing a single minor reckless injury or offensive touching can lead someone to lose his right to bear arms forever, the Court continues to 'relegat[e] the Second Amendment to a second-class right.'") (quoting Friedman v. Highland Park, 136 S.Ct. 447, 450 (2015) (Thomas, J., dissenting from denial of certiorari); Friedman v. City of Highland Park, 136 S. Ct. 447, 449 (2015) (mem.) (Thomas, J., dissenting from the denial of certiorari) ("I would grant certiorari to prevent the Seventh Circuit from relegating the Second Amendment to a second-class right.").

[64] *See* Transcript of Oral Argument at 35–39, Voisine v. United States, 579 U.S. __ (2016) (No. 14-10154); Josh Blackman, *Justice Thomas: Second Amendment Is Not A 'Second-Class Right'*, NAT'L REV. (Dec. 8, 2015), www.nationalreview.com/article/428173/justice-thomas-second-amendment-not-second-class-right-josh-blackman.

[65] Jackson v. City & Cty. of San Francisco, 135 S. Ct. 2799, 2799–800 (2015) (mem.) (Thomas, J., dissenting from denial of certiorari).

[66] Kevin H. Smith, *Certiorari and the Supreme Court Agenda: An Empirical Analysis*, 54 OKLA. L. REV. 727, 743 (2001) ("Positive associations at statistically significant levels repeatedly have been found between the Court's decision whether to grant a petition for certiorari and ... noncompliance, alleged and actual, with Supreme Court precedent...."); *see* Pavan v. Smith, 137 S. Ct. 2075, 2079 (2017) (per curiam) ("Arkansas may not, consistent with *Obergefell*, deny married same-sex couples [legal recognition given to opposite-sex couples].").

[67] *See* Friedman v. City of Highland Park, 784 F.3d 406 (7th Cir. 2015).

Chapter 5, which the Justices overturned in a *per curiam* decision.[68] But given that there have been more than 1,000 post-*Heller* Second Amendment challenges, some outliers are inevitable. By and large, lower courts seem to be engaged in a good faith effort to follow a conflicting and confusing opinion in an environment where mistakes carry significant risks. They have struck down the kinds of stringent gun regulations at issue in *Heller* and *McDonald*, while upholding those that fall within, or are closely analogous to, the kinds of regulations those cases approved.

To say a right is being treated as "second class" or suffering "massive resistance" or being "hollowed out" assumes both a baseline of what the right requires and an examination of what lower courts are doing with it. As to the baseline of what *Heller* requires, it is worth reiterating that the Court's decision approves a non-exhaustive range of "presumptively lawful" regulations. And it is notable that, even with regard to those explicitly sanctioned categories of regulation, legislatures have generally not pressed the boundaries. A wide range of "dangerous and unusual" weapons are not forbidden, for example, and many states have taken steps to *de*regulate the possession of guns in bars, schools, and other potentially "sensitive" places. As a result, the regulatory landscape does not present much of a target-rich environment for Second Amendment plaintiffs.

As to the latter issue – what lower courts are doing – we see little evidence of anything like "massive resistance." To be sure, the vast majority of post-*Heller* Second Amendment claims have failed. But most were deficient from the outset – more than a quarter have been brought by felons, whom *Heller* expressly carves out from Second Amendment coverage. *Heller* not only permits but *requires* an approach to the Second Amendment wherein the right to keep and bear arms has boundaries (entirely excluding certain people, activities, and arms) and is subject to regulation even within those boundaries. Clarifying those boundaries, and accounting for whether particular regulations can survive scrutiny, is precisely the task of post-*Heller* Second Amendment doctrine.

Far from blindly upholding gun laws, lower courts have granted relief when gun regulations are inconsistent with *Heller* and evolving Second Amendment doctrine. In dozens of cases, involving a wide range of regulations – from prohibitions on public carrying, to bans on possession by the mentally ill and felons, to restrictions on high capacity magazines, and others – courts have struck down gun regulations as violating Second Amendment rights. In an article with legal scholar Eric Ruben, one of us identifies and empirically studies these cases.[69]

By way of illustration, take the case of *Ezell v. City of Chicago*. In October 2010, Rhonda Ezell and a group of co-plaintiffs challenged a Chicago ordinance that required a firearms permit conditioned on completing one hour of training at a

[68] *See* Caetano v. Massachusetts, 136 S. Ct. 1027 (2016) (per curiam).

[69] For a full list and explanation, see Eric Ruben & Joseph Blocher, *From Theory to Doctrine: An Empirical Analysis of the Right to Keep and Bear Arms After* Heller, 67 Duke L.J. 1433 (2018).

firing range.[70] That same ordinance also prohibited firing ranges within Chicago.[71] In July 2011, the Seventh Circuit ruled in *Ezell* that the ordinance ran afoul of the Second Amendment and enjoined it.[72] In response, Chicago enacted a series of complex regulations for firing ranges.[73] In January 2017, in the latest chapter of a long legal battle that still continues as of this writing, the Seventh Circuit ruled that Chicago's second attempt also violated the Second Amendment.[74]

Ezell is not unique. State and federal courts, both at trial and on appeal, have held that certain gun regulations violate the Second Amendment either facially or as applied to particular parties. In *People v. Deroche*, a Michigan court ruled that the Second Amendment precluded a prosecution for possession of a firearm by an intoxicated person where the defendant was drunk in a home and the gun was only constructively, rather than actually possessed.[75] In *Palmer v. District of Columbia* (a case set in *Heller*'s old battleground) the court held that D.C.'s ban on public carry of ready-to-use handguns was unconstitutional.[76] In *Wesson v. Town of Salisbury*, a federal court in Massachusetts ruled that, as applied in the defendant's particular case, a state law denying firearm permits to those with old misdemeanor marijuana possession convictions violated the Second Amendment.[77]

One can object that *Ezell* and the like are exceptions that prove the rule, or that the doctrinal rules themselves – and not simply the success rate in Second Amendment cases – are evidence of an under-enforcement problem. This is a hard argument to make or to evaluate, however, and it certainly involves more than a simple nose count of successful versus unsuccessful Second Amendment challenges. Evaluation of the "correct" level of enforcement must necessarily take into consideration other values, including fidelity to the text of the Constitution, compliance with precedent, and the impact on other constitutional and public institutions.

It is far beyond the scope of this book to articulate a meta-doctrine of constitutional law – some legal formula with which one can figure out whether a right is being properly enforced, especially when that enforcement is done by courts through the power of judicial review.[78] Whether the issue is a "conservative" court striking down popularly enacted campaign finance regulations or portions of the Voting Rights Act, or a "liberal" court striking down popularly enacted bans on same-sex marriage or contraception, the basic theoretical problem is the same. How can it be that

[70] *See* Ezell v. City of Chicago, No. 10 C 5135, 2010 WL 3998104 (N.D. Ill. Oct. 12, 2010), *rev'd*, 651 F.3d 684 (7th Cir. 2011).
[71] *Id.*
[72] *See* Ezell v. City of Chicago, 651 F.3d 684 (7th Cir. 2011).
[73] *See* Ezell v. City of Chicago (*Ezell II*), 846 F.3d. 888, 890 (7th Cir. 2017).
[74] *Id.*
[75] *See* People v. Deroche, 299 Mich. App. 301, 303 (2013).
[76] *See* Palmer v. District of Columbia, 59 F. Supp. 3d 173 (D.D.C. 2014).
[77] *See* Wesson v. Town of Salisbury, 13 F. Supp. 3d 171 (D. Mass. 2014).
[78] *See* Richard H. Fallon, Jr., *Foreword: Implementing the Constitution*, 111 HARV. L. REV. 56, 56–57 (1997).

judges – especially unelected federal judges – have the power to override the preferences of a democratic majority? How can we justify this "deviant institution"?[79] And, assuming one accepts this role for the courts, how should judges exercise the power of judicial review so as to minimize the "counter-majoritarian difficulty"?[80]

Finding answers to these questions has been a central task of constitutional law for generations, so it is worth considering how some of the standard efforts to justify judicial review might address the Second Amendment in particular. All such efforts have their flaws, but in recent decades, "political process theory" has been perhaps the most widely accepted.[81] The theory is associated with scholar John Hart Ely and footnote four of *United States v. Carolene Products Company*[82] – regarded as "the most famous footnote in all of constitutional law."[83] The heart of the argument is that judicial review is most justified when the political process cannot be trusted, for example when the channels of political change are clogged by legal restrictions, or when the burdens of legal regulation are concentrated against what Justice Stone (the author of *Carolene Products*) called "discrete and insular minorities."[84] Although no theory is perfect,[85] the attraction of the political process approach is clear, because in theory it keeps judges from imposing their own personal preferences against those of a well-functioning democracy.

It is very hard to see how political process theory could support active judicial review in Second Amendment cases. As Cass Sunstein puts it: "There is no special reason for an aggressive judicial role in protecting against gun control, in light of the fact that opponents of such control have considerable political power and do not seem to be at a systematic disadvantage in the democratic process."[86] In terms of political power, contemporary gun owners are differently – and better – situated than African American school children at the time of *Brown v. Board of Education*.

Some of *Heller*'s conservative critics have made the same point, comparing *Heller* to what they regard as the equally indefensible holding of *Roe v. Wade*.[87] In Richard

[79] Alexander M. Bickel, The Least Dangerous Branch 18 (1962).

[80] *Id.* at 16.

[81] This is not to say, of course, that the theory is without its critics. *See, e.g.*, Laurence Tribe, *The Puzzling Persistence of Process-Based Constitutional Theories*, 89 Yale L.J. 1063 (1980).

[82] 304 U.S. 144 (1938); *see generally* John Hart Ely, Democracy and Distrust (1980). Michael J. Klarman, *The Puzzling Resistance to Political Process Theory*, 77 Va. L. Rev. 747, 748 (1991) (arguing that "important aspects of political process theory have weathered the attack").

[83] *See* Cass R. Sunstein, One Case at a Time: Judicial Minimalism on the Supreme Court 7 (1991); Peter Linzer, *The Carolene Products Footnote and the Preferred Position of Individual Rights: Louis Lusky and John Hart Ely vs. Harlan Fiske Stone*, 12 Const. Comment. 277 (1995).

[84] U.S. v. Carolene Products Co., 304 U.S. 144, 153 n.4 (1938).

[85] J. Harvie Wilkinson, Cosmic Constitutional Theory: Why Americans Are Losing Their Inalienable Right to Self-Governance (2012); Richard Posner, *Against Constitutional Theory*, 73 N.Y.U. L. Rev. 1 (1998).

[86] Cass R. Sunstein, *Second Amendment Minimalism: Heller as Griswold*, 122 Harv. L. Rev. 246, 260 (2008).

[87] J. Harvie Wilkinson III, *Of Guns, Abortions, and the Unraveling Rule of Law*, 95 Va. L. Rev. 253, 303 (2009).

Posner's assessment, "The proper time ... to enlarge constitutional restrictions on government action is when the group seeking the enlargement does not have good access to the political process to protect its interests, as abortion advocates, like gun advocates, did and do."[88]

Some gun rights advocates claim that gun owners are the subject of political and social persecution.[89] But in practice gun owners seem to have ample political support when it comes to the right to keep and bear arms. All branches of the federal government supported *Heller's* central conclusion regarding the right to keep and bear arms for private purposes. Majorities in both houses of Congress filed briefs supporting the plaintiff's reading of the Second Amendment, as did the Department of Justice (while arguing that D.C.'s law was consistent with that right). The decision was rendered in the midst of a presidential election, and both major candidates supported it. These are not the hallmarks of a political process failure.

Perhaps most importantly, as noted above, a strong majority of Americans supports the private purposes reading of the Second Amendment, and only a small minority favors stringent regulation like handgun bans.[90] Almost no one endorses the kind of widespread confiscation of private firearms that the NRA so often claims is the ultimate goal of gun regulation.[91]

Even though they support the Second Amendment, most Americans also support reasonable gun regulation, and support for particular policies – including universal

[88] Richard Posner, *In Defense of Looseness*, New Republic (Aug. 27, 2008), https://newrepublic.com/article/62124/defense-looseness.

[89] *See, e.g.*, Osha Gray Davidson, Under Fire: The NRA and the Battle for Gun Control 300 (1993) (stating that NRA Lobbyist Tanya Metaksa wrote a post in an online forum titled "Gun Owners: The Jews of the 90s in a Fascist America"); Aviva Shen, *Parroting Conspiracy Theorist, Drudge Compares Obama to Hitler and Stalin*, ThinkProgress (Jan. 9, 2013), http://thinkprogress.org/justice/2013/01/09/1423991/parroting-conspiracy-theorist-drudge-compares-obama-to-hitler-and-stalin, archived at http://perma.cc/7NTW-DNR3 (reporting statements by Alex Jones involving Hitler, Stalin, and Mao in the context of the American gun control debate); *Today's Gun Owners: Parallels to Jews in Germany in the 1930s*, GunsSaveLife (Jan. 27, 2013), www.gunssavelife.com/?p=5239, archived at http://perma.cc/4AQM-PRXF ("Propaganda about gun owners has reached a fever pitch in America today, leaving American gun owners feeling like the Jews in Germany before the Second World War."); *see generally* Bernard E. Harcourt, *On Gun Registration, the NRA, Adolf Hitler, and Nazi Gun Laws: Exploding the Gun Culture Wars (a Call to Historians)*, 73 Fordham L. Rev. 653 (2004) (exploring the longstanding argument made by gun-rights advocates that gun control led to the Holocaust); Alex Rosenwald, *Organizer of Gun Appreciation Day Calls out the Racist Outcome of Gun Control*, Equal Gun Rts. (Feb. 25, 2013), http://equalgunrights.com/articles/organizer-of-gun-appreciation-day-calls-out-the-racist-outcome-of-gun-control, archived at http://perma.cc/F6AR-H6DV.

[90] *See* Lydia Saad, *Americans Want Stricter Gun Laws, Still Oppose Bans*, Gallup (Dec. 27, 2012), www.gallup.com/poll/159569/americans-stricter-gun-laws-oppose-bans.aspx, archived at http://perma.cc/T5FN-WUX4 (finding that only 24 percent of Americans favor banning the possession of handguns).

[91] *Id.*, Chris Cox, *Gun Confiscation: An Evil Wind Blows in America*, NRAILA (Oct. 26, 2017), www.nraila.org/articles/20171026/gun-confiscation-an-evil-wind-blows-in-america ("But firearm confiscation and the measures that enable it, including firearm owner licensing and firearm registration, are still the lodestar of the gun control agenda.").

background checks and bans on high capacity magazines – is very high.[92] But these laws were extremely rare even before *Heller*. It has been nearly thirty years since Congress passed any kind of gun regulation, and stringent new gun regulations are generally confined to a dozen or so states (albeit some populous ones like California and New York). Recall the Senate's refusal in the wake of the Sandy Hook massacre to pass a popular compromise gun bill that would have expanded the background check requirement. Indeed, most Americans favor more gun regulation than politics have delivered.[93]

If political process is the metric, then, it seems that the right to keep and bear arms is far from underenforced. In most cases, not only have political leaders declined to use the regulatory room *Heller* provides, they have tacked in the opposite direction, providing statutory protections above and beyond what the Constitution requires. The most obvious example is concealed carry. *Heller* suggests, and courts have held, that concealed carry can be banned without violating the Second Amendment,[94] so long as some alternative is available. And yet, all states permit concealed carry in one form or another, including some states that allow it without any license and with no training.[95] Perhaps even more telling is the proliferation of laws that that specifically *protect* the ownership and use of guns. Such "anti-gun control" laws often give gun owners and manufacturers special protections against regulation or legal liability. Practically speaking, these laws present a more serious obstacle to gun regulation than the Second Amendment itself.

Consider the spread of state level "preemption" laws that limit or prohibit localities from passing gun regulation. Prompted in part by the passage of a handgun ban in Morton Grove, Illinois, the NRA and other gun rights organizations began pushing for state-level preemption laws throughout the 1980s.[96] The campaign was incredibly successful,[97] and by 2002, forty-one states had preempted some or all local gun control.[98] As the former leader of a national gun control organization put it: "There's no question that the NRA's effort to pass preemption laws was a serious setback, and there's no question that whatever the implications in terms of policy, what you do lose at the local level is the ability to rally people around a local issue...."[99] Some preemption laws not only limit regulation, but

[92] *See* Saad, *supra* note 90 (finding that only 24 percent of Americans favor banning the possession of handguns).

[93] *Id.*

[94] *See Heller*, 554 U.S. at 626.

[95] *See* Joseph Blocher, *Constitutional Hurdles for Concealed Carry*, Take Care Blog, Mar. 16, 2017, https://takecareblog.com/blog/constitutional-hurdles-for-concealed-carry-reciprocity/.

[96] Glenn H. Utter, Encyclopedia of Gun Control and Gun Rights 200 (2000).

[97] Kristin A. Goss, *Policy, Politics, and Paradox: The Institutional Origins of the Great American Gun War*, 73 Fordham L. Rev. 681, 706 (2004).

[98] Jon S. Vernick & Lisa M. Hepburn, *State and Federal Gun Laws: Trends for 1970–99*, in Evaluating Gun Policy: Effects on Crime and Violence 345, 363 (Jens Ludwig & Philip J. Cook, eds., 2003).

[99] Goss, *supra* note 97, at 706.

give gun organizations special standing to sue cities over potentially preempted city gun ordinances – even out-of-state groups whose members have not been directly harmed.[100]

The federal government has also exercised its own preemption power. In response to private, municipal, and state lawsuits against the gun industry, Congress passed the NRA-backed[101] Protection of Lawful Commerce in Arms Act ("PLCAA"). That law preempted every state's tort law, extinguished lawsuits by private and public parties that were then pending, and extended to gun manufacturers and dealers a nearly impervious shield against tort lawsuits when their products are misused.[102] Judges who might otherwise be sympathetic to gun regulation have dismissed cases on PLCAA grounds, as they are bound to do by the Supremacy Clause. (As of this writing, a lawsuit filed by parents of the Sandy Hook massacre against certain gun manufacturers has been dismissed for precisely this reason.[103])

These pro-gun efforts challenge the standard narrative of gun owners as libertarians fighting off an over-reaching regulatory state. As mentioned in the previous chapter, at least eleven states have passed laws limiting businesses' authority to exclude guns from their premises.[104] Some of these laws attempt to "hold employers criminally liable for prohibiting employees from storing firearms in locked vehicles on company property."[105] Florida's law, later struck down in part on unrelated grounds, prohibited an employer from "discriminat[ing]" against a worker or customer "for exercising his or her constitutional right to keep and bear arms."[106]

[100] *See* Everytown for Gun Safety, State Firearm Preemption Laws (July 9, 2015), https://everytownresearch.org/wp-content/uploads/2015/06/060115-Preemption-Fact-Sheet.pdf ("The 2014 Pennsylvania law that requires cities to pay challengers' legal fees also expressly gave groups like the NRA the ability to sue local governments. The legislation was a direct response to (and effectively reversed), several court decisions concluding that groups like the NRA did not have legal 'standing' to sue cities.").

[101] The NRA lobbied for the law, and Wayne LaPierre described it as a "the most significant piece of pro-gun legislation in twenty years." *President Bush Signs "Protection of Lawful Commerce in Arms Act" Landmark NRA Victory Now Law*, Nat'l Rifle Ass'n (Oct. 26, 2005), www.nraila.org/articles/20051026/president-bush-signs-protection-of-br.

[102] 15 U.S.C. § 7901–02. This immunity is not absolute, however – the law preserves the possibility of negligence lawsuits when, for example, a dealer sells to someone they have reason to know intends to use it in a crime. 15 U.S.C. § 7903(5)(A) (2012) ("The term 'qualified civil liability action' ... shall not include ... an action brought against a seller for negligent entrustment or negligence per se.").

[103] *See* Soto v. Bushmaster Firearms Int'l, LLC, FBTCV156048103S, 2016 WL 8115354 (Conn. Super Ct. Oct. 14, 2016) ("[T]his action falls squarely within the broad immunity provided by PLCAA.").

[104] *See* Alaska Stat. § 18.65.800 (2011); Ariz. Rev. Stat. Ann. § 12-781 (2011); Fla. Stat. Ann. § 790.251 (West 2011), *invalidated in part by* Fla. Retail Fed'n, Inc. v. Attorney Gen., 576 F. Supp. 2d 1301, 1303 (N.D. Fla. 2008); Ga. Code Ann. § 16-11-135 (2011); Ind. Code Ann. § 34-28-7-2 (West 2011); Kan. Stat. Ann. § 75-7c11 (2009) (repealed 2010); Ky. Rev. Stat. Ann. § 237.106 (West 2011); La. Rev. Stat. Ann. § 32:292.1 (2011); Minn. Stat. Ann. § 624.714 (West 2011); Miss. Code Ann. § 45-9-55 (2011); Okla. Stat. tit. 21, § 1289.7a (2011). Some of these laws (for example, Florida's and Kansas's), however, are no longer valid.

[105] Ramsey Winch Inc. v. Henry, 555 F.3d 1199, 1202 (10th Cir. 2009) (rejecting challenges on takings, preemption, due process, and vagueness grounds).

[106] Fla. Stat. Ann. § 790.251(4)(e).

These policies may or may not be a good idea, but their existence ought to dispel the notion that the right to keep and bear arms is vulnerable to the kind of broad political process failures that justify aggressive judicial enforcement in other constitutional areas or on behalf of other groups. In fact, they underline the notion that the political process is working for the benefit of gun owners well beyond what *Heller* requires.

INACCURATE AND MISLEADING CLAIMS ABOUT THE SECOND AMENDMENT DISTORT THE GUN DEBATE

Our goal in this book has been to understand and explain the Second Amendment as constitutional law. We have attempted to show how taking the Second Amendment seriously as a matter of law means accepting constraints about both the *substance* and *method* of claims that one can make about gun rights.

But our argument is not that the Second Amendment belongs to the lawyers, nor that everyone must master the intricacies of constitutional doctrine in order to participate in a Second Amendment conversation. We do not believe that courts and lawyers are, or necessarily should be, the last word on the Second Amendment or any other constitutional principle.[107] To the contrary, we believe that a broader range of voices in the gun debate should embrace constitutional law and work with it. This is especially true of those on the political left, who are often criticized for a lack of a positive constitutional vision – of having no answer to the ascendance of originalists, for example. Nowhere is the absence of a positive constitutional vision more acute than in the context of the Second Amendment. Until progressives develop a positive account of the Second Amendment, rather than a series of policy objections to it, they will not have an effective voice in shaping the content and future of the right to keep and bear arms.

For the same reasons, there was nothing inappropriate about gun rights activists, prior to *Heller*, making aspirational claims about the Second Amendment or arguing for a change in the way it was interpreted and applied. One can disagree with the substance of their position while recognizing that constitutional doctrine is often formed in a crucible of contested meanings.[108] Claims that were once "off the wall" – whether they be about segregated schools, gay marriage, or the Commerce Clause – can eventually be legitimized and even find their way into doctrine.[109]

[107] *See generally* Robert Post & Reva Siegel, *Popular Constitutionalism, Departmentalism, and Judicial Supremacy*, 92 CALIF. L. REV. 1027 (2004).

[108] *See* Robert Post & Reva Siegel, *Roe Rage: Democratic Constitutionalism and Backlash*, 42 HARV. C.R.-C.L. L. REV. 373 (2007).

[109] *See* Jack Balkin, *The Framework Model and Constitutional Interpretation*, *in* PHILOSOPHICAL FOUNDATIONS OF CONSTITUTIONAL LAW 241, 248–251 (David Dyzenhaus & Malcolm Thorburn, eds., 2016).

Our politics, and our constitutional doctrine, would be impoverished if they did not recognize this process. We do not mean to question it here.

We believe, however, that when partisans in the gun debate invoke the Second Amendment as law, they should do so in a way that respects the substance and method of law. It distorts, rather than enriches, our politics and law when inaccurate statements about the latter are leveraged in ways that shut down the former – when, for example, a discussion about expanding background checks is short-circuited by the claim or assumption that doing so would violate the Second Amendment. Such inaccurate invocations of the Constitution magnify the already-significant pathologies of the gun debate, driving people to extremes and preventing not only compromise but discussion.

Political partisans can dig their trenches wherever they like, but they should not pretend that the Second Amendment mandates the present battlefield. The history of gun rights and regulation in the United States demonstrates that the two can co-exist and always have. When the Second Amendment was ratified, cities had gun regulations more stringent than anything on the Brady Center's agenda.[110] State constitutions have long recognized and protected a right to keep and bear arms for private purposes, while permitting reasonable regulation.[111] Modern politics, not the Second Amendment, have exaggerated the gulf between rights and regulation. If gun debate partisans want to claim the Constitution as legal authority, they should begin with an account of what the Second Amendment actually provides as a matter of law.

Doing so could deliver significant benefits for the gun debate and those mired in it. First, inaccurate claims about the Second Amendment contribute to the extreme polarization and absolutism of the modern gun debate.[112] Some gun rights supporters treat any minor regulation as if it were an assault on the Second Amendment.[113] Their absolutist, constitutional rhetoric helped sink Manchin-Toomey, "no fly, no buy," and countless other gun regulations before and since.[114]

Though such absolutist constitutional rhetoric does occur on all sides of the debate, it is without a doubt far more pervasive among gun rights supporters. Dick Metcalf is a historian and self-described "Second Amendment fundamentalist" who

[110] *See* Joseph Blocher, *Firearm Localism*, 123 YALE L.J. 82, 120 (2013).

[111] *See* Adam Winkler, *Scrutinizing the Second Amendment*, 105 MICH. L. REV. 683, 715–19 (2007).

[112] *See* Andrew Jay McClurg, *The Rhetoric of Gun Control*, 42 AM. U.L. REV. 53, 81–84 (1992); Joseph Blocher, *Gun Rights Talk*, 94 B.U. L. REV. 813, 820 (2014) [hereinafter Blocher, *Gun Rights Talk*].

[113] Bryan Berger, *Why Every (Yes, Every) Gun Control Law Is Unconstitutional*, OFF THE GRID NEWS, www.offthegridnews.com/self-defense/why-every-yes-every-gun-control-law-is-unconstitutional; Bob Owens, *This Lawsuit Could Shatter ALL Federal Gun Control Laws*, BEARING ARMS (Nov. 22, 2016), https://bearingarms.com/bob-o/2016/11/22/this-lawsuit-could-shatter-all-federal-gun-laws/ ("[T]he Second Amendment meant the federal government in Washington had no power to constrain or regulate arms.").

[114] *See* Blocher, *Gun Rights Talk*, *supra* note 112.

wrote a popular column for *Guns & Ammo* magazine.[115] In October 2013, Metcalf wrote a piece arguing that "all constitutional rights are regulated, always have been, and need to be."[116] Metcalf, in other words, simply echoed Justice Scalia's statement in *Heller* that "the right secured by the Second Amendment is not unlimited."[117] Even so, Metcalf's column was met with fury, including cancelled subscriptions and death threats.[118] Metcalf was fired. A former editor of the magazine, Richard Venola, put the matter in constitutional terms: "We are locked in a struggle with powerful forces who will do anything to destroy the Second Amendment. The time for ceding some rational points is gone."[119]

The Second Amendment neither reflects nor requires this kind of absolutism. In fact, post-*Heller* Second Amendment doctrine delivers what the American public says it wants: Protection for a right to keep and bear arms for private purposes, with allowances for reasonable restrictions on that right, especially in cases where the risk to others is high. In part because of overheated claims about constitutional law, gun regulators fear too much from the Second Amendment, and gun rights supporters demand too much of it.

Second, accepting the law of the Second Amendment can lessen some of the unique pathologies that affect the gun debate, in particular its pernicious effects on social trust, and its tendency to treat every issue of gun policy as a Second Amendment problem. In response to the political collapse of some gun safety proposals, supporters of regulation sometimes react by saying that it isn't politics but the Second Amendment that is the obstacle.[120] This leads to quixotic calls to repeal the Amendment. Although these would-be repealers are a vanishingly small minority, they tend to become the focus of mistrust by gun rights supporters, and taint efforts to achieve even popular regulatory changes. Clarifying the constitutional law can help minimize these distortions, sharpen the issues, and perhaps help generate consensus.

For gun rights advocates, the urge to cast every matter concerning firearms as a Second Amendment crisis places too much pressure on the Amendment and leads

[115] Dick Metcalf, *Dick Metcalf Responds, Part II: Confessions of a Gun Guy*, GunsSave Life, www.gunssavelife.com/dick-metcalf-responds-part-ii-confessions-of-a-gun-guy/ ("I have always considered myself a Second Amendment fundamentalist.").

[116] Dick Metcalf, *Let's Talk Limits*, Gun & Ammo (Dec. 2013) at 120.

[117] *Heller*, 554 U.S. at 626.

[118] Ravi Somaiya, *Banished for Questioning the Gospel of Guns*, N.Y. Times , Jan. 4, 2014, at 1 ("The backlash was swift, and fierce. Readers threatened to cancel their subscriptions. Death threats poured in by email. His television program was pulled from the air.").

[119] *Id.*

[120] *See* James Boice, *Inevitability or Pipe Dream?: Meet the Second Amendment Repealists*, Salon (Feb. 16, 2016), www.salon.com/2016/02/15/inevitability_or_pipe_dream_meet_the_second_amendment_repealists/ (arguing "the Second Amendment stands in the way" of reasonable gun regulations); *see also* Bret Stephens, *Repeal the Second Amendment*, N.Y. Times (Oct. 5, 2017), www.nytimes.com/2017/10/05/opinion/guns-second-amendment-nra.html.

to needless friction with other values.[121] Consider the NRA's top legislative priority after the 2016 election: federally mandated concealed carry reciprocity.[122] This policy "would give a concealed-carry-permit holder in Texas the right to carry a gun in a state such as New York, regardless of New York's concealed-carry laws,"[123] essentially forcing states to treat concealed carry permits in much the same way as they have chosen to treat driver's licenses.[124] The NRA has claimed that the ten states which "still refuse to grant full faith and credit to the permits of other states"[125] have "criminalize[d] the Second Amendment."[126] A previous version of such a bill, introduced in 2011, claimed to be enforcing the Second Amendment against the states.[127]

Whatever might be said about the merits of national concealed carry reciprocity, it is deeply misleading to suggest that it is a Second Amendment mandate. *Heller* clearly suggests, and lower courts have almost uniformly held, that the right to keep and bear arms simply does not encompass concealed carry. That of course leaves states free to permit it if they wish. But to suggest that the Second Amendment *requires* them to do so – let alone that it requires the federal government to do so – is simply wrong. Moreover, it puts the Second Amendment into unnecessary conflict with other kinds of constitutional values like federalism, limits on congressional power to enforce the Commerce Clause or Reconstruction Amendments,[128] the First Amendment,[129] and other important features of our constitutional order.[130]

Third, and relatedly, a better understanding of the law may help maintain the line between personal, political, and constitutional disagreements. It is not uncommon

[121] *See* Wollschlaeger v. Governor, Florida, 848 F.3d 1293, 1313 (11th Cir. 2017) ("Even if there were some possible conflict between the First Amendment rights of doctors and medical professionals and the Second Amendment rights of patients, the record-keeping, inquiry, and anti-harassment provisions do 'not advance [the legislative goals] in a permissible way.'").

[122] Nathan Rott, *Following Election, NRA Goes On 'Offense'; Here's What It Could Aim To Do*, NPR (Nov. 15, 2016), www.npr.org/sections/thetwo-way/2016/11/15/502229875/following-election-nra-goes-on-offense-here-s-what-they-could-aim-to-do.

[123] *Id.*

[124] *See* Joseph Blocher, *Constitutional Hurdles for Concealed Carry*, Take Care Blog, (Mar. 16, 2017), https://takecareblog.com/blog/constitutional-hurdles-for-concealed-carry-reciprocity/ [hereinafter Blocher, *Constitutional Hurdles*].

[125] Press Release, NRA-ILA, *NRA Backs Concealed Carry Reciprocity Bill in U.S. Senate* (Feb. 27, 2017), www.nraila.org/articles/20170227/nra-backs-concealed-carry-reciprocity-bill-in-us-senate.

[126] Michele Gorman, *Guns in America: NRA Boosts National Concealed Carry Reciprocity Push*, Newsweek (Apr. 19, 2017), www.newsweek.com/guns-america-nra-national-concealed-carry-reciprocity-586438.

[127] *See* National Right-to-Carry Act of 2011, H.R. 822, 112th Cong. (as introduced to House, Feb. 18, 2011).

[128] *See, e.g.*, Kimel v. Florida Board of Regents, 528 U.S. 62 (2000); City of Boerne v. Flores, 521 U.S. 507 (1997).

[129] *Wollschlaeger*, 848 F.3d at 1313.

[130] *See* Josh Blackman, *Is the Constitutional Concealed Carry Reciprocity Act Constitutional?*, Josh Blackman's Blog (Feb. 15, 2015), http://joshblackman.com/blog/2015/02/15/is-the-constitutional-concealed-carry-reciprocity-act-constitutional/; Robert Verbruggen, *Concealed-Carry 'Reciprocity' vs. Federalism*, Nat'l Rev. (June 1, 2017), www.nationalreview.com/article/448152/concealed-carry-reciprocity-federalism-state-issue; Blocher, *Constitutional Hurdles*, *supra* note 124.

to hear some version of, "Do you believe in the Second Amendment?" There is something odd about this question – it is like starting a discussion of free speech by asking, "Do you believe in the First Amendment?" – and there is a danger that framing the discussion in such a way conflates issues of constitutional law with questions of personal or policy preferences, at risk of distorting both.

The vast majority of Americans, including those who support gun regulation, "believe in" the Second Amendment. The real debates are about what the Constitution permits and protects, just as in so many other substantive areas of constitutional law. People who "believe in" free speech are divided about how much protection it gives to corporate campaign contributions or to transmission of patient prescription information.[131] Those who "believe in" Equal Protection disagree about whether it can or should be interpreted in line with its original expected applications, and whether or how it permits race-conscious student assignment plans.[132] Recognizing the right, it is understood, does not commit one to a package of positions on individual policy matters or even specific conclusions about the right's scope.

"Do you like guns? Do you oppose gun regulation?" are significant and important questions, but they are not *Second Amendment* questions. In constitutional terms, the better question would be, "What do you think the Second Amendment means? What kinds of laws does it prohibit?" These are constitutional inquiries with legal answers. Of course, they might also have significant political salience. But they are not dressed up as binary questions that are more about selecting friends and enemies than generating meaningful exchange. Furthermore, they help force the questions that matter, and can be answered by law: Does the Second Amendment cover concealed carry? Are "assault weapons" constitutionally protected?

The answers to those constitutional questions can, in turn, supply parameters for the kinds of policy questions we should be asking: What kind of training should be required for concealed carry? When, if ever, should nonviolent felons have their firearm rights restored? As we have tried to show, these are the kinds of questions confronting the Second Amendment and the broader gun debate after *Heller*. And

[131] *Compare* Floyd Abrams, *Citizens United and its Critics*, 120 YALE L.J. ONLINE 77 (2010) (offering a defense of the *Citizens United* campaign finance decision) *with* Lawrence Lessig, *Corrupt and Unequal, Both*, 84 FORDHAM L. REV. 445 (2015) (arguing that current campaign finance jurisprudence creates both corruption and inequality); *compare* IMS Health Inc. v. Ayotte, 550 F.3d 42 (1st Cir. 2008) (holding a law prohibiting transfers of physicians' prescribing histories regulated conduct and not speech) *with* Sorrell v. IMS Health Inc., 564 U.S. 552 (2011) (holding such a law was a content- and speaker-based burden on protected expression).

[132] *See generally* Parents Involved in Comm. Schools v. Seattle School Dist. No. 1, 551 U.S. 701 (2007); *compare* Steven Calabresi & Hannah Begley, *Originalism and Same-Sex Marriage*, 70 U. MIAMI L. REV. 648, 695–96 (2016) (arguing for an "originalist" interpretation of the Fourteenth Amendment "instituting a general ban on class legislation") *with* Eric Schnapper, *Affirmative Action and the Legislative History of the Fourteenth Amendment*, 71 VA. L. REV. 753, 754 (1985) (arguing that "the framers of the amendment could not have intended it generally to prohibit affirmative action for blacks or other disadvantaged groups").

they can best be answered using the legal tools described and applied throughout this book.

This does not mean an end to the gun debate. To the contrary, what we have described here is a way of maintaining the boundaries around that debate – preserving an arena in which the hard questions about gun policy can and must be addressed. As we have tried to show, that is no problem for advocates of reasonable gun regulation. The vast majority of gun regulation supported by the largest gun safety groups – expanded background checks, permit requirements for public carrying, even increased restrictions on assault weapons and high capacity magazines – are fully compatible with *Heller*.

For some absolutist gun rights supporters – those who, ironically enough, invoke the Constitution most often – there may be less incentive to accept and embrace what the law actually says. After all, apocalyptic rhetoric has been a common and useful tool for groups like the NRA. Why give it up now? And yet the world is changing, and it may be time for the message change along with it. Support for the right to keep and bear arms is strong, but it overlaps with support for gun regulation. And with gun ownership at its lowest level in decades,[133] a dwindling and demographically unrepresentative membership,[134] policy positions that apparently diverge from the preferences of the rank-and-file,[135] and its fortunes increasingly tied to only one of the two major American political parties,[136] NRA leadership may need to find allies among the non-absolutists in the coming years.

We do not suppose that the gun debate's intransigent partisans will be changing their tunes anytime soon. We hope, however, that the political debate will draw more heavily on the substance and method of constitutional law. The Constitution is on the side of those who believe in the right to keep and bear arms, and also those who believe in gun regulation. The coexistence of rights and regulation is not forbidden by the Second Amendment, but is – and always has been – a part of it.

[133] *See* Ingraham, *supra* note 22.

[134] Adam Winkler, *The NRA Will Fall. It's Inevitable*, WASH. POST POSTEVERYTHING (Oct. 19, 2015) www.washingtonpost.com/posteverything/wp/2015/10/19/the-nra-will-fall-its-inevitable/.

[135] Stu Bykofsky, *NRA Dumps Toomey: That is Good News For Him*, THE INQUIRER (Philadelphia) (Oct. 10, 2016), www.philly.com/philly/columnists/stu_bykofsky/20161010_NRA_dumps_Toomey__That_is_good_news_for_him.html.

[136] *See, e.g.*, Nate Cohen & Kevin Quealy, *Nothing Divides Voters Like Owning a Gun*, THE UPSHOT: NYTIMES.COM (Oct. 5, 2017), www.nytimes.com/interactive/2017/10/05/upshot/gun-ownership-partisan-divide.html.

Index